# CAP MỘT

## The Story of a Marine Special Forces Unit in Vietnam, 1968–1969

# War and the Southwest Series

Series editors: Richard G. Lowe, Gustav L. Seligmann, Calvin L. Christman

The University of North Texas Press has undertaken to publish a series of significant books about War and the Southwest. This broad category includes first-hand accounts of military experiences by men and women of the Southwest, histories of warfare involving the people of the Southwest, and analyses of military life in the Southwest itself. The Southwest is defined loosely as those states of the United States west of the Mississippi River and south of a line from San Francisco to St. Louis as well as the borderlands straddling the Mexico-United States boundary. The series will include works involving military life in peacetime in addition to books on warfare itself. It will range chronologically from the first contact between indigenous tribes and Europeans to the present. The series is based on the belief that warfare is an important if unfortunate fact of life in human history and that understanding war is a requirement for a full understanding of the American past.

## Books in the Series

*FOO—A Japanese-American Prisoner of the Rising Sun*
*Wen Bon: A Naval Air Intelligence Officer behind Japanese Lines in China*
*An Artist at War: The Journal of John Gaitha Browning*
*The 56th Evac Hospital: Letters of a WWII Army Doctor*

# CAP MỘT

## The Story of a Marine Special Forces Unit in Vietnam, 1968–1969

## BARRY L. GOODSON

v. 5 War and the Southwest Series

University of North Texas Press
Denton, Texas

© Barry L. Goodson
First published in 1997
Manufactured in the United States of America
5  4  3  2  1

Requests for permission to reproduce material from this work should be sent to:
Permissions
University of North Texas Press
PO Box 13856
Denton TX 76203

The paper used in this book meets the minimum requirements of the American National
Standard for Permanence of Paper for Printed Library Materials, Z39.48.1984.
The LaserVietnamese® for Windows® font used to print this work is available from
Linguist's Software, Inc., PO Box 580, Edmonds, WA 98020-0580
USA tel (206) 775-1130.

Library of Congress Cataloging-in-Publication data:
Goodson, Barry L., 1949–
    CAP Mot: a marine special forces unit in Vietnam, 1968–1969 / by Barry L.
Goodson.
        p.    cm.
    ISBN 1-57441-004-0
    1. Vietnamese Conflict, 1961–1975—Commando operations.  2. United States.
Marine Corps. CAP—History.  3. Vietnamese Conflict, 1961–1975—Regimental
histories—United States.  I. Title.
DS558.92.G66   1996
959.704'3373—dc20                                                96-5940
                                                                    CIP

cover and interior design by Amy Layton
interior and cover artwork by Barry Goodson

To my wife, Cindy

# Table of Contents

# Preface

This book is based upon actual occurrences and events that took place during my tour of duty in Vietnam, from July of 1968 to June of 1969.[1] Even though the entire book is written from memory,[2] I feel confident of its accuracy because the events of that period of time will remain etched into my mind for the duration of my life.

CAP[3] was a Special Forces unit which the United States Marine Corps developed in Vietnam as an answer to the never ending question, "Why am I here?" CAP was the abbreviated version of the name Combined Action Program, which was a nebulous title for a unique, specially trained unit of men. Generally, each unit consisted of six to eight men including one radioman and one corpsman (medic). These men lived in the jungle with no compound or firebase to offer security and no place to lay one's head. The only time a CAP Marine left the jungle was when he was rotating home, wounded or dead.

My unit was CAP One, and the number "one" in the Vietnamese language is "Một," hence the title of this book, *CAP Một*.

As the plot of the book unravels you will discover that the CAP Marines were responsible for two primary functions, each of which involved multitudes of equally important responsibilities. We were first and foremost to become deeply involved, on a personal basis, with the Vietnamese people; helping them throughout their daily lives in whatever small way we could. We were to help the sick to heal, the starving to survive, those in fear to be comforted and the orphaned to find a home. We were to teach the farmers how to improve their farming methods in simple ways. Basic tools were brought in to decrease their workload, while at the same time enhancing our purpose and communicating our friendly intentions to everyone.

The Vietnamese were very proud people with many ideas and beliefs which created an invisible and, in some cases an impenetrable, barrier. Yet if you approached them with sincerity, with your heart on your sleeve and with a desire to "become one of them," they would accept you, follow you and learn from you. As long as you were willing to accept and become involved in every phase of their life and do, say, eat and drink everything as they did, your mission would succeed and, most of all, you would survive.

Having gained acceptance, our second responsibility was to train new warriors in each village, young men ages fourteen and up, who were willing and eager to learn how to seek out and to destroy the enemy that plagued their villages, who unquestionably understood the oppression by the forces of Communism that plagued their homeland.

Side by side with these Vietnamese we fought enemy forces ranging from a single Viet Cong to untold numbers of the enemy including the NVA (North Vietnamese Army). Our unified effort destroyed them and drove them from the villages and from the area.

Initially, I entered the CAP Marines with the misconception that I would be training a bunch of jungle natives who knew nothing about the methods and strategy of true combat. It only took a few short days being a member of an actual CAP unit to realize that the person who really needed to listen and learn was the new kid on the block—yours truly. Even the youngest of the men in the Popular Forces[4] had experienced far more combat than most American soldiers. The PFs only needed training in respect to the use and maintenance of American-made weapons—a skill each man could be taught within a matter of hours.

The PFs taught us, especially me, far more about jungle warfare and survival in the bush than the Marines ever hoped to accomplish. The Vietnamese were adept at living in the harshest conditions. They could spot booby traps on the darkest of nights. They could teach us how to actually smell the presence of the enemy.

After living among the Vietnamese people and fighting beside them in numerous battles I began to realize that other units throughout Vietnam were, speaking metaphorically, "fighting in the dark"; unnecessarily risking and losing lives because they never took the time to get to know the people they were trying so desperately to help. I grieved for American lives lost to booby traps that even the smallest Vietnamese child could have spotted.

During my brief time as a "grunt"[5] with Alpha Company, II Marine Amphibious Force, I had virtually no contact with the South Vietnamese soldiers. The only things I knew about them were the rumors other Marines passed on from their own personal experiences, rumors which portrayed the South Vietnamese soldier as a weak, unreliable coward that no one could trust. That, I soon discovered, was far from the truth.

Another of our responsibilities was the care and protection of an artillery firebase[6] known as "Fat City."[7] It stood right in the middle of our APR (area of prime responsibility). Our small unit of six men was responsible for recon and protection for a base of over 400 men who never understood how we managed to survive outside a compound.

The CAP Marines had an important mission. A special purpose. Many of them gave their lives in an effort to help the people of Vietnam. This book portrays their story and true feelings. The renditions portray actual events . . . hopefully revealing the sorrows, the agonies, the sincerity, the joy and the hopes of their daily lives. This is their story . . . a true one, retold from the haunts of my mind.

In spite of countless hours, days and years I have spent trying to remember the names of those men with whom I fought, my mind still refuses to cooperate. Because of this, the names of my fellow marines as used in this book are fictitious, with the exception of Earl Jones and John Ciminski, for whom I have documentation to prove their names.

If, as you read this story, you discover you are one of the men who shared the jungle with me, or you know someone who might have been there, please contact me. (It is for this reason I have described the men as "black," "white," or "Puerto Rican," thinking it might help to locate them.) A reunion is long overdue. Together we could create an even more accurate picture of our life in Vietnam.

CO—Commanding Officer of our platoon
Colonel Andrews—CAP Battalion Commander

*Squad Members*
Jésus Rodriguez—Puerto Rican, rifleman
Elano Mendez—Puerto Rican, rifleman
"Doc" Bob Johnston—Australian, corpsman
Earl Jones—Black, machine gunner
Jerry Lackey—White, rifleman (Smith's replacement)
Sergeant Alberto Rivera—Puerto Rican, squad leader after Everett

Sergeant Steve Rogers—White, squad leader (when I first arrived)
Corporal John Everett—Black, squad leader (Rogers's replacement)
John Ciminski—White, rifleman/radioman (hit in leg night of Tết)
"Doc" Robert Bradley—White, corpsman (when I first arrived)
Gary Smith—White, rifleman (killed night of Tết)
Frank Thomas—White, rifleman
Paul Speck—White, rifleman
Barry Goodson—White, assistant squad leader

*Vietnamese:*
Taan—My counterpart in charge of PF (Popular Forces) squads
Naum Tôu—Taan's protégé
Mamasan Tôu—Vietnamese friend and informer (no relation to Naum Tou)
Lín Tôu—Mamasan Tôu's daughter
Sergeant Shôu—Sergeant in charge of Chu Lai Company PFs
Ton—"Kit Carson" scout

---

1   Barry Goodson served a thirteen-month tour of duty, including the time he spent in the hospital. This was the standard length of service in Vietnam for soldiers, about thirty percent of whom were involved in combat. The one-year tour of duty and the practice of individual replacement had a significant impact on fighting the war. For example, U.S. combat soldiers tended to reach peak fighting efficiency after six to eight months in Vietnam and were transferred out after acquiring valuable combat experience. Their replacements, of course, went through the same indoctrination period. In addition, some soldiers experienced "short-timer's syndrome." They became anxious and timid as they approached the end of their 365-day tour and were often considered a liability by other soldiers. Ronald H. Spector, *After Tet: The Bloodiest Year in Vietnam* (New York: Free Press, 1993), 46–67.

2   I was able to listen to a couple of tapes that I had sent home while I was in Vietnam, but they contained no actual names or places, so they were of little help. The letters I sent home to my parents and other family members no longer exist, so I could not rely upon those. I was too busy while serving in the CAP unit, unfortunately, to keep a journal. The official correspondence I've received from the Marine Corps has so far yielded no other names.

3   The Combined Action Program or CAP was organized by the U.S. Marine Corps in August 1965. At that time and up until 1968, General William C. Westmoreland, commander of the Military Assistance Command, Vietnam (MACV) pursued a strategy of attrition, actively searching out the enemy and attempting to destroy him. Despite Westmoreland's later denial, MACV took a negative position toward the CAP program, one of the most innovative approaches to pacification. From experience in

other civil wars in Haiti, Nicaragua, and the Dominican Republic, the Marine Corps believed that firepower alone would not subdue the enemy and that the people had to be won over. The Combined Action Platoon consisted of a Marine rifle squad and a Navy medical corpsman (all volunteers) and a locally recruited platoon of Popular Forces (PF). The Marines and the PF forces lived among the villagers for an indefinite period and were responsible for village security. Unlike other forces in Vietnam, the CAP forces did not arrive by helicopter in the morning and leave at night. They became part of village life and aided the local residents in many ways. The Marines became familiar with the local terrain, could bring in heavy firepower when necessary, instilled discipline and confidence in the PF forces, and won the loyalty of many Vietnamese villagers. They also protected the local area from indiscriminate heavy bombardment. The Marines often provided medical assistance to the villagers and helped out in various community projects. By 1968, there were 79 CAPs operating in I Corps Tactical Zone (I CTZ). Marine casualties were substantially below that of regular infantry units. Despite the demonstrated success of the program, General Westmoreland refused to adopt the CAP program. Spector, *After Tet*, 189–96; Guenter Lewy, *America in Vietnam* (New York: Oxford, 1978), 116–18; Neil Sheehan, *A Bright and Shining Lie: John Paul Vann and America in Vietnam* (New York: Random House, 1988), 634–37; William C. Westmoreland, *A Soldier Reports* (Garden City, New York: Doubleday, 1976), 166. Francis J. West, Jr., provides an excellent account of a Combined Action Platoon in the village of Bình Nghĩa, Quảng Ngãi province in *The Village* (New York: Harper & Row, 1972). See also Francis J. West, Jr., "The Fast Rifles: A Strategy for Grassroots Pacification in Vietnam," *Public and International Affairs* 5:1 (1967), 99–109 and Francis J. West, Jr., *Small Unit Actions in Vietnam, Summer 1966* (Washington DC: Government Printing Office, 1967).

[4] Popular Forces (PFs) were South Vietnamese men recruited and trained to fight the Viet Cong and North Vietnamese in the villages in which the PF lived. Regional Forces (RFs) were similarly recruited and responsible for a larger area. Americans usually lumped the two together and referred to them as Ruff-Puffs.

[5] Grunt was the most frequent nickname given to infantry troops in the U.S. Army and Marine Corps ground forces. On the Marine role in Vietnam, see *A Chronology of the United States Marine Corps, 1775–1969*, 4 vols., (Washington DC: Headquarters U.S. Marine Corps, Historical Division, 1965–1971). Volumes three and four cover the Vietnam years.

[6] A firebase is a temporary artillery firing position often secured by infantry.

[7] Fat City I believe must have been in the area of Diêm Phô. (See map on page 22.)

# Acknowledgments

First and foremost, I wish to thank my wife Cindy for her undying devotion to helping me see this book to its completion. Without her support its writing would still be only a dream.

In addition, I wish to thank my children, Brad and Haley, for their continual support even when it took time away from them. Their faith in their father renewed my resolve many times.

To Taan, whom I hope is somewhere alive and well, I express my thanks for the many times he saved my life. Maybe someday I will be able to deliver a copy of this book to him.

Last, but not least, I dedicate this book to the memory of a good friend, a comrade in arms, John Ciminski. Had he not been cut down in the prime of his life by a drunk driver, we might have co-written this book. I will miss him always.

I sincerely appreciate the relentless pursuit by Fran Vick and Charlotte Wright to see this book to its completion in spite of the numerous obstacles hindering their progress . . . one of which was me. I appreciate the efforts of Professor John M. Carroll at Lamar University for providing most of the historical and explanatory footnotes.

Thanks to all of you for making a dream come true.

MCRD San Diego Basic Boot Camp graduation. Goodson on top row, fifth from right.

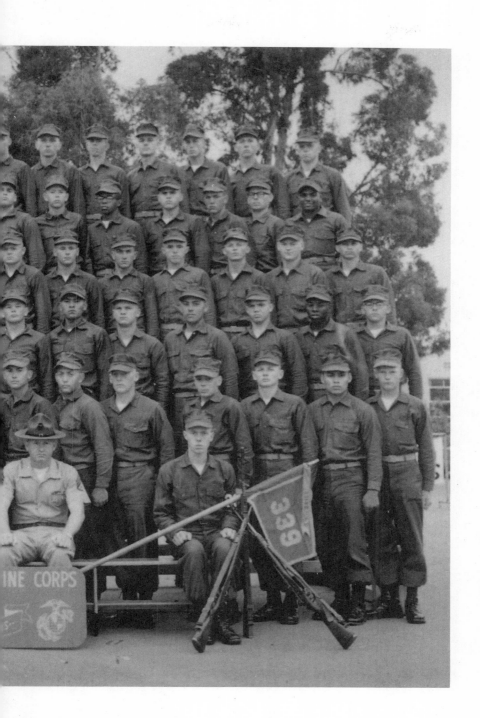

Intensive Infantry Training at Camp Pendleton. Goodson on top row, third from left.

## Chapter 1

# Mead River

**T**he ominous cloud of the reality of "Operation Mead River"[1] was still shadowing me the day I received word that Top Sergeant Bentley wanted me to report to his quarters. As I left my tent and started the short walk to the Top's quarters, the shadow overwhelmed me and I drifted into the endless memory of the first battle of Mead River.

The operation had started during the waning days of the monsoon season, a season with an awesome ability to inflict our already haunted lives with constant miseries. To begin with, there wasn't one inch of dry land left to stand on and you remained constantly drenched, soaked and chilled to the bone. You slept (when you could sleep) with your head lying against a soggy rice paddy dike while your body endured an unending bath in the stagnant, leech-infested waters of the paddy. As if to assure you that misery could be worse, hordes of mosquitoes possessing the bite of horseflies descended upon you like squadrons of fighter planes.

Perhaps some good evolved from the whole scene, however; patience and/or willpower, whichever label you chose to slap on it. In normal situations you would simply get up and leave such situations behind. Therein lies the catch. One quick move, one snap of a twig or slap at a mosquito could bring a bullet to your brain. You had to remain virtually motionless, or become impervious to the sucking of the leeches, the bites of mosquitoes and the itching knowledge that jungle rot was attacking all parts of your body. To live, you had to set aside all these nagging problems.

The Vietnamese claimed that rubbing buffalo dung all over your body would ward off any and all pests. I had my doubts, because I knew the VC also packed buffalo dung into homemade booby traps and laced the tips of pungi stakes with it. This process nearly always led to blood poisoning, gangrene, and death within twenty-four hours. So the idea of purposely rubbing it on my body, even if it did repel mosquitoes, seemed an invitation to suicide.

It was on a dreary, rain-soaked day in November that they heli-lifted my company about fifteen miles southwest of Đà Nẵng, into the depths of a jungle area we had dubbed Death Valley. Appropriately dubbed, too, since we figured there was always a ninety percent guarantee of being dismembered by a booby trap or shot in the back by Viet Cong hiding in "spider traps."[2]

As the Chinook[3] started chopping in between the trees surrounding the paddy we were to leap into, rounds began cracking from all directions, impacting the thin shell of the Chinook with a quick thud and then continuing on a brief ricochet until each bullet found its mark. Casualties were instantaneous. A lump grew in my throat and my gut knotted into a small, yet ominous ball. Death and destruction engulfed me. A guy I hardly knew screamed, clutched his head and fell from the helicopter as it passed about twenty feet over the elephant grass below. He never felt the ground as his lifeless body disappeared in the depths of the razor-sharp grass.

I froze momentarily, watching the dead man fall, wondering if a round had my name on it.

Scared? Hell yes, I was scared. The CO's[4] yell to jump suddenly jolted me back to reality and I found myself leaping from the hovering Chinook. The drop to the ground seemed like eternity as other death-screams bombarded my brain. My body fell heavily against the rice paddy dike, momentarily loosening the grip I had on my M-16.[5] The enormous fear I had of losing my weapon in the depths of the rice paddy forced my hands to develop a white-knuckled grip on the rifle. A sudden burst from an AK-47 in the hands of a VC hiding in a nearby tree line sent me rolling and tumbling into the nearest cover: a rotten, stench-filled log.

A handful of other marines followed me to my temporary haven where we all sat simply staring at each other as we forced our racing minds to regain control and plan our next move. God! Next move! Where?! How?! The gooks were everywhere! Surrounded by death, no one even noticed the leeches as they stretched their way through our clothing searching for a tender spot to start sucking away our blood.

Sounding out quickly, quietly, I located my squad, which was still intact and had incurred no casualties.

"Take that tree line to the north," the CO's voice had bellowed through the radio. Re-mobilized, we struck out toward our assigned objective.

Rapidly spreading out, we advanced "on line," ripping the tree line apart with a continuous, deadly spray of lead and grenades. An occasional LAW (the military's replacement for the bazooka)[6] would burst with a tremendous roar as someone fired at what he thought he saw. The jungle was ungodly thick. The knee-deep water and muck clutched at our legs like a thousand hands trying to slow us down. In all this muck and dense growth we could barely see each other, much less the Cong. How could we possibly "seek and destroy" something we could not see? Automatic fire hit us like a tidal wave from the tree line on our right. We turned instantly and retaliated with answering fire.

Suddenly, one marine panicked with a spray of lead in all directions. His initial burst caught the First Sergeant in the back, sending him sprawling face forward into the waters of the rice paddy, never to move again. The panic-stricken man vomited all over himself and fell into a dead faint.

The gravity of the situation momentarily stopped our assault, allowing the VC an opportunity to increase their attack with hellish intensity. Men started dropping like flies as the lead and shrapnel tossed their bodies in various grotesque positions. Everywhere men were groping in pain trying desperately to find shelter, while others were simply begging God to let them live.

As suddenly as our assault had begun, it ended. Men not mortally wounded or in total shock were running in all directions in a last-ditch effort to gain cover before another barrage of bullets and shrapnel ripped them apart.

A man beside me screamed, dropped his rifle and grabbed his left arm, staring at a gaping hole that had once been his elbow. Quickly, I shoved him to cover. The corpsman had his hands full elsewhere, so I removed two bandages from the pouch on my belt. Using the first as packing, I wrapped the second around it and tied it tight. The bleeding would not stop. Using my last bandage I fashioned a tourniquet above the wound.

"Aieee . . . ," he screamed in pain.

I had nothing to offer the tortured man. Only the corpsman was allowed to carry medicine.

"Sorry, man. I'm sure it hurts like hell," I said as I finished patching the wound. "Let's pack you up." The bleeding had slowed but refused to be stopped. The wounded man groaned through clenched teeth as I hoisted him to a fireman's carry.

Momentarily staggering under the load, I searched the skies for the medevacs[7] and saw them descending behind some trees on the opposite side of the paddies. The journey across was a good hundred yards with no cover—that is, unless you were a leech.

What rotten luck. To attempt a crossing unencumbered would have been dangerous, but a trek carrying a wounded man was suicide. Then again, so was simply standing there with a wounded man on my back. Besides, with half his arm blown away he might bleed to death if I decided to wait until the battle subsided to a safe level. Tightening my cinch and my nerve, I leapt from cover and began a staggering, labored weave pattern across the rice paddy, with the wounded man draped across my shoulder.

"Who is this man?" I thought. I didn't even know him. "Surely I recognize him." I studied his face. No, not even an inkling of his name. Not that it made any difference, I just felt that I should know his name.

The knee-deep, fetid water and muck gripped my legs, slowing my progress to a seemingly hopeless effort as the opposite side loomed far into the distance. The hundred yards seemed more like a mile. A burst of fire from my left sent water spraying all around me. Suddenly, I felt or actually heard a "thud" which catapulted us both behind the safety of the tree line covering the rice paddy dike. I set the wounded man against the dike for a moment to see if I could locate our attackers. He groaned with pain. I studied the area we had just crossed. Nothing. No movement, gunfire, nothing. Momentarily we were safe. I turned and checked the wounded man over and was shocked to discover he had been hit again through the same arm, the bullet lodging in his gut. We were both soaked in his blood.

Ignoring the arm, I applied a pressure bandage from his own pouch to the torso wound and helped him slowly to his feet. We had another hundred yards to go to reach the choppers and a fireman's carry was out of the question due to the chance of aggravating the gut wound. With his body leaning heavily against mine, we woodenly approached the medevac area, keeping a strained eye on every bush, tree, and blade of grass. I wasn't sure how I would or could react if we were attacked again, but I had resolved not to let the Viet Cong kill the man after getting him that far. The battle behind us still raged with full fury.

We stumbled into the medevac area, which was strewn with dead and dying men. I tried to settle him on the soggy ground as gently as possible but he gasped heavily despite my efforts. Chopper wash hammered us as the Hueys lifted off with their wounded.

"I need a cigarette," he moaned.

"No way," I answered. "Cigarettes are out with gut wounds."

He smiled a weak, pleading smile. "Aw, come on. It's probably my last one anyway," he said.

I studied his face and searched my soul for a plausible argument, a reason why he should not have a cigarette. He was right. Normally, gut wounds were a promise of death. I could not argue with him.

"Where are your cigarettes?" I asked, my eyes searching for a tell-tale bulge that would reveal the hidden pack.

"In . . . in my left chest pocket," he stammered as the pain stabbed through his body.

I slowly pulled out the cigarettes, making sure I didn't cause him any more pain. Removing one from the pack, I reluctantly gave in and lit the *first* cigarette of my life, possibly *his* last, and handed it to him with a prayer. "God, I hope he makes it," I thought.

I gently shook his uninjured hand and promised to kill the VC that had nailed him. Some promise, when you could not even *see* the enemy, much less destroy him. Gathering my weapons and my nerve, I started my trek back to the waiting, gut-wrenching hell of the fire fight.

The CO, Captain Roll from Alpha Company, was hovering behind a protected knoll a safe hundred yards from the battle, surrounded by a squad of lucky marines. He yelled me over. "What's going on out there, Goodson?" he yelled.

"What's going on?!" I screamed. "We're being destroyed! What the hell does it look like?" I waved my arm back towards the battle scene and the uncountable bodies of dead and dying marines.

Luckily, Captain Roll ignored my snide comment, or maybe he realized my present mental state was borderline psychotic. Anyway, he calmly asked, "What do you suggest?"

My mind raced with recollections of the battle I had just left. I tried to remember if I had even an inkling of our enemy's position.

"All I can say is that the gooks are hiding somewhere in this tree line." I pointed to a position on the map that lay before him. "I think you should pull us back and call in every piece of artillery, Cobras,[8] jets or tanks that you can. There are not enough men left in my platoon to even hope to oust those gooks!" With that comment, I turned on my heel and went to rejoin my diminished troops, leaving him with the decision that meant life or death to us all.

I wished that I had been a seasoned veteran with the right answer for the CO. Unfortunately I was not. I had been in a number of firefights, but none of them lasted more than a few minutes. I had previously seen wounded and dead men, but never so many. This battle had lasted hours. My fellow marines lay scattered before me. The veterans, the old-timers I had depended upon, were among the dead and wounded, so now my survival— and that of others—depended solely on my own expertise. We were unable to pinpoint the enemy's exact location. All we knew was that they were somewhere in that tree line. I felt ashamed that I could not give the CO more information than that, but I was also upset that we had been thrust into such a hopeless situation.

As I reached the dike where the man I carried had been hit a second time, I cautiously peered through the trees to see if there was any sign of the enemy. The rattling gunfire sounded like a string of firecrackers inter-rupted by an occasional boom from grenades.

I studied the expanse of terrain, looking for a safe way across. The smell of death hit me like a whip, making my hands sweat profusely and fear settle somewhere in a small corner of my brain. I simply couldn't take my eyes off the countless bodies. No, not just "bodies," but *dead marines* lying in the stench of the rice paddy.

I don't know how long I squatted there in an uncontrollable stupor. Seconds, minutes, an eternity. A hand on my shoulder jolted me back to reality. It was Danny, leader of the Third Squad, returning from dropping off another wounded soldier. It could just as easily have been a gook sneak-ing up on me. I had to gain control over my mind before I joined the list of dead marines.

"Hey, you're gonna grow roots if you don't move from that spot," he whispered.

A feeling of guilt crept into my mind and I hoped he hadn't noticed the trembling racing through my body during the momentary stupor. I feared the label of a coward much more than I feared the dangers of the rice paddy. Danny threw a cautious glance in the direction we had to go. I anticipated his thoughts.

"Danny, let's set up a zigzag pattern from different approaches. That may create some confusion," I suggested. "You set up about twenty-five yards over there." I pointed toward a nearby clump of bamboo growth just south of our position. "I'll go first," I whispered. "You follow about five seconds later." He sauntered off toward the bamboo clump. "Good luck," I thought, as I watched him disappear behind the slender arms of bamboo.

Once he was settled, I bit my lip, leaped over the dike and started a zigzagging pattern across the paddy. Smoke from gunpowder and explosives hovered over the water, giving it the foreboding look of an old foggy swamp in a horror movie. The only problem was that this fog was laced with real bodies—real death.

As the muck sucked at my legs the corner of my eye caught a glimpse of Danny following off to my left. It was working! They couldn't sight in on both of us or couldn't decide who to concentrate on. With luck we'd both make it. I felt sick from the slow-motion feeling of the muck sucking at my feet, the bullets spraying water in my face, the fear gripping my body.

"Surely I'm a sitting duck," I thought, and wondered if each step would be my last. But God was with me. As I neared the opposite side a few of the marines lying in the paddy started waving wildly at me. "What the hell?" I thought.

All at once I knew why they had been waving. The muck of the rice paddy had given way to a mound of earth that I assumed to be part of the dike. As I ran up, the gently sloping mound abruptly opened into a large water-filled crater created by a bombing run sometime in the past. It was too late to stop. My body flew into the air towards the pool of water, then belly-flopped into the manmade pond.

Suddenly the noises of battle subsided to a mute rumble as the weight of my gear pulled me to the bottom of the crater. Strangely, for a moment I felt peaceful rather than panicky, overwhelmed with the silent tranquillity. Then a burning desire for air hit me at the same time I realized that any explosion under this water would rupture my eardrums. Pulling my way through the vegetation, I finally reached the surface and gasped for air.

"Boom! Rat-a-tat-tat!" The sounds of war rushed back as my head cleared the surface. I had spent only a few seconds in my underwater refuge. I settled behind a mound of earth formed by the forces of some previous bombardment and systematically disassembled and cleaned my weapon the best I could.

Harry Goad, one of my fellow machine gunners, scuffled over to me. "We tried to warn you, man. You okay?"

"Yeah, fine," I assured him. "How are things back here?"

"They suck, man. They've had us pinned down behind this mound since you left. Tell me where to set up this 'pig,'" he said, pointing to his M-60, "and I'll give 'em hell. So far we just can't locate the bastards."

"Sorry. I'm no help," I said. "I didn't see a thing during the trip there and back. I told the CO he needed to call in the Phantoms or something."

We were getting low on ammo and it would soon be dark. A bullet slammed against a rock above our heads and ricocheted into the crater. Just then the radio in the hands of the man nearest us crackled. We saw him turn and say something to Staff Sergeant Bledsoe, who came running over to us.

"We're moving back," he said. "The CO's calling in the artillery and the Phantoms."

"Thank God," I thought. I looked around, searching for Danny. "Hey, Larry, have you seen Danny?" I asked the marine closest to me.

"Yeah, man," he answered, "he's back in that tree line behind you." I sighed with relief that we had both made it unharmed.

"We'll have to pick up the dead tomorrow morning," Bledsoe continued.

"We can't leave them here!" someone behind me argued. "They'll be mutilated."

"We have no choice!" Bledsoe screamed. "Now, move out!"

He was right, of course. The rice paddy was literally covered with bodies. There were only a handful of us left as we started our retreat. God! Retreat, like dogs with tucked tails while our slain buddies lay in silence waiting for the inevitable.

That night I recalled the sermon or prayer that one of our men had given for us before we entered the battle. A very devout minister, he had pleaded with us to refrain from killing.

*"Thou shalt not kill," he quoted. "God will make the bullets miss you," he said. "Have faith."*

*Little did he know that was one bit of scripture that constantly plagued my mind. I knew we weren't supposed to kill; we all knew that. But we only had two choices as I saw it—kill or be killed. I looked around at my fellow marines, some outwardly mocking the minister and God, others simply standing there, frozen expressionless faces dutifully listening to the man. A few others secretly wiped away a tear that somehow fought its way to the surface.*

*When the sermon was over, I made my way over to the pastor. "There's one part I simply don't understand, sir," I stated.*

*"What part is that, Lance Corporal?" he asked.*

*"Thou shalt not kill!" I half yelled, emotion swelling up inside of me.*

*He looked me over for a minute as he searched his brain for what he thought was the right answer. "That's God's law, Lance Corporal. There are no exceptions."*

*I couldn't accept that. I refused to be condemned to hell for fighting for my country. It was my turn for brain searching. "Well, sir," I began, making every effort to control the emotion bursting inside of me, "I've never been a big Bible reader, but I've got to believe that somewhere in that book of yours, God must say that if I go my fifty percent, He'll go His." I paused for a minute, then committed my soul to hell. "Sorry, Preach," I snapped, "I'm pulling that trigger." I turned and walked away, disappearing into the darkness, hoping against hope that I had indeed made the right decision.*

*The next day "Preach" was the first man to die.*

Once back with the main unit, Captain Roll reassigned those of us who were unharmed to new squads. Harry Goad and I were re-assigned to Second Platoon. Along with a few others, I took the first watch, since sleep was out of the question anyway. The night was dark and still. Not even a leaf stirred. For some reason, even the mosquitoes were quiet. The only sound was an occasional sigh from one of my fellow marines, no doubt rehashing the day's battle through his mind. It was around midnight. The silence was deafening.

A twig snapped. Silence. Then shuffling footsteps.

The others heard it, too. Footsteps echoed in the dark as an unseen enemy attempted to sneak past our right flank. I readied a grenade, pulled the pin, and let the handle fly into the darkness, the noise alerting everyone to my intent. They waited. I counted the seconds—one, two, three, four— I let it fly in the direction of our intruder. The grenade's flash illuminated the VC as they tried to sneak through our positions. Immediately, flashes, cracks and booms broke the silence of the night as death's arms reached for our enemy.

I picked out one man, squeezed the trigger repeatedly and watched every tracer round pass through his body. He kept running! "My God!" I thought. "What are we up against?" It was the first evidence of what I had heard from other soldiers was common practice among the VC: before every battle they would "dope up" to make themselves impervious to pain. That, coupled with their belief that they would be reincarnated, made them an awesome enemy that would fight until the last bit of drugged-up blood drained from their mutilated bodies.

"Come in, Goodson." Top Sergeant Bentley's voice brought me back. Unbelievable. A complete battle had passed through my thoughts during the short distance to his quarters. I shook my head to clear my thoughts.

"Reporting as ordered, sir," I stated.

"At ease, Goodson. Your orders are in."

"Orders, sir?"

"Yep. It looks like you've just joined the CAP marines," he said.

"CAP? I forgot all about my request, sir."

"Well, pack your gear," he answered. "You're in it now."

"In what?" I wondered. My mind briefly scanned the months before when a fellow marine, Marcelo Gomez, and I first heard about the CAPs.

"Instead of just killing the enemy," the recruiter had said, "you'll have a chance to work with the local people and help take care of them. You'll be a real part of their lives."

We signed up immediately, without question and without going through proper military channels. Our sergeant jumped us severely over that one. Afterward I forgot the whole idea until Marcelo had shipped out to CAP Command about two weeks before.

"You're scheduled to leave at 1400 hours," the sergeant stated, bringing me back to the present once again. "Oh, and leave your weapons with the armory. You'll receive new issue from the CAPs."

"Yes, sir," I answered, turning to leave. I stopped momentarily as the realization of his last statement sank in. "Turn in my weapons?" I thought. "Surely not!" The look on his face assured me that he was not kidding. I gathered up my gear, shook hands with my fellow gunners and headed for the armory.

"Whatcha want?" A burly looking sergeant stood behind the dark green counter in the armory. Behind him stood row after row of M-16s, M-60s and a multitude of other weapons.

"I'm shipping out to another unit, so I'm turning in some old friends." I laid my M-16, and my .45[9] on the counter. My M-60 stayed with First Squad guns.

The sarge simply stood there looking at me. "Need that knife too, boy," he ordered.

". . . but."

"No buts. All weapons must be turned in."

Reluctantly I loosened the scabbard and laid the knife alongside the other weapons that had been my friends for so long. With a sigh, I picked up my sea bag, turned and left them behind. An empty feeling settled over me.

A jeep was waiting outside. "Goodson?" the driver asked.

"Yes," I answered. He nodded for me to climb in. I tossed my sea bag into the back, grabbed the side of the jeep and plopped into the seat beside the driver. Without a word, he jammed the shifter into gear. The tires spun up a cloud of dust as the jeep responded with a jolt. It sped past the front gate, leaving the rows of concertina wire and Hill 10 behind.

I cast a look back as my home in the jungle disappeared in the dust. "What now?" I wondered. It was a warm, humid, 110-degree day as I sat in the jeep—weaponless—rolling toward a new unknown, the CAP marines.

The driver said nothing. He only peered ahead into the depths of the jungle, a massive green of towering Palms engulfed by an Army of undergrowth that was interrupted only occasionally by a rice paddy or the narrow brown ribbon of earth we called a road.

---

[1] On Operation Mead River, see Ronald H. Spector, *After Tet: The Bloodiest Year in Vietnam* (New York: Free Press, 1993), 306–10.

[2] A "spider trap" is a small, well-camouflaged hole that can be used by a soldier to conceal himself from the enemy. It is called this because of a species of spider that does the same thing.

[3] A Chinook is a CH-47 transport helicopter.

[4] CO refers to commanding officer. The M-60 was the standard U.S. 7.62-mm machine gun. The AK-47 was the Russian-made, and later Chinese-made, standard assault rifle of the North Vietnamese Army (properly the People's Army of Vietnam). It was also used by the Viet Cong. The terms VC, Cong, or Victor Charley (Charlie)

were used by U.S. soldiers in reference to the Viet Cong. These South Vietnamese Communist soldiers were members of the People's Liberation Armed Force which was formed in 1961. Ngo Dinh Diem, South Vietnam's first president, coined the term Viet Cong, a contraction of the phrase, "Viet-nam Cong-san," meaning "Vietnamese who are Communists." See George Donelson Moss, *Vietnam: An American Ordeal*, 2nd ed., (Englewood Cliffs, New Jersey: Prentice Hall, 1994), 98.

[5] The M-16 was the standard U.S. rifle in Vietnam beginning in early 1967.

[6] The LAW or LAAW was a U.S. Light Antitank Assault Weapon. A one-shot, throw away weapon, it was used mostly in Vietnam against bunkers.

[7] Medevac refers to medical evacuation. In Vietnam, often, but not always, it was done by helicopter.

[8] The Cobra was a Bell AH-1G fast attack helicopter, armed with machine guns, grenade launchers, and rockets. Gooks was a derogatory term, brought to Vietnam by Korean War veterans, for anyone of Asian descent.

[9] The .45 was the U.S. standard automatic pistol in Vietnam.

## Chapter 2

# CAP

The monsoons were over and the 100-degree plus temperature, coupled with the suffocating humidity, returned with the same intense fury it had when it left. In silent protest the jungle vegetation drooped and seemed to sweat. Nothing moved, no animals or insects, short of the biting flies and mosquitoes. Those little pests seemed impervious to everything.

The jeep we were in looked like a relic from the Korean War, complete with bullet and shrapnel holes, and a driver so doped out that he continually swayed into bushes, chug holes or anything else he could find to hit.

The driver held his silence no longer and began raving about some "broad" he had banged while on R and R[1] in Saigon. I didn't really care for his rambling but it somewhat subdued my nervous feeling. I was afraid, not of the surrounding jungle but of the unknown ahead of me. The bums had taken away all my weapons and now here I was with a drugged-out idiot rambling along a jungle road as if the war was millions of miles away. For crying out loud, I thought, don't those fools know there are gooks out there, snipers, sappers[2] or even some kids with a satchel charge.[3] They wouldn't even let me keep my knife. Damn good knife, too. So sharp it could slice you open if you just stared at it too hard.

I sat like a coiled spring in the jeep and studied the passing jungle with the intensity of a cat hypnotizing its prey. If anything moved, I was at least not going to be caught chewing my cud.

"What the hell? Watch where you're going!" I screamed. The bastard almost drove us off into a rice paddy. I wasn't too excited about flipping over into that stench. Besides, it was a long walk to Đà Nẵng, and to be honest, being lunch for a bunch of leeches didn't turn me on either. The driver mumbled something about loose steering and jerked the jeep back onto the road. Amazingly, we rumbled into Đà Nẵng just around sunset without encountering a single VC. "Life has its little pleasures, doesn't it?" I said to myself.

I didn't report the driver, although I probably should have. Guys like him always end up getting somebody else killed. The joy of reaching the "rear" safe and sound, along with my extreme curiosity of what I had gotten myself into, overwhelmed my desire to have the doper caged up.

"Lance Corporal Goodson?" It was obviously the man who had been sent to lead me to my new home.

"Yes sir, Sergeant. Here and ready to find out what I've gotten myself into."

He laughed. "You'll find out soon enough. Grab your gear and follow me. You're the last one in and just in time for the orientation session. By the way, what's your MOS?"

MOS was an abbreviation of a long-winded title for a Marine's specialized training. "Got a couple of them," I answered. "My primary MOS is 0331." Every marine was an 0311, a rifleman, right out of boot camp. ITR, Intensive Infantry Training, and all future training added to your list of MOSs.

"Good," he beamed. "We need more machine gunners. It's hard to keep enough on hand."

"Thanks for the encouragement," I said. "Are things that rough?"

"Have been here lately," he answered. "We lost two complete squads this month."

"Two squads?" I repeated. "Wiped out?"

He nodded.

"Why don't we just forget the whole thing and cut my orders for Cowtown, USA?" I said in a feeble attempt to quell the sick feeling rising in my gut.

He smiled knowingly. "Cowtown, USA? Where's that?"

"Why, that's Fort Worth, Texas!"

"Thought you sounded kind of funny," he chuckled.

We were approaching a small building well lit inside and out. A sign was posted on the door. COMBINED ACTION PROGRAM ORIENTA-

TION SESSION was painted on it in bold red. "So that's what CAP stands for," I said to no one in particular. Of course, that didn't tell me any more than the abbreviation did. Total squads wiped out! Machine gunners on the hit list. "Oh, God, what am I in for?" I wondered.

"What was your other MOS?" he asked.

"What?" I jumped, wondering if he could read minds. "Oh, uh it's . . . explosive/ordnance."

"Didn't mean to startle you," he mused.

"Thought you read my mind."

"Let's go on in," he said. "They're waiting on us."

The inside of the building boasted the typical Marine Corps decor, good old basic green, with steel folding chairs and rough wooden tables. But it wasn't the decor of the room that caught my attention. It was the tables—or what was on them. They were all lined up in a neat row at the front of the room. Each table had numerous odd-looking items sitting on it.

The table on the far left contained items I was well acquainted with, various kinds of booby traps. There were bamboo pungi sticks tipped with that lethal poison more commonly known as buffalo dung. There were assorted types of the "Malayan gate"—a simple framework of bamboo that had a multitude of pungi sticks tied to it with strips of hemp or wire—also tipped in the appropriate manner. The gate was either spring loaded by fastening it to a larger, flexible bamboo pole or tree, or it was weighted down in some fashion and hoisted into a hidden position in the vegetation above. When the trip wire was released the gate would spring up or drop from above to impale its unsuspecting prey. The victim had barely a second to realize his mistake and react. Death rarely was instantaneous. Instead, it was purposely slow and painful. The remaining traps were types I had heard of and seen the effects of, but had never seen intact, such as "Bouncing Betties," mines that sprang into the air about face high before exploding; trip-wired bombs and glass jars packed with explosives, rocks, glass, barbed wire and other items. In some cases the homemade explosives were packed with buffalo dung so that when the device exploded every little piece carried some of the dung. When it entered the body, it guaranteed blood poisoning, gangrene and a painful death.

The second table contained an assortment of glass jars containing a variety of menacing looking insects; spiders; snakes—from the small but deadly "Two-step" Bamboo Viper to the awesome giant King Cobra; foot-long centipedes; scorpions the size of crawfish and many others equally ugly. The third table contained an assortment of camouflage gear and makeup. Table four contained a massive group of weaponry: knives, gre-nades, rifles, shotguns, machine guns, pistols and a multitude of home-made devices. I wasn't sure what each could do but my imagination conjured up all sorts of gruesome pictures that I hoped never to experience. The last table contained a scale model of Vietnam.

To the rear of the tables stood a podium, behind which stood a full-blown general. "Well, I'll be," I said to myself. I couldn't believe there were actually generals in our war. I hadn't seen one up to this point. Regardless, there he stood as fully decorated and as brazen as Patton.[4] Alongside this general stood another. "Not two in one night," I thought, "and one is Viet-namese!" He was dressed in the typical South Vietnamese pale green uni-form but was as decorated and brazen as the American general.

"Welcome, Sergeant McGuire, Corporal Goodson," the American gen-eral stated. "Please be seated and we will begin the orientation."

I followed the sergeant to the left side of the room, which was filled with about twenty other marines already seated and awaiting the general's speech. I assumed they had come from units stationed all over Vietnam, since a prerequisite to joining CAPs was at least three months of combat in-country. As we took our seats in those hard metal chairs it suddenly struck me that the general had referred to me as "Corporal Goodson."

"His eyesight must be bad," I thought. "I'm only a lance corporal."

Sergeant McGuire was reading my mind again. "Congratulations," he said as he passed the packet of double stripes and crossed rifles to me. "I almost forgot to tell you. Your CO with Alpha Company passed on a rec-ommendation for a combat promotion for you."

"You're kidding!" was all I could say. All of a sudden, I was a noncom-missioned officer. The elation I felt was tremendous.

The General noticed my moment of elation, smiled and began the open-ing speech for the orientation.

"Gentlemen, you have joined the most unappreciated, yet most elite fighting force in Vietnam. We are known as CAP Marines and boast a quiet reputation that, within our own thinking, more than equals that of the Green Beret."[5]

"Oh, my God," I thought. "I've joined a Special Forces unit."

The General continued. "The other armed forces, even some of the marine units, are virtually unaware of our existence, partially due to size but mainly due to our efforts to maintain a low profile. We operate in a manner that differs drastically from any other unit you have ever seen or heard of. We are the 'silent warriors' of the bush. Our duties as CAP Marines are two-fold, or actually multi-fold.

"First of all, we are . . . well, a police force, if you will. By that I mean you and your team of seven or eight men will be responsible for training all of the local militia in each village in your area, as well as assisting your Vietnamese counterparts in seek-and-destroy missions[6] that will rid the area of the Viet Cong."

"There's that seek-and-destroy bullshit again," I thought. "Searching for something we couldn't even see . . . Mead River all over again." I shivered as flashes of the battle filtered through my mind.

The General continued. "I'm sure each of you has had your share of seeking and destroying . . ."

"Great, another mind reader," I thought.

" . . . and the thought of it doesn't exactly make you happy. However, we are going to provide you with sufficient training over the next couple of weeks that will make its gruesome burden somewhat easier and hopefully somewhat less deadly. In addition to being warriors of the bush, you will shoulder the responsibility of living with your Vietnamese counterparts and helping them improve their lives and the lives of all the villagers in whatever small way you can think of. The improvements must be small so that you can be assured that the gesture is understood and accepted. To shower the Vietnamese with lavish gifts, weapons or any other paraphernalia will only intimidate and alienate them. We will teach you how to approach this situation with the same amount of diligence and concern as the destruction of the Viet Cong. We want to help these people in whatever small, direct manner that we can. Nothing dramatic. Just simple gestures that will assure them that we are totally on their side." He stopped, allowing his statements to sink in.

I could not believe my ears. An American general standing there telling us that his main goal was to simply help the Vietnamese people, not to kill them! Boy, that blew the lid off everything I'd seen, heard or done before. Yes, I was a part of the action that destroyed villages, rampaged throughout rice paddies, burned huts and performed hundreds of other

wantonly destructive deeds. I wasn't proud of it either, but in the marines
. . . yours is not to reason why. The next few days, as well as the remainder
of my stretch in 'Nam, would reinforce my realization of how terribly I had
wronged the Vietnamese people in my previous service.

The General ended his speech by introducing his Vietnamese counterpart, General Na Pinh Ton. I wasn't sure I heard his name right, but I
didn't worry. Experience had proven I would not see him again anyway. His
contribution was to conduct a comprehensive, short course on Vietnamese
history, social mores, and other basic information about the people we would
be helping.

"It's about time," I thought. "Up until now we only thought of the
people as simple idiots, or animals we could slaughter without a second
thought."

"Your training," said General Na Pinh Ton, "commences at 0400 in
the morning. In fact, your schedule will be intense from 0400 until 2100
hours every day for the next two weeks. Good luck, gentlemen. Until that
time," he looked around the room, "you are dismissed." As we filed out of
the room I glanced around to see if Marcelo was among us. He was nowhere
to be seen. He obviously had already completed his training and shipped
out to his CAP assignment.

The training was brief, but thorough. Banging of trash can lids announced the arrival of 0400, as Sergeant McGuire sauntered through our
hut letting us know how lazy and ungrateful we were, sleeping to such an
ungodly hour. He was right. It was an ungodly hour, but we were all fairly
used to lack of sleep anyway.

The first week we concentrated on learning about Vietnamese culture—
the social mores, religious beliefs, basic entertainment, family organization
and general information about attitudes and mannerisms. We also studied
the language intensely, or at least I did. I was beginning to feel a strong
devotion towards helping these people, and I knew that to help, I had to
communicate.

The Vietnamese people had interesting attitudes. In fact, some were
hard for me to accept without being judgmental. For instance, people from
one village would steal from the people of another village, or from strangers. If fact, you were socially judged by how well you carried out your
thievery. Another attitude, one I could more readily understand, was that
the Vietnamese would accept you, as well as your efforts, only if you showed

them that you could do everything they could do at least as well, if not better than they could do it. You were viewed with disgust if you failed to measure up.

The first week, with all its intensity, fell far shy of the rigorous training we endured throughout our second and final week. It concentrated on hand-to-hand combat, special weaponry, explosives, guerrilla strategy and most of all . . . survival techniques. All of the paraphernalia I had seen sitting on the tables became basic everyday knowledge to me. No longer did I wonder about the specific use for each weapon. No longer did I marvel over the assorted variety of snakes and insects. The intense training had embedded their reality into my brain forever.

Training complete, CAP Command decided to give us a treat. A USO show was traveling through our area so they set aside our last night to allow us a little time of celebration and frivolity.

I was excited! Girls were going to be there . . . "good old American round eyes," as we called them. I showered and scrubbed until my body screamed in protest, slapped on some aftershave I borrowed from one of the instructors, donned my gear and headed off in search of the USO show and *the girls*. For some reason, though, I felt very uneasy.

As I arrived, the show was already underway. There they were, three girls in the shortest skirts I had ever seen, dancing and singing "We Gotta Get Outta This Place" as loud as they could. Each swayed and throbbed in her own sensuous way.

Suddenly, tears were forcing their way to the corners of my eyes. I fought them back, yet they returned. At first, I didn't know why. Then the realization struck. All a soldier dreams about—longs for—are things, places, people and women from home. The girls on that stage were, unknowingly, teasing us with all that we longed for, but could not have. Not so much for sex, although that was a part of it, but for just a moment to share with an American girl. Someone from home, from the "real world." Besides, the reality of the war was too fresh in my mind and somehow the idea of our women in such a foul place was a combination I simply could not handle. Our girls did not belong in Vietnam . . . not in this hell!

The pain was too much. I walked away, back to the barracks to get shed of the pain. I couldn't allow my mind the freedom of the moment. Back in the barracks, I readied my gear for the early morning departure to Chu Lai,[7] my new home.

Everything packed, I hunted up a pencil and settled down to write my parents another letter. I didn't write that often. Somehow I could never bring myself to talk about what was actually going on in my part of the war. "Dear Mom and Dad," I began. "You'll never guess what has happened during the past two weeks."

A short while later, I set the pencil down, folded the finished letter and set it aside for mailing in the morning. I laid in my rack studying the ceiling for some clues about what my new home, Chu Lai, would bring.

Sleep overtook my weary mind as I drifted into dreams I wanted no part of. I tossed and fought throughout the night, my last night to spend in a bed of any kind for a very long time.

---

1   R and R meant "rest and recuperation." In Vietnam, it was the only escape from the war afforded the troops. It usually lasted five days.

2   Sappers were enemy engineer troops who were trained and equipped to assail a fortification.

3   A satchel charge is a quantity of explosive in a bag or satchel, which, along with its detonating device, is placed or thrown against a fortification in order to destroy it.

4   Patton refers to General George S. Patton, Jr., who led the U.S. Third Army in Europe during World War II.

5   The Green Berets were the U.S. Army Special Forces. They were trained in counterinsurgency warfare at Fort Bragg, North Carolina. The origin of the Special Forces dated back to World War II. After taking office in 1961, President John F. Kennedy became a champion of these counterinsurgency forces and overruled Army generals in allowing them to wear the distinctive green beret headgear. Kennedy first employed the Green Berets in Vietnam in May 1961. They later became early heroes of the American intervention in Vietnam partially as a result of a popular song and film about their exploits. The Green Berets' mission in Vietnam was similar to that later carried out by the CAP Marines. Andrew F. Krepinevich, *The Army in Vietnam* (Baltimore: Johns Hopkins, 1986), 100–12; A.C. Weed, II, "Army Special Forces and Vietnam," *Military Review* 49 (August 1969), 63–68; Christopher S. Wren, "The Facts Behind the Green Beret Myth," *Look* 30 (November 1, 1966), 28–36.

6   Seek-and-destroy missions refer to the "search and destroy" strategy associated with the U.S. commander in Vietnam, General William C. Westmoreland (1965–1968). The strategy essentially called for a war of attrition against the Viet Cong and North Vietnamese regulars. In retrospect, this approach to the war has been criticized because of the general devastation it brought to South Vietnam and the failure to locate and kill enough of the enemy to make it effective. See George C. Herring, *America's Longest War: The United States and Vietnam, 1950–1975* 2nd ed. (New York: Alfred A. Knopf, 1986), 150–154 and William C. Westmoreland, *A Soldier Reports* (Garden City, New York: Doubleday, 1976), 83–84.

[7] Chu Lai was a U.S. Marine base, including an airfield, constructed in 1965 in the northern part of the Republic of Vietnam in Quảng Tin province near the border of neighboring Quảng Ngãi province. The area surrounding the base was also referred to as Chu Lai. Chu Lai was not a Vietnamese word, but the Vietnamese translation of the Chinese characters for the name of Marine Lieutenant General Victor Krulak, who selected the location for the base. The positioning of the base in Quảng Tin province was part of a Marine Corps strategy for pacifying the five most northerly provinces of South Vietnam which included a population of 2.6 million people, 98 percent of whom lived within twenty-five mile of the South China Sea. If the strategy were successful, the Communist forces in the jungles and mountains inland would be deprived of supplies and support from the coastal population and wither without the sustaining flow of food, recruits, and intelligence from the local peasants. At minimum, Hanoi would have to supply all the provisions for North Vietnamese forces in the I Corps region (the northern provinces). The Marine Corps approach to the war differed from that of the "search and destroy" attrition strategy employed by General Westmoreland and the Army. The Marine CAP units played an important role in trying to root out the Communist infrastructure and win the loyalty of the peasants. Otto J. Lehrack, ed., *No Shining Armor: The Marines at War in Vietnam, an Oral History* (Lawrence, Kansas: University Press of Kansas, 1992), 16–32; George Donelson Moss, *Vietnam: An American Ordeal*, 2nd ed., (Englewood Cliffs, New Jersey: Prentice Hall, 1994), 199; Neil Sheehan, *A Bright Shining Lie: John Paul Vann and America in Vietnam* (New York: Random House, 1988), 632–35.

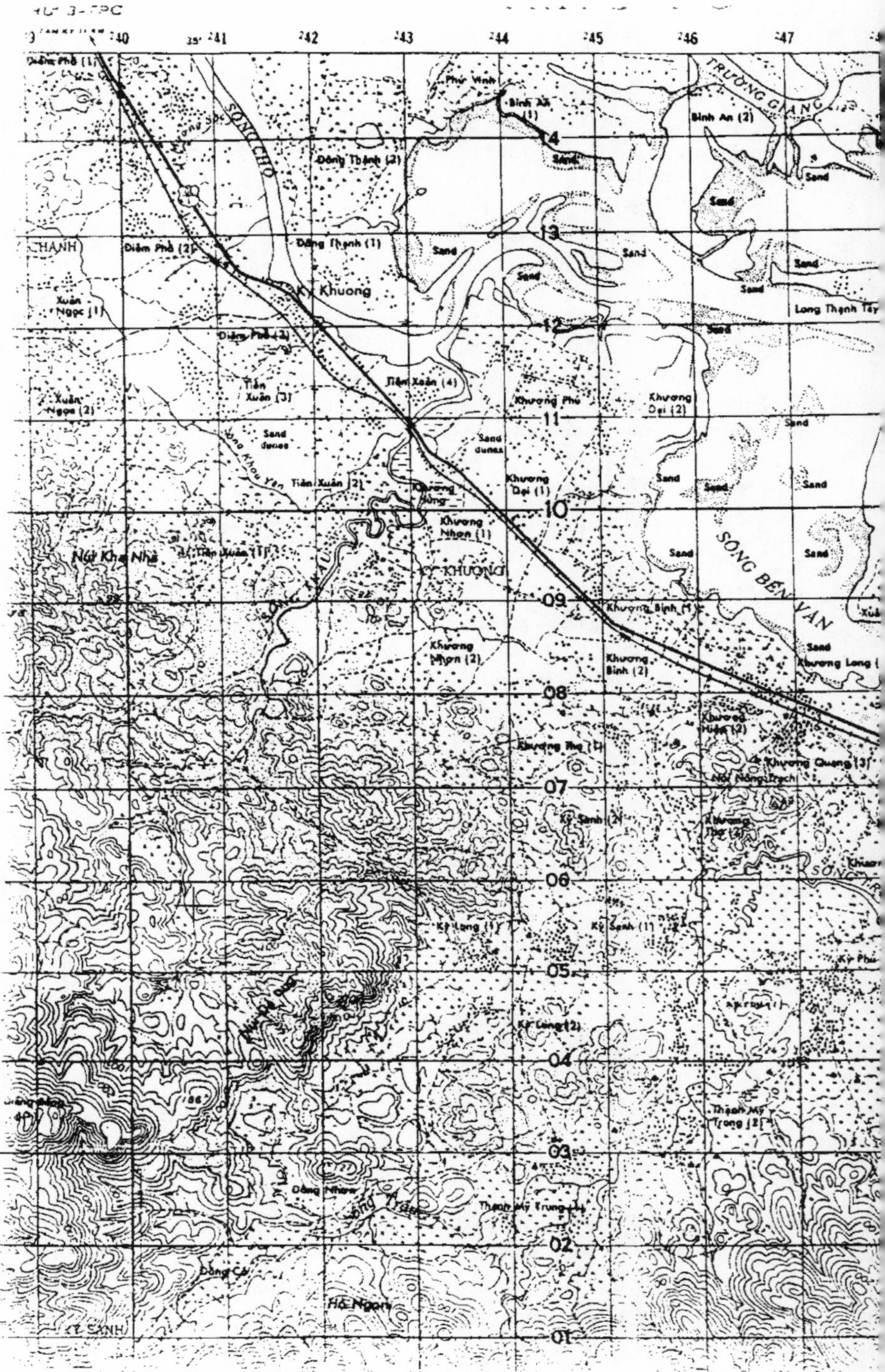

Phư Vinh
Bình An (1)
Bình An (2)
TRƯỜNG GIANG
SÔNG CHỢ
Đông Thạnh (2)
Đông Thạnh (1)
Diêm Phổ (2)
Kỳ Khuong
Xuân Ngọc (1)
Long Thạnh Tây
Tiên Xuân (4)
Tiên Xuân (3)
Xuân Ngọc (2)
Khương Phú
Khương Đại (2)
Sand dunes
Tiên Xuân (2)
Khương Đại (1)
Khương Nhơn (1)
Núi Khe Nhè
KỲ KHƯƠNG
SÔNG BẾN VÂN
Khương Bình (1)
Khương Nhơn (2)
Khương Bình (2)
Khương Long
Khương Hiệp (2)
Khương Quang (3)
Kỳ Sanh (2)
Kỳ Long (1)
Kỳ Sanh (1)
Kỳ Long (2)
Thạnh Mỹ Trong (2)
Đông Nhơn
Thạnh Mỹ Trung
Đồng Cả
Hố Ngoni
Sand

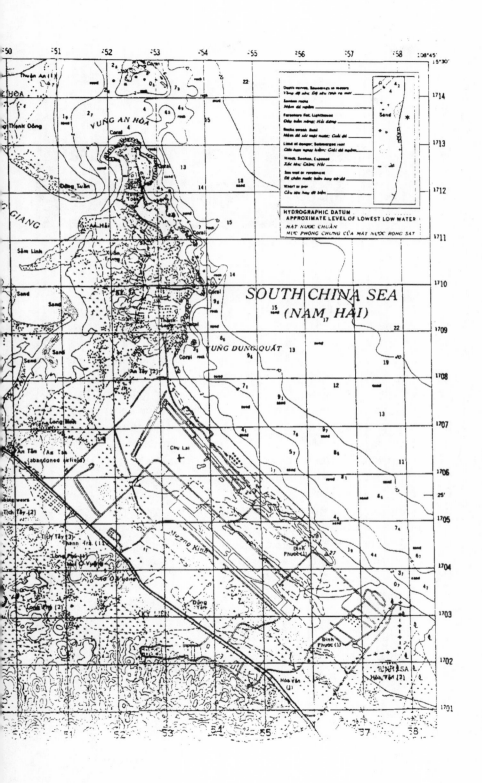

SOUTH CHINA SEA
(NAM HẢI)

## Chapter 3

# Chu Lai—Day One

**T**raining was over. Every possible bit of information needed to increase our chances of survival had been crammed into our minds during those two short weeks. Now I found myself sitting on a seat in an old transport heading for my new destination, Chu Lai, simply a spot on the map to me. As the plane bounced through the air pockets, I studied a map of the jungle area that possibly held the key to my death. Fear attempted to grip me as the plane and my thoughts brought me closer to my new home. The realization of the importance of my CAP assignment was weighing heavily on my mind. How could I possibly expect to do any good in this foreign world with just a handful of knowledge and a spattering of the language? Would the Vietnamese people accept me? What about the existing squad? Would they accept the new kid on the block? The answers to some of my questions would be answered that very day. I looked around at the handful of other men, each heading toward his own place in hell. Their faces told me nothing. We all sat in silence, staring into the jungle below.

As the pilot swung the plane into its final approach, my mind drifted back to the events and reasoning that led to my joining the Combined Action Program.

*Marcelo and I shared our frustrations over the senseless destructions of the war. "What is our purpose? Our goal?" we used to ask, and "What about the people? Isn't the war to protect them from Communist aggression? Are we any better than the Communists? Are we not indiscriminately destroying villages, animals and people?!" The questions were endless, as was the destruction.*

*One day Marcelo came running up to me waving his hands in excitement. "Barry . . . Barry!" he yelled.*

*"Whoa, slow down," I urged him. "You're gonna bust a gusset!"*

*He laughed. "No way, man. Listen to this."*

*Within moments he had me believing that there truly was a unit in 'Nam dedicated to fighting the war for the people, dedicated to helping the people. A unit called CAP. Before I knew it, ignoring chain of command and all, we were standing in front of a CAP recruiting officer, volunteering for duty, something I promised myself I would never do as long as I was in the Marines and especially in Vietnam.*

The plane bounced over an air pocket. I reached down and turned up the CAP insignia now pinned on my chest. "Combined Action Program" was written across the top. Across the bottom were the Vietnamese words "Lục Lương Hỗn Hợp,"[1] with identical meaning. The insignia was shaped like a badge about an inch-and-a-half tall by two inches wide. The background color was a pale blue with a silver bald eagle, wings outstretched, commanding the center. Over his head was a silver star. Crisscrossed behind the body and wings of the eagle were South Vietnamese and American flags adorned in full color and equal in size. The insignia was our key to the jungle. We were to wear it twenty-four hours a day. It told all who saw us that we were CAP Marines and that they were in CAP territory.

I let the insignia fall back into place. I was proud to wear it, proud to be a part of a unit called CAP.

The aged transport landed with a loud "thunk" as the wheels dug into the sod of the dirt runway. I peered out the window, taking in what I thought to be my new home. The rebuilt French airfield was located right on the ocean, adjacent to a small Vietnamese village known as Chu Lai. A "bush hospital" was located at one end of the airfield. The jungle had been dozed down to create a 100-yard clearing. Wooden towers, manned with snipers and 50-caliber machine guns, guarded all four corners of the base. As we taxied to a stop, I readied my gear for transfer to my next form of transportation. A jeep met us as I climbed down out of the plane, gear over the shoulder, orders in hand, and anticipation in full control. My mind was racing.

"Corporal Goodson?"

"Yep," I replied. The driver was a tall lanky dude with a look right out of the hill country of Arkansas.

"Name's Private Johnson." He grinned as he extended his hand. "I'm here to take you to your new home. Climb in."

I grabbed his hand and returned his firm grip. "Where you from?" I asked.

"California," he answered. "And you?"

"Texas!" I said aloud and beamed with pride, as I chided myself for being a poor judge of people's hometowns.

"Thought so." He smiled back.

Small talk over, he jammed the jeep into gear and stabbed it onto the road leading from the base into the jungle interior. The jungle road suddenly opened up onto an honest-to-God paved road. Noticing my shock, Johnson stated, "We call it 'Ho Chi Minh Highway.' Obviously, it's not the renowned enemy trail, but we call it that, anyway.[2] It runs clear down to Cam Ranh Bay and somewhere near Đà Nẵng. It's labeled on the maps as Highway One." He swung the jeep onto the blacktop.

We fell into silence as we sped toward our destination. After about a half hour of dodging Vietnamese pedestrians who insisted the road belonged to them, we arrived at my new "Humble Abode." Johnson was obviously nervous.

"Something wrong?" I asked.

"Yep. I'm a 'rear man,'" he replied. "I get a little jittery every time I have to drop one of you guys off."

"I know the feeling," I said, knowing that "rear man" is the common label for a soldier who spends his entire tour in a rear area base camp far away from most dangers of combat. However, even the rear area wasn't safe. They too had to worry about rockets, mortars, and snipers, or being overrun by a sapper unit.

We drifted back into silence as Johnson slid the jeep to a stop. I sat there momentarily, studying what I was to call home. Fear began to creep up on me again. The place looked like an old compound with a large official-looking building guarding its center. The perimeter of the building was haphazardly protected by bits and pieces of rusted concertina wire and a few strands of common barbed wire. A 300-pound woman with fifteen kids could have run through the perimeter unscathed. "Great," I thought, "these guys must be pretty sloppy." Even the bunkers, if that's what you wanted to call them, were so run down, the sand was pouring out of the bags. In fact, none of the bunkers even looked safe enough to enter.

Old French Headquarters building in the center of the CAP Một's compound.

A view from the center of the compound towards a shrine still being used by the Vietnamese. Iron stakes surrounding the compound had previously held concertina wire, but in 1968–69 held only common barbed wire. Loose concertina wire visible in lower right hand corner.

Remains of old French bunkers. White trails show footpaths through perimeter wire. The outhouse is on the extreme right, and behind the tree on the left is the place where the well and the shower were.

My eyes focused on a group of guys squatted at the foot of the steps of what looked to be an old French Headquarters building, all shabbily dressed, unshaven and covered in what had to be a month's filth. Johnson drove the jeep up to the perimeter's outer edge and tossed my gear to the ground. I jumped out as he spun the wheels in eagerness to leave. "I've got to get back to headquarters," he yelled over his shoulder as he sped back down the blacktop.

"That man was as nervous as a jackrabbit," I thought, gathering my gear and heading for the group. I had a feeling Johnson was right to be afraid.

The bunch of soldiers turned out to be only five men, all of whom seemed anxious for me to join them.

"Hiya. I'm Sergeant Steve Rogers." A medium-sized dark-haired man extended his hand. "You must be Corporal Goodson, our new machine gunner? This here is Private Jésus Rodriguez, our token Puerto Rican and rifleman. And this is Corporal John Everett, the man you'll replace as Assistant Squad Leader in a couple of months. He's going home."

I exchanged handshakes and greetings with each man.

"This man is known as Doc," Rogers continued. "And this little guy here is Private John Ciminski, another rifleman and radioman. Ciminski will show you where to stash your gear. Then come back out and we'll brief you as much as possible." Rogers nodded toward the building.

Ciminski helped me with my gear and we locked it away in some old footlockers in a back room. Mission accomplished, we returned to the group where everyone was already rigged up for the bush. Sergeant Rogers handed me an M-60 and six belts of ammo.

"Strap these on," he said. "Out here all we carry is ammo and medical." Signaling an exit from the decrepit compound, Rogers began to brief me. "That old compound back there used to be one of the French strongholds during their hitch over here," he said. "We use it simply to store our gear and ammo."

"You mean we don't have a compound to hide in case of attack?" I asked, unbelieving.

"You'll have to rearrange your thinking out here," he replied. "A compound for only six men, especially that dilapidated rat trap, would only invite suicide."

"We just live in the jungle then?"

"Yep. You heard of guerrilla warfare?"

"Uh-huh," I nodded. "But I thought that's what we were *all* doing over here."

"In a sense you're right," he said. "Except in our situation, to stay alive we have to be able to hit and run—or simply run. If we fence them out, we fence ourselves in. You'll get used to it."

The jungle trail we were on was covered with typical vegetation so thick that our eyes could not penetrate more than a couple of feet. That Old Man Fear crept silently back into the private corners of my mind with a snicker as he readied for the moment he could possibly gain control.

"Oh, God," I silently prayed. "What have I gotten myself into?" Here I was with only five other men, only four of whom were actually fighters (one being a corpsman), and Rogers tells me that we have no place to hide. The *jungle* was our home! Fear said, "Howdy!"

"Back off," I said aloud.

"What?" Rogers turned with a questioning look on his face.

"Oh, nothing," I said. "I was just talking to myself."

I settled back into my own thoughts as we continued our trek through the jungle. Rogers seemed like a nice enough guy, but there was something about him that bothered me. I couldn't put a handle on it, not totally, anyway. He had a certain look in his eyes, and the other men seemed to maintain an aloofness from him and only speak when he spoke to them. "Not more strife," I thought. The problems we'd had in Alpha Company had been bad enough.

I began to study each man. Rodriguez was a short Puerto Rican about eighteen or nineteen years old. He saw me looking at him.

"What you looking at, man? You never seen a Puerto Rican before?" He shoved his chest forward. "You're looking at the baddest dude in this outfit."

I laughed. "I hope you *all* are the baddest," I said. I had little doubt that Rodriguez, being a veteran in a CAP unit, could hold his own in any fight.

Corporal Everett was a fair-sized black man about my height, but he outweighed me by fifteen or twenty pounds. His body and face held visible signs of previous battles. His eyes held a stern, yet understanding, look.

Corporal "John Everett" on the left and Corpsman "Robert Bradley" on the right.

John Ciminski on the left. The
man on the right is unidentified. Ciminski was not included
in any of the CAP Một photos,
but Ciminski's mother was kind
enough to provide a photo
taken of her son close to the
time when he served in the
CAPs.

This was a man I felt could be trusted, but at the same time shouldn't be
crossed.

Robert Bradley, or "Doc," as he was known, was a big white man around
six foot four and probably weighed 230 or 240 pounds. He had a clean,
friendly look and I like him instantly. Doc, of course, was our Corpsman
and he carried mostly medical supplies. However, even he was draped with
a couple of belts of M-60 ammo and a few grenades, as well as an M-16.

Ciminski was an average-size white guy with a long hollow face filled
with the effects of the war. His eyes were constantly checking the jungle.
Not that the rest of us weren't, but Ciminski's concentration was feverish.
His nervousness was contagious. A chill ran up and down my spine. I had
no doubt that he had good reason for his nonstop inspection of the jungle
around us.

The jungle trail suddenly gave way to a beautiful valley covered with
rice paddies laced with dikes to help contain the stagnant water needed for
seedling growth. Strange, though; the paddies were empty, obviously
vacant of the people needed for grooming and harvesting the ripening rice.
The scene was like a graveyard: silent and foreboding.

No command needed, we instantly spread out and backed into the
cover of the jungle area we had just left to await the inevitable gunfire. It

was hard to believe that just a few short hours before this, I had been safe in the rear. I studied the terrain. A tiny village dotted the hillside across from us, with crude huts constructed from bamboo, banana tree leaves, and palm tree leaves. Frail looking dogs and chickens wandered about aimlessly, impervious to the impending doom. Death hung in the air like the stench from an outhouse.

Suddenly a burst from an AK broke the silence. We all tensed, searching desperately to locate its owner. Then silence settled back in place as we peered across the paddies. The shots had come from the village. It seemed hours, but in actuality, it was only minutes before Sergeant Rogers gave the order: "OK, Gents, let's head for the village. Keep low and fast."

Rogers, Rodriguez and I leaped onto a dike and began the long journey across the checkerboard of paddies. Corporal Everett, Doc and Ciminski struck out toward another dike to break the concentration of fire from the Viet Cong, if it should come. Cold sweat trickled down my forehead, stinging my eyes. I quickly wiped them clear and fixed my concentration on the approaching village. The stillness was so profound we could hear our hearts beat.

Suddenly, another sound interrupted the solitude of the silence. We all dove for the rice paddies. As the muck and stench oozed up around my waist, I realized that the sound we'd heard was a scream! No, not a scream, but a wailing sound like you'd expect from someone being tortured in a horror flick.

We kept to the paddies, struggling our way through the muck, impervious to the searching leeches and biting flies. We finally reached the opposite side where a trail led into the village. There was still no sign of the enemy. I looked at Rogers. He had a chilling grin on his face. I turned and searched for Everett and his group. They were climbing out of the paddies about 100 yards south of us. Rogers waved them up.

As Everett's group arrived, Rogers whispered, still fostering that grin, "We got Cong here, guys. Get ready for the kill!" His eyes were ablaze. I shivered at his lust for blood. Rogers sent Everett and his group down the trail to the village and we struck off through the jungle.

As we started into the bush, movement to my left froze me in my tracks. I tapped Rogers with the barrel of my M-60 and stabbed my head in the direction of the movement. He understood. We started to take position when a squad of Vietnamese soldiers stepped into a clearing heading for the village. I breathed a sigh of relief. They were PFs (Popular Forces), our

South Vietnamese counterparts, equal to us in number. They, too, had heard the AK burst and had been waiting for us before seeking out the Cong.

Rogers nodded them onward toward the village. The wailing was incessant now and growing louder with our every step. We passed through a banana tree grove and entered the village which, with the exception of the wailing, was quiet, still, and desolate. The wailing pierced the air from the direction of a large hut located in the center. We headed that way, eyes searching every corner. Dogs tucked their tails and cowered away from us with menacing growls rising from their throats. The chickens had to be kicked out of the way.

Once inside the hut we found the source of the wailing. Approximately twenty Vietnamese villagers were crouched in a circle around two blood-soaked bodies, dressed in beautiful silk clothing of multiple colors, that had been riddled with bullets and gutted. The villagers were all swaying to and fro with tears streaming down their faces and arms stretched out toward their slain friends. We interrupted the wailing and found a guy who seemed to be in charge. Through our Vietnamese counterparts we discovered that the two bodies were those of the village elders, or chieftains, if you will. They had adamantly hated the Viet Cong and had long resisted their Mafia-type, strong-arm tactics.

The Cong always offered villagers "protection" in return for food, clothing, storage for arms and ammo, and hiding places from us. If the villagers refused, the VC simply began a systematic elimination of one person at a time until they found a leader who would agree to their demands. Sometimes complete villages were wiped out. The Viet Cong considered that their methods were "for the common good." We called it murder.

Such was the case here except these VC knew where to start their murderous rampage. The murder of the two chieftains had the villagers in total turmoil and fear, giving them a strong incentive to submit to VC demands. Our interpreters advised us that the Viet Cong had come from a farm about two miles down the valley, south of our present position. According to them, one of the Cong was a son of the farmer who lived there.

The grin returned to Rogers's face. "Let's move out," he ordered. "We're going to pay a farmer a visit."

Our counterparts advised the villagers that we were off to pursue the Viet Cong and then followed along behind us. The trek to the farm was uneventful and we arrived just before dusk. The farmer, his wife and two small children were calmly, innocently, planting rice seedlings in a new paddy. As we reached the farmer, Rogers, without warning, reached out and grabbed him by his shirt, threw him brutally to the ground, and thrust the butt of his rifle into his gut. The farmer rolled with pain. The Vietnamese counterpart in charge of his group, known as Tin Thanh, joined Rogers in systematically beating and questioning the farmer. My stomach turned as the farmer's face turned into an unrecognizable bloody pulp.

"Ở đâu VC!" Rogers screamed. The farmer just mumbled something about not understanding and collapsed to the ground. Rogers turned away from him a few steps as if to leave him alone. Suddenly, the sarcastic grin returned to his face as he spun on his heel and emptied his M-16 into the farmer, whose lifeless body sank into the rice paddy with steam rising from the gaping wounds, his lifeblood turning the stagnant water red. The farmer would speak no more. Tin Thanh released his own barrage of rounds into the already lifeless body, as if to say, "Me, too!"

I was sick. I couldn't shake from my mind the look on the dead man's face as my ears were bombarded with the screams from the farmer's wife and children. "Oh, Lord God, what in hell have I gotten myself into," I thought. Rogers ordered a search of the farmer's huts and sheds. Nothing turned up, neither any spent shells or cigarette butts, nor a hint of a trap door or tunnel hiding the VC for whom we searched so desperately.

The murder loomed in the back of my mind as tears fought to surface in my eyes. I fought them back as condemnation attacked my very being for having even been a part of such a horrid event. Rogers's evil grin haunted the very depths of my soul. The man seemed immune to any humane feelings. He even wanted to blow away the woman and children. "God, help us!" I thought. The rest of us managed to convince Rogers to leave the farmer's family alone as we gathered our gear and our thoughts and headed off to some other village Rogers wanted to visit.

We reached the village right after dark. Finding it peaceful and quiet, we continued into the jungle about 100 yards where we silently set up an ambush based on a tip our counterparts had received from the village of the slain chieftains. Night closed in around us and so did the mosquitoes. Silently, we launched our counterattack against the little devils as they fearlessly sucked away on every exposed portion of skin. I was relieved to discover that these men didn't risk unnecessary noise in slapping at mosquitoes. They simply traced their fingers up the sides of their bodies and silently squashed the miserable creatures.

The night seemed to loom into eternity as our eyes searched the jungle around us for any signs of movement or unnatural sounds. The hour of 0200 slid into history, and suddenly I thought I heard a twig snap. For a minute then, the only things I could hear were my heartbeat and my breathing. Surely the enemy can hear it, too, I thought. Fear grabbed hold as I subconsciously held my breath. There it was again, that telltale "snap." We all quickly, quietly readied ourselves with grenades, armed and positioned for the toss.

Not ten feet away, a figure stepped from behind a tree, followed close behind by another. Grenades flew in their direction. Explosions illuminated the bodies, and we opened fire with everything we had. Screams penetrated the night as lead found its mark. Banana and bamboo trees crumbled under the hail of lead and shrapnel. Minutes passed as we exchanged fire and grenades. An RPG[3] round exploded against a palm tree behind me. It crumpled to the ground and coconuts fell like hail on top of us.

Suddenly it was over. The gunfire and explosions ceased as abruptly as they had started and silence regained its rightful position in the night as our ears and eyes searched the jungle for signs of movement. Rogers passed the word to move out.

"Good idea," I thought. "Those gooks definitely have our position now." We left the smell of gunpowder behind and circled around to the back side of the hill about 200 yards from our previous position. We settled in to wait for daylight.

Sunlight danced through the thickness of the jungle as dawn brought a partial release from the tension of the night. We had all escaped injury, but the radio had taken a couple of rounds and refused to transmit. Ciminski didn't care, though. In fact, he was obviously more than happy that his radio was dead instead of him!

We cautiously left our positions and struck out for the battle scene to make sure the dead were dead and collect any paraphernalia we felt important to our survival. Gunpowder still hung in the air as we closed in on the area. Anticipating gruesome sights, I strengthened my stamina and searched for bodies. There were none. Not even any parts or members typical of explosions, only occasional blood stains. There had to have been at least a dozen dead or wounded Cong, yet not one single body remained, not even a weapon.

The VC strategy worked. It was unnerving to know that you had killed the enemy but were unable to find his body. They didn't just walk off; they couldn't have! Or did they?

---

[1]  The author has endeavored to use the properly accented letters in Vietnamese words and phrases, but admits that his knowledge only goes as far as his Vietnamese dictionary, maps, and notes and documents from 1968–69.

[2]  The Ho Chi Minh Highway remark is in reference to the Ho Chi Minh Trail, which was the major infiltration route for North Vietnamese troops and supplies entering South Vietnam. Cam Ranh Bay and Da Nang were U.S. coastal military bases, the former south and the latter north of Chu Lai.

[3]  An RPG was a rocket-propelled grenade. It was mainly an anti-armor weapon used by the North Vietnamese Army.

## Chapter 4

# Bounty

The days following the murder of the farmer were pretty much the same as my first day. The humidity forced us into the ritual of cleaning our weapons every morning, regardless of the previous night's activity. We traipsed through the jungle by day, and set up ambush by night.

I was more than a little curious about Sergeant Rogers. He kept to himself for the most part. Ciminski was the first to provide any insight into the strife.

"You thinking about home?" he asked me one day while I was inspecting the bore of my .45 to make sure the cleaning rod had brought it to a polished finish. I held it up towards the sun, peering through as I slowly turned it between my fingers. Satisfied, I looked over at Ciminski.

"Naw," I answered, and looked around at the village we had chosen for our spot for the morning. There were only a handful of small huts nestled in a palm grove bordering the east side of the farmers' rice paddies. The murky water of the paddies glistened in the early morning sun. The palm trees swayed with an occasional breeze from the ocean. The villagers were all out working in the paddies, except a few curious children hanging around to watch us clean our weapons. The PFs had vanished into the jungle to take care of their own chores.

"Just wondering what kind of strife has y'all so torn apart. I mean, y'all hardly even talk to each other."

"Yeah," Ciminski said quietly. "Rogers keeps us in turmoil." He looked around and I followed his gaze to Sergeant Rogers napping under a palm tree well out of hearing range. "The man's a bloodthirsty killer who doesn't care about life. Anyone's life." He glanced back towards Rogers.

"Why doesn't someone report him?" I asked.

"Everett just did," he said.

We fell back into silence, working on our weapons and gear.

A few days later a message came over the new radio requesting that Sergeant Rogers pay a visit to headquarters. We all figured he was up for promotion or something, but we never found out. The CO radioed back later that day and promoted Everett to sergeant and squad leader and me to assistant squad leader. We were now down to five men, total. Considering the loss versus the gain, we considered ourselves fortunate. The obvious lifting of the tension had an equally lifting effect on our attitudes.

Everett encouraged our participation in the daily chores of the Vietnamese people. I took an immediate liking to the idea because it gave me a sense of purpose and took my mind off the inevitable nightfall. One of our Vietnamese counterparts, Taan, sort of took me under his wing after I displayed a strong interest in helping his fellow villagers.

Taan, posing for a Popular Forces formal dress photo.

On one particular day in the middle of January (we were never able to keep precise track of the passage of time), we set up our day base near a farmer's hut in the eastern-most sector of our area of primary responsibility. We had just established a guard watch schedule and settled in when Taan found me.

"Corporal Barry." He nodded in the typical Vietnamese fashion.

"Chào anh," I answered, in an attempt at his language.

He understood. "Come."

I looked around. Doc was already tending to the local villagers along with his PF, a corpsman-in-training. The villagers had formed a line to await their miracle cures. One man in particular drew my attention. He had weather-beaten skin that looked gray in color and seemed to be thick as leather. There was no question as to the reason for his visit. A fish fin protruded through the back side of his left hand. The wound was engulfed in rot and gangrene.

A woman held a small, crying boy in her arms. Black, burnt holes in his right thigh reached all the way to the bone and out the other side. He was one of the victims of our war. Although we didn't wound him directly, we felt indirectly responsible. He had been hit by what we called "Willy Peter" or "WP," a white phosphorous shell used by our artillery units for spotter rounds. Exploding WP would illuminate the immediate area and produce silhouettes of anyone standing near it. Hundreds of burning globs would fly in all directions, igniting and burning anything they touched. Each glob continued to burn until all the oxygen was exhausted or it burned itself out. The boy would in all probability lose his leg, if not his life. My heart went out to him. He was truly an innocent victim of our war.

"Okay, Taan," I said. "Let's go."

We took a path that closely followed the edge of the jungle and meandered down the hill until it opened abruptly into a clearing in the surrounding valley. Taan seem at ease so I relaxed, too. It felt great to let the tension subside, if only for a short while.

As we approached the edge of the clearing, I caught a glimpse of a small group of villagers hacking away at something on the opposite edge. Taan started towards them.

"What are they doing?" I tossed my question at Taan. The tension returned.

"They chop trees." He clarified his meaning with a karate chop movement into the air. Each of them had a machete and was chopping away at trees about six to eight inches in diameter. I studied them for a few minutes and made a mental note to notify the rear to send out a case or two of single blade axes. Even though the trees were small, the progress of each man was painfully slow. Once the axes arrived, I could show them how to really cut down trees.

Without attempting to explain my plan, I picked up a lonesome machete and joined in with the farmers. At first, the men were suspicious. I didn't blame them. Who was I, anyway, but a foreigner trying to impress them with my ability to chop wood? I studied their faces as I hacked away. Some showed disgust. They all showed curiosity. Regardless, I was elated with the opportunity to pitch in.

Taan explained as we chopped. "Farmers cut trees to build new huts and pens because monsoons blow away old ones."

"Tell them I appreciate them letting me help," I said, "and tell them we'll help as long as they need us."

Taan and I spent the rest of the day working with the farmers, chopping down trees and hauling off the trimmed logs to the proper site for the huts and pens. Setting my machete aside, I wiped the sweat from my brow with the back of my hand and glanced westward. The sun was settling into the tree tops, so Taan and I bid our adieus and headed back for the base area. As the sun faded behind the distant horizon, Taan's face lost its cheerfulness and our tension increased with every lengthening shadow.

At the camp, Sergeant Everett was gathering up the rest of the men in preparation for the rapidly approaching darkness. Our strategy for the night was to move out before dark and vanish into the jungle so none of the villagers could report our exact whereabouts to the Viet Cong. As soon as shadows melted into darkness we were to cross the blacktop and search out an area just south by southwest of "Fat City," the Army artillery base located in the very heart of our APR. The commander of the base had reported harassment mortar fire from that general area. Their efforts to snuff it out had failed and it was now our duty to seek out and destroy that mortar and whoever was behind it.

The night had no moon and in spite of the stars you could not see your hand in front of your face. Silently, we started our trek across the maze of rice paddy dikes, searching with our feet for the ground our eyes could not see, taking care to change our course at random to set up a zigzag pattern across the open area. This, we hoped, would confuse the Cong if they caught

Some typical rice paddies across which the CAP Một unit and the PFs would zigzag to reach their destinations.

a glimpse of our outline against the ever-darkening sky. Every step seemed like eternity. Every small sound radiating from our loose ammo and the crushing of vegetation under our boots seemed to resound against the jungle walls. In spite of the night coolness, sweat trickled down the back of my neck. "What will the night bring?" I wondered. "Ambush? Booby traps?"

Suddenly, I was falling face forward.

Fear jolted my memory to instant recall of a pungi pit I had fallen into during a full Alpha Company sweep I took part in when I had only been in the country a couple of weeks.

*We were walking through a dense growth of elephant grass in an area dubbed "Elephant Valley." Elephant grass looked to me like a giant mutation of the Johnson grass we had back home, with one exception; this grass grew about twenty feet tall and every blade was razor sharp. The grass grew so dense that you had to force your way through, despite the sharp blades. I was grateful for the long-sleeved utilities they had issued us.*

*On that particular day back in August, members of Alpha Company were stretched out across the valley, "on line," as they called it. We were pushing our way through the grass, maintaining approximately fifty feet between ourselves and the man on each side of us and relying strictly on visual contact since the Colonel had ordered "silence." The man must have thought we all had mental telepathy, because the growth was so thick we could not see two feet on any side of us, much less fifty feet. We continued to move in, straining our ears in both directions.*

*I had gone about a hundred yards into the grass when suddenly the ground underneath me collapsed. I remember vegetation ripping past, and then the sight of pungi stakes. I wanted to scream, but the echo of the colonel's command of "Silence!" stayed with me. I felt the pointed stakes brush past my body as I plummeted to the bottom of the pit. Abruptly, all was quiet again. I lay there in a pool of stench that seemed alive. Half in shock, I began to check my body to see where the stakes had driven through. Nothing! Not even a scratch! The stakes had simply crumbled under my weight. I had never known bamboo to crumble as this did, until that moment in the pit. It was evident that the hole I had stumbled into was an ancient one, left over from the war with the French or maybe even in WWII. "Another one of God's little miracles," I thought, and offered a silent prayer of thanks.*

*Motivated by the little critters crawling all over my body, I forced myself to stand and then pull up the remaining stakes as I began searching for a way out. The pit was roughly ten feet deep by four or five feet in width. I looked upward. The grass and vines at the surface almost completely covered the mouth of the pit, allowing very little light to filter through. I shouldered my weapon and dug my fingers into the walls. With finger holds secure, I searched with my feet for possible holes or projections to begin my climb out. The soil, pebbly and loose, constantly collapsed under my weight, sending me falling back to the bottom.*

*When I was within a few feet of the top, I felt the entire right side of the hole give way, and I plummeted back down. I wanted to scream with frustration, but I bit my lip, dug fresh hand- and footholds with my bayonet and once again hoisted my body upwards. This time I succeeded. Stopping with my head right at the edge of the pit, I checked in all directions to make sure I was alone. Nothing stirred. With one final heave, I lifted and rolled out onto the ground. Breathing a sigh of relief, I checked my watch; over an hour had passed. I stood up, searching the depths of the jungle with my eyes and ears. Nothing! My unit was gone—long gone. I was all alone—totally alone . . . except for God and the silence of the jungle.*

Splash! My body sank into the shallow leech-infested waters of the rice paddy we were crossing. Anger shoved aside the fear as realization sunk home: Rodriguez had forgotten to wait and redirect me onto the next dike, an unspoken rule on pitch-black nights.

Two men were instantly beside me, helping me to my feet and re-positioning my M-60 and the belts of ammo. The cool night became cold as the drenched utilities clung to my body. "I'll have to let the critters suck until tomorrow," I thought as I briefly searched for leeches.

"Sorry, thought we lost you there," Rodriguez whispered. "Come on. The gooks heard that splash, for sure."

Fortunately, we were just a few yards from the jungle edge so only moments passed before we could once again melt into the "security" of the interior. The checkerboard of paddy dikes stretched into the darkness behind us. We briefly gathered under the cover of a banana grove. As we sat on our haunches, each man studied the depths of the jungle for signs of movement. Searching with our eyes was nearly futile, but search we did, straining our eyes and ears in every direction. I caught myself holding my breath for fear of missing a sound, or worse—being heard. Minutes seemed like hours as we waited, the silence of the jungle night consuming us.

Sergeant Everett crawled over to my position. "Are you okay?" he whispered.

"Just frozen," I whispered back. "Let's get moving before I catch my death."

When he turned away into the darkness, I followed. Silently he touched each man on the shoulder as we passed, signaling it was time to move out. They fell into step behind us, keeping a safe distance of fifteen or twenty feet— "keeping interval" we called it. Taan took point.

The trek through the jungle warmed me. I was just beginning to relax when Taan brought us to a halt. We had reached Highway One, the only paved road between Chu Lai and Đà Nẵng, and one of the most dangerous nighttime areas of our APR. The Cong liked to patrol up and down the road until they found a lost American patrol or a late night convoy attempting to gain ground under the cover of night.

We spread out in the jungle alongside the road and crossed over two at a time to decrease the possibility of discovery and minimize the noise of our crossing. As quietly as possible we faded into the tree line bordering the road. Our boots seemed to resound against the night air. Blacktop crossed, we reunited and set out for our final destination—find that mortar! Like creatures of the night, we crept down the jungle trail, each one straining to catch that fleeting telltale sign or unnatural noise that would warn us of our enemy.

"Wonder what Mom and Dad are doing right now?" I thought, allowing myself to slip into a sense of longing. I shook my head to shake loose
the thoughts. It was dangerous to allow yourself such a luxury. You had to
keep your senses tuned to the present and its dangers, or risk walking into
a trap. Many squads, even companies, were wiped out because of a relaxed
moment of daydreaming.

The night dragged on as we continued our search for the "phantom
mortar," as we had dubbed it. "Surely they will drop a couple of harassment
rounds on the base," I thought. "Then we could pinpoint their location."
Instantly, remorse hit me as the significance of my thought sank into the
conscious side of my brain. "God forgive me!" I thought. "I certainly don't
wish a mortar attack on anyone—any American soldier, anyway."

If the Cong did choose to launch an attack on Fat City we would be
able to pinpoint their general location by simply listening to the distinctive firing sounds of their mortar. Mortars and artillery shells produce fright-
ening sounds as they pass over your head and so do bullets. Bullets sound
like the crack of a bullwhip. Mortars and artillery produce a unique sound
all their own, kind of a "woove-woove-woove" sound. The way you distin-
guish between the two is that the artillery shell produces a much greater
magnification of the sound. Also, the artillery cannon produces a loud boom
as it fires, while a mortar fires with a distinctive "pfoomp." In reality, as
long as you could hear the "crack" of the bullet or the "woove, woove,
woove" of incoming rounds you could rest assured that you were relatively
safe. The deadly rounds hit without warning.

Eternity seemed to pass as we slowly moved northward, searching but
not finding the elusive mortar. 0200 rolled around as we paused on the
crest of a hill overlooking a small village, or "vil," known as "Xuân Ngọc
Hai." We had visited it a few weeks earlier. It consisted of half a dozen
crudely constructed bamboo huts with thatched palm leaf roofs and lay just
west of the sand dunes of Diêm Phô Hai along the foothills of Núi Hỏn
Ro's limestone mountains. Small lean-to type sheds sheltered water buffalo, the Vietnamese farm tractor.

From our position roughly 500 feet above the "vil," we could see dancing shadows created by candlelight radiating through the openings of two
huts sitting right in the center of the village. Light. It suddenly struck us.
I checked my watch. The red beam from my flashlight illuminated the
hands: 0215 hours. Sergeant Everett passed word for me to join him. As
quietly as possible, I crawled to his position, making sure of my every move.

He was waiting in the protection of a termite mound that stood roughly six feet tall and covered at least that much ground at the base. It offered little true protection but did allow us to stand and observe the "vil" without fear of detection. "Remember, this is the only Viet Cong-controlled village in our APR. And those lights spell trouble," he whispered, pointing towards the dancing shadows. "They could be our mortar guys," he continued. "There are two trails leading into the village from the base of this hill. We'll split up and meet right here." He risked the beam from his red-lens light to faintly illuminate a spot on his map which portrayed the village as tiny black dots in the midst of green ink representing the jungle. "We'll choose our positions once we reach that point." He folded the map, returned it to one of the large, button-down pockets of the right thigh of his utilities, then gave the pocket a quick pat to assure himself the map was safe. He whispered, "Let's go."

A chill tickled its way down my spine, and it didn't come from the dampness of my clothing. "How many are we going to face this time," I wondered, "and what kind of weapons will they use?" I had no answer. All I knew for sure was that we had to be ready for anything.

Everett took Ciminski and Taan and left me with Rodriguez and Doc. With Taan taking point, Everett took his team down the trail to the left of the termite mound. "Taking point" was a nebulous title for the most unwanted position in the squad, by most anyway. It meant "take the lead," meaning you had to walk a good fifty to one hundred feet ahead of everyone else. You were usually the first to uncover booby traps, and in most cases the first to see or encounter the enemy. Worst of all everyone behind you was depending on your alertness to protect them from falling into a trap of any kind. Your decisions, your steps, could mean life or death to everyone behind you.

I took point in my group and led my two men down our side of the hill. Walking point was no big deal—that is *if* you were some kind of maniac with a strong masochistic desire and a yearning for the thrill of the sudden attack. Well, I wasn't one of those, so I was scared, simply scared, and every step was a nightmare.

"Watch out for booby traps and especially for guards," Everett had whispered. "This must be some kind of pow wow." Booby traps. God knows I hated and feared those things. You never knew when your number might be up. Even worse than the death and destruction they caused was the fact that you simply could not fight back. I promise you that there is no thrill in shooting at a pungi stake or wrestling with pieces of shrapnel left from an exploding mine. Another disconcerting thing about booby traps—they let everyone know where you were!

We slowly made our way down the hill and as quickly as possible crossed the sandy clearing separating the village from the jungle. Reaching the edge of the village, we stopped to get our bearings. "Wonder where Everett is?" I thought. I strained my ear in his direction. Nothing but silence, deadly silence.

Passing word by touch, we moved out in search of those two huts. Rodriguez chanced a quick sigh to release some of his tension. Somewhere to our left a dog barked. "We're discovered!" I thought. Fortunately, the dog only had one sharp bark in him before he was satisfied that he was in control.

We continued past a hut, silent and dark, on our right. We turned a quick 360 degrees as we checked for Cong hiding in the shadows. None were there. Minutes passed as we progressively and systematically investigated and eliminated each hut as a potential danger. Just as we rounded a buffalo shed, I heard a faint noise echoing from the shadows of the adjacent hut. The darkness was overwhelming. "Good and bad," I thought. Using hand contact I motioned Rodriguez and Doc to stop. I'd only gone about five steps when I risked a quick look over my shoulder to reassure myself that Rodriguez and Doc were still there. Nothing but blackness stared back at me. The only thing reassuring me that the shed was definitely behind me was the familiar odor of buffalo dung hanging in the moist night air. "Sure could make a man trigger happy," I thought.

I had walked a few more steps when I heard a clicking noise like a good old Texas grasshopper. It was Everett's signal. I clicked back with a definite Texas accent. "He'll like that Texas click," I thought. I made my way in his direction.

Everett and his gang were nestled under a clump of bushes roughly fifty yards from the now brightly-lit huts. The sounds of laughter and unintelligible conversation filled the night air. I still could not see sentries of any kind. Due to the darkness of the night, hand signals were not an option. Everett whispered, "There's a trench running from this spot to within twenty feet or so of the front doors of those lighted huts. Go get the rest of your brood and we'll spread out in the trench with you in the middle." We always protected our machine gun this way. It also allowed the gunner to strafe a wide radius without fear of hitting his own men. "We'll wait until those gooks break up from the meeting and hit them as they leave," he continued. "God only knows how many we are up against. You drop a WP into the hut on the left. I'll take the other."

I squeezed his shoulder to let him know I understood and silently disappeared back into the night to fetch my "brood."

Rodriguez and Doc were still waiting by the buffalo shed. Suddenly, a lesson I had learned early in 'Nam returned to my conscious mind: water buffalo hate the smell of Americans and usually go into a frenzy, tearing the place apart in an effort to trample one to death.

"The shed is empty," Doc whispered, seeming to read my thoughts.

I nodded and then laid out the plans Everett had communicated. As we started back to Everett's position in search of that trench, I reminded them, "Watch for guards, and for Pete's sake, don't scare any animals or we're dead meat."

We moved forward a step at a time, testing the ground with each step before we shifted our weight down lightly to make sure that a twig, mud puddle, or sleeping animal would not betray our presence. We reached the trench and spread out in it with about ten feet between each one of us. Settling down, we concentrated on controlling every body function and movement. A growling stomach could easily give us away. Our eyes were fixed on the huts and the area surrounding them. As we waited, we concentrated only on the shadows and darkness surrounding the huts, looking for guards and keeping our eyes away from the light. Light, especially on a dark night, can create an instantaneous, momentary blindness that can cost you your life, or worse, someone else's.

There were no guards. "Boy, these gooks are cocky," I thought. Then I remembered that Fat City rarely sent out patrols, day or night. Those guys feared the bush more than anything. "Who didn't!" I thought. No one but fools—or CAP Marines—would spend the night in the jungles of Vietnam.

We sat in the trench readied and coiled for combat. I could sense the tension in each of the men even though I couldn't see them. I checked my watch: 0330. Over an hour had passed. Waiting was part of the hell we went through. Knowing our last minutes on earth might be spent right there in that trench, time passed slowly. We sat poised like cats, ready to pounce yet knowing that we could just as easily be the prey. "God, help us," I thought.

Twenty more minutes slid into history before movement caught my eye. In the hut on my left men were all shuffling around as if preparing to leave. "Sounds like a whole army," I thought.

Everett's command reverberated in my brain, "You lob a 'Willy Peter' at the hut on the left," he had said, "and I'll lob one at the hut on the right." I readied the deadly egg.

The cloth covering the door of "my" hut suddenly opened. A man stepped into the opening, silhouetted against the candle light behind him. "These guys are extremely sloppy," I thought. They obviously were not afraid of Fat City firebase and thought that we, too, were afraid to "test the jungle at night."

The silhouette melted into the darkness toward the other hut, leaving the doorway of my hut wide open. I could make out at least a half-dozen men, all dressed in green fatigue uniforms with red and yellow insignia. Two of them boasted the typical black PJs of the Viet Cong. "My God," I thought, "these guys are NVA Regulars."[1] NVA—North Vietnamese Army—troops held a well-earned reputation as the most deadly "enemy" fighting force in Vietnam, as well as the most ruthless. My prayer returned in hopes that God was not asleep and, more so—that he was on our side.

The men in my hut were exchanging good-byes and donning their gear and weapons when the cloth covering of the doorway of the hut on the right, Everett's hut, opened. The silhouette from my hut stuck his head inside and let loose a line of unintelligible words that were evidently a command to prepare to move out. We could then hear giggles from the prostitutes inside the huts. "Hope you enjoyed it," I whispered. "It will be your last."

The door of Everett's hut swung wide open and men began to saunter outside, adjusting their gear and tossing words back at the women. Our silhouette lit a cigarette. "Probably an American one," I thought. About a dozen men milled around in a little group, keeping in front of Everett's hut. Then the men in my hut came out in one little bunch.

That Texas grasshopper let out one little quiet "click click." Everett and I tossed our Willy Peters into the doorway of each respective hut. Simultaneously, Doc, Rodriguez, Ciminski and Taan let fly their own "frag grenades"[2] into the bunch of men. Instantly, I readied my M-60 to strafe the huts as I knew Everett and the others were doing.

Seconds seemed like hours as the gooks stopped talking when the grenades bounced onto the ground around them. You could see realization slap them in the face as the Willy Peters lit up the night with massive balls of flame which instantaneously turned each hut into a bonfire. My stomach turned and tears welled up in my eyes as I heard the screams of the prostitutes inside the huts. Crying was a luxury one could not afford. Tears blurred your vision and the emotions blocked logical thinking. Both could spell death. You had to become impervious to the death and horrors around you. Your life, as well as the lives of your remaining friends, depended upon instant reactions.

"I pray there are no children in there." Shuddering at the thought, I fought back the tears and opened fire at the body of men in front of the huts. Just as my M-60 broke the silence of the night the frag grenades added light to the already illuminated scene with a rapid "boom, boom, boom." The grenades had been accurately tossed to the outside of each clump of men, keeping them corralled in front of the huts. They scattered back and forth as the deadly shrapnel from each successive grenade found its mark. They went wild, firing their AKs in every direction. Green tracer bullets cracked overhead, creating a momentary break in the black of the night. We continued to concentrate our fire, in rapid five-round bursts, into the crazed group of men. One jumped up and ran toward us, unaware of his impending doom. Everett dropped him cold. Three remained. Suddenly they all three jumped up and sent a hail of lead in our direction. Their shots snapped over our heads into the foliage of the trees above us. Ciminski, using his M-79 grenade launcher,[3] popped a couple of grenade rounds in front of the escaping Cong as we followed them with our fire. One more met his maker as his riddled body flopped around on the ground. The M-79 rounds ripped the other two to pieces. I turned my attention to the bodies strung out in front of the flaming huts and fired one long burst into them. Silence regained its foothold in the night as we waited for movement, any movement. In the silence, I quickly slipped a new belt into my M-60. Clicking noises in the dark reassured me that others were renewing their weapons as well.

We settled in for the wait. Experience had taught us to hold our position for a good five minutes to give any Cong "playing dead" the opportunity to give themselves away and also to allow the heroin they may have taken to drain out of their bodies along with their lifeblood.

As we waited I recalled that once, during Operation Mead River, I had emptied twenty rounds into the chest of a Viet Cong and he kept running just as if I had been firing blanks. We found him the next morning about a hundred yards or so deeper in the jungle, his body riddled with bullet holes.

The five minutes passed without a hint of movement. Even the dog had nothing to say.

Everett gave the command to advance, verbally this time. Everett and Doc kept their positions as the rest of us moved, in a low, crouching trot, to inspect the scene. The stench of death hung in the air. My stomach turned again. "I'll never get used to this," I thought. Systematically, we inspected each body. Before we touched one, we fired a few rounds into it to make sure it was indeed dead. Then we searched them all for possible information and plans that would reveal their purpose and intent for meeting at that hour. We continued from body to body, keeping a watchful eye for movement and searching the surrounding jungle with our ears for telltale signs of Viet Cong reinforcements that might be heading in our direction. We took great care not to move the bodies or to turn them over. NVAs specialized in arming their bodies with some form of booby trap as they gasped for their last breath of air.

"Corporal Goodson," Ciminski tossed a quiet yell in my direction.

I followed his pointing finger to a body lying directly in front of the huts. "My God," I said. "It's an NVA lieutenant colonel."

"Yeah," answered Ciminski, "and look what else." He held up an AK-47. We typically destroyed all enemy weapons. I was not normally impressed with VC weapons, but this one was beautiful. It had a smooth, well-finished dark wooden stock and grip and boasted an all stainless steel body, barrel and bayonet. It was absolutely beautiful. "You've got yourself a keeper there," I assured him. Ciminski beamed from ear to ear. You would have thought that someone had just given him a million bucks.

"Let's search him," I ordered. "But be careful." The colonel was lying on his back. I forced my hands under him and searched his pockets. The first one revealed a map of the area. "We'll study this later," I stated to no one in particular and stuffed it into my breast pocket. I noticed a thin leather strap wrapped around his shoulder and disappearing under his back. I stopped. Ciminski, sensing my thoughts, said, "Don't turn him over, man."

"Not to worry. Get back a few feet and hit the deck," I ordered. "I'm going to try to pull it out from under him."

Ciminski didn't argue. He backed off a few steps and dropped to the ground. I tugged at the strap. It gave a little and then jammed against his belt. Testing, I lifted his body just far enough to free the strap with a quick jerk. A pouch came flying out at me and I grabbed it in flight, letting the dead colonel settle back onto the ground. A quick look inside and I took Ciminski's million dollar look away from him. The pouch was loaded with money. Thumbing through the bills, I estimated there to be around twenty thousand dollars of Vietnamese money in the pouch. Along with the money was a little ledger book listing Vietnamese names with dollar signs scribbled beside each one. "We've hit a North Vietnamese paymaster and his team," I told Ciminski. "Just look at this money."

He beamed. "Wow!" was all he could get out.

Taan and Rodriguez came trotting up. Their hands were full of jewelry and other useless treasures. Taan tossed a small object at me. Barely seeing it in the light of the fire, I managed to catch it before it hit the ground. It was a tooth, or filling anyway—a gold one. Memories of old war movies popped into my head as I recalled soldiers bashing jaws in search of pieces of gold. My stomach complained once again.

Ciminski and Rodriguez caught a glimpse of the filling. "Hey, these guys could be hiding a fortune," Rodriguez said eagerly.

"Yeah," Ciminski answered as they both started toward the bodies.

"Hold it," I ordered. I wasn't about to take part in such a rampage. "Forget the idea. We've stayed here too long already. Let's move out."

Momentarily, they checked my face to see if I was serious. I was.

"Okay," they shrugged, and we headed back to Everett's position carrying our possessions along with us. Along the way, Ciminski spotted something in his path. "Hey, look at this," he yelled, "a spare." He held up a leg that had been blown off at the hip and waved it in the air. No order was needed as the sudden realization of what he had done sunk home with him. He dropped the leg and brushed off his hands in a futile effort to push the reality aside.

We all gazed at the leg as it plopped back onto the ground and surrounded itself in a cloud of dust. For a moment, we all stared, transfixed, as if awaiting an answer to the question that continually haunted us—why? The remains of our mortal enemies remained silent—they too, had no answer. Everett turned and started down the trail with his own private burden. One by one we broke the power holding our gaze and slowly followed him. The silence was unbearable yet inevitable.

Once again, a tear fought its way to the corner of my eyes. This time, I left it there. It was a normal reaction after a "firefight," normal to us anyway. The profoundness of our situation, the reality and our closeness to death, coupled with the need to know "why" always engulfed us, each one of us, as we wrestled with our own inner selves to force our minds to a mental state that could cope with the hell in which we lived.

Even as a kid back at my grandparents' farm in Texas where my Dad took me hunting, I never could really get used to killing something. It just never felt right taking any kind of life. We justified it, though, for food. But this was different. This was a fellow human being who in another situation, a different time, might have been a good friend. "Why?" we continually asked ourselves. The answers never came and the question never left.

I checked my watch: 0525. "Sun up in about thirty more minutes," I thought. "We'd better be alert."

The most dangerous times in the bush were dusk and dawn. Dusk was tough due to the many groups of people scurrying about to gain cover before nightfall. Such random, hurried movement confused the typical routine and offered easy cover for the enemy we sought so desperately. In addition, our eyes played tricks on us as the shadows deepened, and the spots of reflected light played havoc with the pupils of our eyes as they tried to adapt to the oncoming darkness. Bushes began to look like men hunkered down waiting for the opportunity to kill. The imagination proved to be a dangerous enemy, if you succumbed to its seductive ways. Dawn was dangerous for many of the same reasons. In addition, however, we were extremely weary, especially after a long night in a fire fight. It was very easy to allow ourselves to get caught up in the false security of the morning sun, a new day promising new hope.

This particular morning was uneventful. We stepped onto the blacktop just as the sun began reaching through the trees. A fresh breeze from the ocean[4] filtered its way through the jungle and filled our lungs with the hope of new life. The smells brought by the breeze assured us that the villagers were already well into preparation for their new day. Odors from morning fires told of the typical cooking of rice. Somewhere a pig squealed. The villagers built their pigpens against their huts and actually continued the pen through the exterior wall into the hut. They ate their meals huddled around a cooking fire and simply tossed the leftovers into the pigpen.

"Here comes a meal on wheels," I said. They all looked up. During the day it was a treat to be on the blacktop, normally filled with people heading to and from Chu Lai or Đà Nẵng. It was like watching a parade back in the States. Most of the people were very polite and bowed to us, some through fear and some simply out of respect. We always tried to greet them in their own language, making sure to use the correct title. Children were acknowledged with "chào con," men with "chào anh," unmarried and young girls with "chào cô," and married and older women with "chào bà" and "chào bà an." Older men were greeted with a bow and a "chào ông." Failing to recognize them properly was considered a grave insult.

"Think I'll help myself to a good old sourdough fish and pork sandwich soaked in the 'Nước Mặn' sauce," I said.

"Don't know how you can eat that stuff," Everett responded. "You have to pick out all the bugs from the bread, the meat is raw, and that *sauce* is made from vinegar and fermented raw fish. Gross, man."

"Hey, it tastes great. Besides the meat is pickled, I think, and the sauce adds to the flavor." I didn't add that it also covered up the taste of the raw meat. I didn't much care, because eating it was a simple way to strengthen my bond with our Vietnamese counterparts. Of course, it also offered me the opportunity to eat something besides rice. I was interested in trying every type of food the Vietnamese diet included in any shape or form, unless I suspected it would bite back.

Taan excused himself and trotted off due east, in the direction of a village bordering the ocean and surrounded by coconut palms. Due to the severe loss of its own men in 'Nam, the South Vietnamese government had issued a polygamy law. Taan took exceptional advantage of the law. He had one girl in each of the three primary villages in our APR, and he was constantly attempting to entice others to join his list of lucky women. Only one of the women had blessed him with children, but Taan kept trying. He was a good soldier. I smiled as I watched his silhouette fade into the jungle. "God be with him," I thought.

Everett had the rest of us set up day camp at a roadside "hooch"[5] which we frequented on a random schedule. Mamasan Tôu and her daughter of about fifteen lived in the place and had set up a trading post for us. We all loved her, and she waited on us hand and foot during each visit. In addition, she put on alert all the people within a hundred yards in any direction of the hooch, to act as our perimeter warning system. They would send runners to us—usually children—if VC activity was spotted.

When I first got there, I had distrusted her. Her husband and two sons had been Viet Cong and I simply could not believe in her loyalty. But as the

Taan with one of his
wives and children.
Notice the potatoes
drying in the circular
plate on the roof.

time passed, she had repeatedly proven her sincerity toward us and her
disgust for the Viet Cong. She blamed the VC for the death of her husband
and her offspring and had her heart set on helping us in every feasible way.

Her daughter, Lín Tôu, was beautiful. Her skin was olive color and so
smooth you could hardly take your eyes from her. She spent her every moment dancing around in a multicolored silk outfit that enhanced her beauty
even more.

Mamasan Tôu's hut was constructed of a framework of bamboo poles
with walls and a roof made from palm leaves interwoven and neatly tied to
keep out the weather. The door opening was covered with a drab, brown
drape weighted at the bottom with a bamboo pole. The windows were
covered in a similar fashion. The interior was one small room except for a
sleeping area that was nothing more than a bamboo framework covered in
silk cloth to create a comfortable enclosure. The silk was extremely thin,
allowing air to pass through but shielding against most nuisance insects.

Lin Tôu, Mamasan
Tôu's daughter.

The floor was a provision from Mother Nature, good old dirt. Mamasan kept it swept clean with a broom she had cut from a nearby date palm tree. She was very meticulous, constantly batting us with her broom in protest if we dropped the slightest crumb on her tidy dirt floor. Her only source of light, heat or cooking fire was a small fire built close to one wall of the hut. A hole in the roof allowed a quick escape route for the smoke. She had an interior hog pen which boasted one fat, happy pig.

The exterior of the home was surrounded by a variety of bushes typical of the jungle nearby, each bush in full bloom. A water well stood just a few feet away, and a crude picket fence built from split pieces of bamboo surrounded the immediate area.

After our meal, our first duty was to clean our weapons and check our ammo count. We were definitely low on everything. Ciminski radioed in

for a chopper drop for fresh ammo. The battle of the night before had taken
its toll, not only on the ammo, but also on us. Although elated with our
success, we were mentally and physically exhausted.

As we sat in the shade of Mamasan Tôu's thatched roof, Doc, Ciminski
and I began systematically disassembling our weapons while Everett and
Rodriguez kept watch. Bore and mechanism cleaned, I glanced over at
Ciminski. He had his thumb stuck in the breech of his rifle to reflect light
up the bore.

"Got her all clean?" I asked.

"Yeah, guess so," he answered.

"What about your prize?" I asked. "Going to clean it?"

"Naw man, she's pretty just as she is." He picked it up. "I'm just going
to pack it up and ship it home." He held it out for me to admire one more
time.

"She's sure a beauty," I assured him. "What are you going to do when
you get out of this hell hole?"

"Well, I've been giving that some thought. I'm sending all of my money
back to my mother in Little Falls, Minnesota, and when I get back there,
I'm going to buy a four-wheel drive truck to help cars out of ditches in the
winter. It's a big problem up there, you know."

"No kidding," I answered. "Sounds like a noble venture."

"What about you?" Ciminski asked. I looked at him for a minute then
dropped my eyes to the disassembled weapon that lay before me.

"I don't know," I answered. "I honestly don't know. I can't seem to look
past today, anymore."

"Yeah, I know what you mean."

I brightened up. "There is one thing, though."

"What's that?" he asked.

"Well, I've promised myself that if I make it out of the bush, I'm going
to get myself a college education. You know, with the GI Bill and all."

"You'll make it, Corporal," he urged. "You'll make it."

Weapons clean, we settled in for a well deserved rest. I took first watch,
hoping for a peaceful day. I found myself a shady spot in the shelter of a
nearby palm tree. The breeze from the ocean felt good. I relaxed a little bit,
watching the sky and listening for the distinctive "chop" of the carriers of
our ammo.

Everett had completed his radio report to CAP Headquarters and was
heading in my direction. "Looks like we'll get a medal out of this one," he

said as he walked up. "The CO is sending out a jeep to pick up the twenty thousand and drop off our ammo." He stopped momentarily, as if studying his next thought. "Another thing," he said, almost hesitantly. "The CO wants all confiscated weapons sent back with the jeep."

"Ciminski's going to be livid!" I answered back, glancing over to his position. "And I don't blame him. The CO has no right to do that."

"I agree," Everett said, "but it was a direct order. What about the map?"

"Oh, yeah." I had completely forgotten about it. I dug into the pockets of my utilities until I found it. "Here it is." We spread the map onto the ground and began studying it. The map only revealed a few crudely marked Xs. A chill danced down my back as I recognized their meaning. The largest X revealed the location of Fat City. Another X, similar in size, portrayed our base camp area, the old French compound.[6] The remaining Xs were much smaller and were scattered around the area due west and north of the French compound.

"Do you realize what those small Xs stand for?" Everett asked, pointing to the smaller ones.

I studied them more intently. Suddenly my heart sank. "Why, they . . . they . . ." I couldn't get it out. I swallowed—hard. "They portray every ambush site and every place we've set up in that area over the past two months!"

"Right." Everett's face was somber. "That means somewhere around that compound we have ourselves an informer. I'm surprised our goose hasn't already been cooked with that informer running loose." He folded up the map. "Better send this back to CAP Command along with the CO's toys," he said. "The intelligence group may be able to make more out of it." He put the map into his pocket, turned and set out to find a place to settle down to clean his weapon, rest and await the jeep's arrival.

The map haunted my mind even though the jungle surrounding us appeared quiet. The ocean breeze tried to relieve my tension, but my eyes kept searching the jungle. I half expected to see little beady eyes staring back at me as their owner marked down another crude little X.

The day passed rapidly. The jeep came and left. Ciminski threw his fit and threatened the driver within an inch of his life. Finally we settled him down, and the jeep—complete with a shaken driver—returned home with the CO's new toys in tow.

The following couple of days and nights were basically free of activity, which in a way was its own little hell. Inactivity meant the enemy was planning something we definitely were not going to like.

A week passed by and the jeep returned with two new men. Doc was being rotated to another unit and was being replaced with a tall, lanky Australian[7] named Bob Johnston. I took an instant liking to him. He had a great sense of humor and brought new life to our little group. The other man was an addition to bring us closer to true squad strength. The second man was a black man named Earl Jones, about five-foot-nine or so, stocky build, and a somber, yet trustworthy, look on his face. Both Johnston and Jones had good hand shakes.

"Welcome to our haven," I said. They both smiled, then followed Ciminski off to stash their gear. I remembered the jeep ride that had brought me in a few months before. I smiled at the memory, at the fear I'd had of the unknown, the worry over fitting in.

Suddenly, Taan burst upon the scene waving a fistful of papers in the air and jabbering away like a chicken caught with a leg wire.

"Bob Johnston," the Australian corpsman.

"Whoa! Slow down!" I yelled. "We can't understand that fast talk." He didn't smile at my attempt at humor. He just shoved one of the papers into my hands, stabbing a finger at the picture and the writing below it.

As I unfolded the paper, my heart joined my feet on the ground. It was a Viet Cong propaganda pamphlet which portrayed a picture of mutilated bodies of Vietnamese women and children. Under the picture was a caption written in English and Vietnamese, "You Marines are rapists, murderers and baby killers. You are destroying our country." Then there was an appeal in Vietnamese: "The men you are sheltering attacked the Xuân Ngoc Hai village last week and killed all the villagers. Yet you protect them." The pamphlet was referring to our battle with the VC paymaster, although we thought there had been no villagers involved except the prostitutes. "Oh, God, I hope there were no children in those huts," I thought. I read on. "We will pay $500 American dollars for the head of each of the Marines you are now sheltering." That was it.

I sank back against a palm tree as the meaning of the pamphlet sank home. The Cong had placed a bounty on our heads. They wanted us dead and were ready to offer hard cash, a good couple of years of their income, for the death of each one of us.

Taan put his hand on my shoulder. "Not worry," he smiled. "Villagers not want money anyway."

I prayed he was right. I returned the smile.

"Let's find Everett," I said, "and don't tell the rest of the men yet." Taan understood. He nodded his head and followed alongside me.

Everett was just as shook up as I was. "We've got to break it to the men," he said, "but let's not show them the flyer. We have enough trouble with morale as it is."

I agreed. We all wanted desperately to be able to go home. More than that, no one knew better than we that memories of the women and children caught up in the death and suffering from our war ate at us more than anything. We rounded up the men. Rodriguez, Ciminski, our new Doc and the other new man, Jones. (The old "Doc" had already hopped his jeep out of there. He hadn't wasted time with formal goodbyes. He simply climbed in his jeep, waved and yelled out "Give 'em Hell guys." In a moment he was gone.)

Everett, Taan and I gathered our little group together. "Men," Everett began, "we have just received a late news bulletin." He tried to take the humorous approach, but his tension was obvious. He held the pamphlet up, but from that distance they couldn't see the details. He continued, "It boasts the same bull about us being rapists and baby killers that their pamphlets always try to perpetuate. However, this one poses a new challenge."

Everett paused for a moment and fixed his gaze on the ground as if searching the dirt for a better way to let the men know. A sobering silence hovered over us. You could have heard a tree growing. Cautiously, Everett transferred his gaze from the ground to the men. He let out a deep sigh, straightened his shoulders and said: "There is simply no other way to tell you guys. We are in big trouble. This pamphlet also boasts a reward for the head of each man in this squad. Evidently our attack against that paymaster and his little group of heathens had a major impact. We now have a price on our heads, which means every Tom, Dick and Harry will be laying for us. So we need to remain twice as alert from now on."

"How much is the bounty?" Ciminski asked.

"Five hundred American dollars," Everett answered. "Each." The squad grew quiet again. Each man turned to the other with silence. Unspoken questions hung in the air.

Rodriguez let out a long, low whistle. "American dollars?" he asked incredulously.

Everett nodded.

"Hey! That kind of makes us a legend in our own time, doesn't it?!" remarked Ciminski. The idea took hold, as if a torch had been lit under us. We were electrified with the thought of being "legends." Suddenly, the fear was gone. Everyone was happy. Even the new guys, though they had no idea what had happened, got caught up in the jovial atmosphere. Jones strutted around like a game hen doing John Wayne imitations.

"How 'bout a beer?" he asked.

"Sure, but only one," I said. "We don't want any drunk heroes. By the way, that's one of our standing rules here. One beer a day, no drugs, no one man ventures into the bush, and trust no one."

"Sounds like a pretty tough set of rules," Jones said.

Everett joined the conversation, "You can live by it or die by it," he said.

"Meaning what?" Jones answered, angered at Everett's remark.

I jumped in. "Meaning there is only one way to guarantee the safety of our unit. We all must stay at 100% alertness at all times, twenty-four hours a day. Without it, we don't stand a chance. Those gooks fear us right now, but if they find one of us in a weakened state, they'll hit us with everything they've got."

"One final thing," I continued, "that rule is a direct order. Either you obey it or we ship you out or kill you, depending on the circumstance. We simply cannot allow one man the opportunity to jeopardize the entire unit."

Jones stared at me for a moment, then at Everett, then dropped his gaze to the ground. "Must be pretty tough out here," he said.

"Yep," Everett said, "and it's liable to get a lot tougher."

"Let's get that beer," I said. "And that's an order."

Jones looked up, checked my face again. I gave him my Texas grin. He laughed, "Yeah, let's get it while we can."

The rest of the men were already heading that way. I thought about how I had felt when I first arrived in CAP—pretty scared. "That Jones will make a good man," I thought.

We all bought a dollar beer from a local street vendor, checked it for visible signs of penetration, stabbed holes in the tops with our knives and toasted to our future, the America that awaited our return, and to our "legend," bounty and all.

---

[1] North Vietnamese Army (NVA) regulars, or officially the People's Army of Vietnam, had taken over a larger portion of the Communist war in Vietnam by 1969, in part due to the heavy losses suffered by the Viet Cong during the 1968 Tết Offensive. American soldiers, like Goodson, had a healthy respect for the NVA motivation and skill. North Vietnamese soldiers were easier to spot because of their distinctive uniforms and fought more predictably because of their professional training. Many American soldiers had less respect for the Viet Cong, who some viewed as treacherous and dishonorable, because they often looked and acted like civilians and fought in a more unpredictable fashion. Ronald Spector, *After Tet: The Bloodiest Year in Vietnam* (New York: Free Press, 1993), 199–201.

[2] "Frag grenades" refers to fragmentation grenades.

[3] An M-79 is a shoulder-fired 40-mm grenade launcher.

[4] Ocean refers to the South China Sea.

[5] A "hooch" is a hut or simple dwelling.

[6] The old French compound refers to a former French military installation dating to the French colonial rule of Vietnam, most likely used during the French Indochina War, 1946–1954.

[7] Australia, New Zealand, Thailand, and the Republic of Korea sent forces to aid the Republic of Vietnam in the war. Arnold W. Braeske, "Aussies on the Allied Team," *Army Digest* 24 (April 1969), 45-46.

## Chapter 5

# Tết Offensive of 1969

**D**ays slid into weeks and still there was minimal VC activity. Everett and I were worried. Inactivity meant the VC were regrouping for some form of attack—but what? Another thing that worried us was that the men had grown lax with inactivity. A false security was setting in. To fight the inevitable, we set up a daily training program. We had target practice twice a day and a regimented practice of our hand-to-hand combat. These seemed to work. The men maintained their combat readiness, but the mental alertness worried me.

January 28, 1969, at 0600: a jeep rolled in with our once-a-month mail call. We always met him at random locations in hope of keeping the enemy confused. The jeep was loaded with mail and packages—late Christmas arrivals, a dozen axes and one cistern water pump I had ordered, and a set of orders for me.

"Orders," I thought. "What are they up to now?" As I opened them I began searching for the bottom line.

"Whatcha got?" Everett was just as curious as I was.

I read the orders aloud. It read: "Subject: Birthday—Corporal Goodson—29 January 1949. These orders provide you with one full day in the rear starting at 0600 on 29 January and ending at 0600 on 30 January." At first, I was excited. "Yahoo!"

Everett smiled weakly.

"What's wrong?"

"Well," he began, "It's great to get out of the bush for a day but we sure need you here at night."

"Yeah," I agreed. "Let's call the CO and get him to bring me back at 1600 hours."

Everett liked that approach.

The CO nixed the whole idea. "My orders stand as they are," he said. "You will come in for a full twenty-four hours. It's SOP. Besides," he continued, "I am not about to send a jeep out at that time of day."

"Standard Operating Procedure," I snapped as I placed the radio back on the ground. "Big deal!"

Everett just murmured something and walked away.

We spent the rest of the day distributing axes to the local villagers Taan and I had helped when I first arrived. Using Taan as an interpreter, I demonstrated the use of a single-edged ax. They were definitely impressed with the effectiveness of the ax in comparison to their machetes. The women and children stood around, peering out from behind bushes and trees. They were a little leery of these strange tools from the good old USA.

The men took their first swing. Most of them had accurate aim and the blades dug deep into their respective trees. A couple of them missed not only their marks but their trees, losing their grip on their axes and sending them flying into the jungle. People scattered like BBs on ice. The women and children screamed. The men who had succeeded laughed while the two men chased after the runaway axes.

Before long, every man had mastered the art of chopping wood with axes rather than machetes. They were natural born woodsmen and were simply amazed at how fast they could chop down a tree. We set up a Paul Bunyan contest to see who was the best. All the other men in the squad were diehard city boys, so the boy from Texas won the contest hands down. The sore losers began hurling all sorts of profanity and derogatory Texas jokes. Undaunted by their harassing jeers, I shouldered my ax, picked up my coconut (the prize) and marched around the fallen trees.

"Remember the Alamo!" I shouted, "Viva la Texas."

Further obscenities were hurled in my direction, along with more coconuts. I dodged the incoming fire and found security behind a palm tree. Peering in their direction, I gave them my old Texas taunt: thumbs in my ears, waving hands, I let fly— "Nana nana naa na." The men circled out after me in an attempt to cage me in. Trapped! I growled and leered at them. They laughed and moved in for the kill. With a loud scream I burst from my protected area and threw myself into the clump of men. We all

Barry Goodson, Texan,
winner of the ax-
swinging contest.

tumbled to the ground in a heap of laughter and giggles. The Vietnamese
were elated. They had never seen Americans act so foolishly. "Keep watching," I thought. "You ain't seen nothing yet." We all lay back for a moment, catching our breath. Momentarily, our tension was gone.

Taan assured the villagers that we were not "beaucoup điên kiện đầu"
(very crazy), suppressed a laugh, and continued to tell them that the axes
were theirs to keep. We left them marveling over their new prizes. I prayed
that the axes remained as tools, not weapons.

Mission accomplished, we gathered our gear and set out to pick up the
cistern pump. Due to its bulky size and weight, we had stashed it in the
jungle near the area where the jeep had met us earlier that day. Because we
were breaking a cardinal rule by returning to the same place in the same
day, the tension returned.

We approached the area slowly. About a half-mile away we split up
into two groups, each one following a tree line to the hidden location.
"We'll need to organize this better in the future," I thought. The area seemed
secure. Not a sign of life—well, at least as far as the eye could see, which
was only a hundred yards or so. Everett set up a perimeter guard with

Goodson and "Everett."
There were times when
even marines had to
release some tension by
acting silly.

Ciminski, Rodriguez, and Doc Johnston. Jones and I dug up the hidden pump. I stared down at it. "Must weigh a hundred pounds or so," I said.

Jones smiled, handed me his rifle, and easily hoisted the pump to his shoulder. Just as gingerly, he picked up the two sections of pipe and shouldered them as well. "Lead the way, boss," he smiled again.

"Smart aleck," I said. I waved the others over and showed off my strongman.

Everett wasn't pleased. "He's a sitting duck, man!" He motioned to Rodriguez, "Take that pipe from him." Rodriguez grumbled and shouldered his load. "I simply don't like this," Everett continued. "We're burdened enough as it is."

"My fault," I offered. "I should've had the jeep drop the pump off at Lín Tôu's house."

"Oh, well," he murmured, "let's get at it."

Fortunately, we were only about half a mile from the blacktop. As we reached the edge of the jungle opening onto the road, Everett called a short rest for Jones and Rodriguez.

The blacktop was teeming with people, all hurrying to get somewhere so they could hurry back. I always marveled at the endless amount of energy and strength the Vietnamese possessed. A barefoot man clad only in black PJ bottoms came by, carrying two huge woven baskets loaded with rocks. The baskets were suspended from each end of a bamboo pole and yet he was *trotting* down the road. With each step the loaded baskets would sag toward the ground with increased heaviness. Undaunted, the man never slowed his pace.

"Think I'll stick to pumps," Jones remarked as he followed my gaze.

"Yeah," was all I could get out. Still trotting, the man disappeared into the crowd of people.

Off to the north a "xe tắc-xi," a half-motorcycle, half-van type vehicle, lumbered towards us with a "pop and bang" followed by an occasional puff of smoke spiraling from the exhaust. "Hey! I've got an idea," I said.

Everett followed my gaze. "And a good one," he agreed.

I sent Taan to flag down the driver and negotiate our fare with him. The "taxi" slowed to a stop. The driver and Taan broke into a steaming argument which ended as quickly as it erupted. Taan smiled and motioned us over. "No charge," he beamed. "He let marines ride for no money."

We loaded our gear and the pump onto the waiting vehicle while Taan gave orders to our driver. The man was not as happy about the idea as Taan, who obviously had powers of persuasion. With a jolt and a barrel of smoke the xe tắc-xi nosed its way forward in search of our destination.

Along the way the driver, hanging out the window, released his frustrations against us, onto the local folks and any and every thing or animal that got in the way of his vehicle. His dialect was somewhat different than I was used to, so I caught only pieces of his conversation with Taan and even less of the gibberish he unleashed on the people in his way. Taan helped him navigate by hanging off the side of the vehicle and yelling at everyone, continually prompting the driver when he thought he saw a better route to take. Finally we reached our destination. Jones and Rodriguez carried the pump and pipe over to the cistern.

I attempted to pay the driver something, but Taan gently shoved me away and ordered the driver to leave quickly—"để đi mau" as he put it. As it turned out, "soldiers" never pay for rides, or for anything. "Not good for villager morale," I thought, but I knew better than to interfere. It was their way.

Mamasan Tôu was glad to see us and was obviously curious about the pump. Jones and I unpacked the tools and accessories that accompanied the unit. The rest of the men scattered into various shady locations. Mamasan passed out one beer to each man—this time on the house.

Jones and I, under the leadership of Taan and Lín, constructed a crude bamboo platform and placed it over the mouth of the cistern. Jones was obviously enjoying himself as he let go with a song. Taan and Lín laughed and egged him on. I joined in. With a song on our lips and jeers and laughter from our peers, we completed the installation, primed the pump, and sent Lín on a run after her mother.

Everyone gathered around. I gave the pump a few good strokes and the water came flowing out of the spout and onto the ground around the cistern. Lín was elated, clapping her hands, and dancing for joy. It obviously had been her chore to fetch the water. Mamasan Tôu was more dignified and simply bowed to each one of us. To further show her gratitude, she invited us to join her family in their noonday meal. We obliged.

After the meal Jones and I decided to complete the finishing touches on the platform. The others cleaned weapons and sharpened knives, a daily routine regardless of the night before. Although we all were weary from the long night, sleep came only when opportunity allowed the luxury. Usually half the squad would nap while the remaining half maintained a watchful eye. On this particular day, with chores done, everyone but Ciminski, who stood a lone watch, took a nap while Jones and I worked. Our nap would have to wait a couple of hours. Everett and I planned that night's patrol and ambush based on input from one of Taan's sources. Since tomorrow was my birthday, Everett decided to patrol the blacktop that night and set up an ambush in an area just north of the old French compound. According to Taan the Viet Cong had infiltrated the village "Kương Bìhn Một," and were attempting to recruit the local kids as well as infiltrate our PF troops.

Jones and I completed strapping down the platform to secure it against theft and the fury of storms. Jones wiped his brow. Weariness showed in his face. He looked at our creation, patted the pump gingerly and laughed. "Looks like Mamasan Tôu's in business now."

I checked my watch. We had just enough time to catch a couple of hours of Zs.

"Let's wake the others," I said. Jones readily agreed. Quietly we made the rounds, making sure to awaken each man gently so as not to create undue alarm. Just a touch brought every man instantly awake.

Doc Johnston relieved Ciminski on watch. John laid his poncho liner underneath the shade of a clump of banana trees. "I hope the gooks leave us alone long enough for some decent shut eye," he remarked.

"Yeah," I agreed. Jones, who answered with only a mumble, was already drifting away. I followed suit.

It seemed like I had just closed my eyes when I jolted awake, reaching for the M-16 by my side. Rodriguez crouched beside me. "Didn't mean to startle you man, but it's time to rise and shine," he said.

My nerves settled back as I realized he had awakened me in the middle of dreams of a previous battle.

"You okay, man?" Rodriguez added.

"Yeah," I stammered. "Just fine." I walked to the pump and showered my head with water. The coolness cleared my head. I turned to gather up my gear. Most of the others were already prepared to move out.

Everett turned to me: "You've lost that fear haven't you?"

I was taken aback. "What? I, uh, . . . *fear?*"

"Sure," he added. "Remember when you first arrived? The very idea of not having a compound to hide in was hard to swallow . . . right?"

"Yeah, it was."

"And now the fear is gone, man!" Everett said.

I was embarrassed at the memory. "Sorry about that," I stammered. "I guess I was just too pre-programmed."

He laughed. "Not to worry old man. We all had to face it. Welcome to the club." He extended his hand. We shook hands the old way, then I made a feeble attempt to throw in the "Brother" rhythm that I had seen the Blacks do so many times. I failed miserably. Everett rolled in laughter. "Keep practicing, White Boy. Keep practicing."

I laughed with him. "Don't know how you guys do it."

"It's all in the wrist," he offered as he slapped me on the back. "Come on. Let's gather the others. It's time to leave."

It was 1800 hours. We bid Mamasan and Lín good-bye and disappeared into the jungle behind her hut. The two women kept on talking as if we were still there. I smiled at their efforts. If anyone was listening, we would be long gone before they discovered that Mamasan and Lín were talking to thin air.

Our journey was short. We arrived at our ambush spot at 1930 hours and set up our perimeter. Not a soul or a sound. We chose a trench between a tree line and a dried-up rice paddy as our home for the night. We placed the machine gun in the center of the trench facing the dried rice paddy. The rest of the men flanked either side of the gun with alternating positions to cover both directions. We set up Willy Peter booby traps at both ends of the trench at approximately 100 yards either side of our position, to forewarn us if anyone attempted to sneak into our ranks from the shadows of the trench.

Night closed in around us. The stars and moon seemed to illuminate the entire area. We hugged the shadows and smeared mud all over our faces and arms. Time moved slowly.

At around 2100 hours, we were all jolted into full reality with a sudden burst of AK fire. We hugged the ground awaiting another burst, but nothing happened. Moments passed. Then the AK, accompanied by RPG and mortars, opened up into a full battle—but not with us. The mortar we had been searching for was attacking the artillery base! We prepared to move out, our hearts resounding in our ears. Suddenly, silence settled back into its rightful place. Nothing stirred. Even the radio was silent. The attack ended as abruptly as it had started. We settled back down into position and peered into the surrounding tree lines. Nothing! Not even a breeze. "That's good," I thought. "At least when a leaf moves we'll know to blow it away." We kept our position. There was no sense in trying to locate the Mortar Gang. They had no doubt disappeared underground anyway. Besides, the bright moon made such an effort not only stupid, but also downright suicidal.

Hours dragged by. Shortly after 0500 we were startled by a rustling noise at the north end of the trench. We tried to blend in with our surroundings. "Act like a tree," I thought. "I don't want to miss that twentieth birthday."

The Willy Peter trap ignited in a flash. "Kaboom!" The white phosphorous lit up the night with a ball of flame, sending lethal goblets of flaming gel in all directions. A surprised yelp penetrated the darkness and suddenly a dog burst from the flames and smoke in a rampage towards our position. We checked for other movement. Nothing. Nothing but a yelping dog scared half out of its wits by a massive ball of flame that rudely interrupted his morning venture. Amazingly enough, the unscathed dog vanished into the jungle, leaving nothing but a continuous yelp to follow him.

Once my heart settled back to normal, I made a mental note to set those trip wires just little bit higher.

Everyone laughed at the situation except for Everett. "Goodson." He motioned me over. "Let's readjust the height of those trip wires from now on. If those gooks had been anywhere near our position, we would have been sitting ducks for a mortar attack."

"Yeah, I thought about that," I agreed. "I'll be more careful."

"Add one dog to the VC list," he stated with a smile.

The jeep arrived at 0615. I climbed in, carrying a list of orders for various items for each of the men, for Mamasan Tôu and Lín, and with a request from Everett to check on his stateside orders. "What a bummer," I thought. "The man is a short-timer,[1] has only a few weeks left and one of them includes Tết."[2]

The driver of the jeep was a young man of eighteen or nineteen, frail looking with nervous eyes. He had absolutely nothing to say. Silence was fine with me. My mind was still with the CAP unit anyway. What would they do today? Where would they go?

Why was I going to the rear? I had never really celebrated birthdays anyway. It just wasn't a family tradition. Besides, if I was going to celebrate, then strangers wouldn't help. Heaviness overwhelmed me. What if the gooks unleashed their Tết fury early and wiped out my squad tonight? I longed to be back in the bush with them. "If only I could have traded places with Everett," I thought. "His time was so short anyway."

The jeep continued to lumber down Highway One.

In an attempt to take my mind off my men, I began studying all the people traipsing to and fro down the blacktop. "An artery of life," I thought. We passed a man herding a bunch of pigs to God knows where. Off to the right a group of small children were playing chase. Another small boy, probably around six or seven years old, was tugging and kicking at a water buffalo. I smiled. The way those kids could manhandle those beasts amazed me.

The jeep motor produced a monotonous hum. My mind rolled back to the children playing along the roadside. Taan and I had discussed at some length the various games they played, but the discussion had been difficult at first because the word "play" was almost absent from the Vietnamese language, at least in respect to organized games. Toys simply did not exist.

"What games do they play?" I had asked.

"P . . . lay," he had stammered back.

"You know, have fun," I said, pointing to a group of kids milling around at the edge of the jungle.

"Ah," said Taan. I was finally getting through to him. "You mean 'choi đùa.' No play. No games. Only goof off from work."

I went through a long list of games that I felt might be international, but Taan didn't recognize a one. It was pure and simple. The Vietnamese worked from sun up to sun down with very little idle time. The children, as soon as they could stand and walk on their own two feet, were given specific chores to complete. When they were not working, they rested or chased each other around. In some cases, they did play combat with each other— or were they playing? To the Vietnamese, it was actually more of a prompting or training for real combat. The children were simply emulating their parents in a mock effort to reproduce the war on their own scale. Their actions reminded me of how the young of such animals as wolves, lions and other predators play in mock combat, unknowingly preparing themselves for mortal combat or, to simplify it—to kill. My heart longed to teach the kids some of the simple games kids played back home, but something warned me to leave them alone.

A jolt from the jeep as it turned into headquarters brought me back to the situation at hand—my birthday. "I'd just as soon forget the whole idea," I murmured to myself.

Headquarters looked like a city to me. There were hooches and buildings everywhere. The base was surrounded by row after row of concertina wire[3] and had only one entrance and exit, unless you had a boat, because it backed right up against the ocean. Every 100 feet or so were watchtowers boasting floodlights, 50 Cals[4] and M-80 mortars. A couple of the towers revealed silhouettes of 106 recoilless guns.[5] 106s were awesome weapons that fired a projectile in a somewhat similar fashion to that of a bazooka, or LAW as we called them in this war—"Land to Air Weapon." A 106, however, was a literal cannon with an open breech. When a shell was fired, a twenty-foot flame would flare out the back side of the gun. They were very effective in close range combat, but they were extremely visible even when they were covered up, because 106 towers were always surrounded by safety

Two of Taan's children playing with Goodson's M-16 rifle.

nets to catch men dodging the flame or hunks of metal from an exploding chamber due to "cook offs," created by the overheating of the chamber to the point that the explosive in the projectile would ignite before the gunner had time to fire it. Many times the gunner and his crew were severely injured or killed. The effectiveness of the gun far outweighed the number of our men it killed, so our leaders decided to keep it around.

The compound was fairly typical of any other marine compound, with the mess tent and clubs centrally located while sleeping quarters formed a perimeter around them. The ammo bunkers, CO's quarters and medic quarters were also inside the perimeter of buildings. This compound did have one other thing that I had never seen before, a bakery. The smell of fresh bread taunted my senses, and I knew I'd have to pay them a visit.

Chu Lai rear. Photo taken on Goodson's birthday, 29 January 1969.

Another corporal was waiting for me in front of the CO's tent. "Corporal Goodson? Welcome to the rear." He smiled and extended his hand. "And happy birthday. The CO asked me to tell you to do what you want for the next twenty-four hours. Get drunk, sleep, write letters or whatever. Just don't tear the place up." Under his breath he added, "The man is fanatic for maintaining a perfectly clean base."

I just smiled, waved him away and set off toward—what? I had no idea. As I wandered aimlessly around, my thoughts turned back to my first days in 'Nam and the CO—or actually the Top Sergeant—we'd had to put up with then. He was absolutely fanatic even to the point of having us line up rocks in front of all the officers' and NCOs' tents and paint them white. In addition, we had to rake the dirt around the hooches, which gave them a look of neatly plowed miniature fields. "This man went to the same school," I thought as I passed a similarly groomed area. "Never thought of it before, but it sure makes it easy for the gooks to pick out targets."

My wandering led me to the ocean. There were no beaches, just mound after mound of coral reefs randomly protruding above the waterline to create natural pools of captured life and sufficient footsteps to allow an extensive study of just about all the pools. I was fascinated by the abundance of marine life. Everywhere you looked something was crawling or swimming. An octopus loomed in the depths of one pool and we spent a better part of the morning simply staring at each other. He won the staring contest. I moved on. I captured a starfish and tried to motivate it into action. It ignored my prodding so I plopped it into a nearby pool.

A sea snake darted in and out of the many small caverns hidden in the depths of one of the pools. I watched him in awe. "Heard a lot about you," I told him. "Silent, but deadly, right?" I recalled my CAP training. "Sea snakes are more deadly than king cobras, so beware of them." The snake came up for air. We exchanged stares. I moved on.

Morning traded with afternoon and hunger directed my attention back to the base. "Might as well get some good out of this day," I thought as I headed in search of the mess tent. "A hot meal and fresh baked bread might help." My stomach growled in eagerness and anticipation of a hot American meal.

I was not disappointed, but as I ate eyes stared through me as if I were some ravenous dog they had found hiding in the shadows of the mess tent. With a hunk of raisin bread protruding halfway out of my mouth, I stopped and leered back at them. The eyes turned away. A typical looking mess sergeant came lumbering over to my table.

"Looks like you've missed that fantastic American cooking," he said with a smile.

I smiled back through chomps on the bread.

"You make the bread?" I asked in a muffled tone.

"Sure did," he answered. "What do you think of it?"

"You could make a fortune on this stuff in the bush," I returned.

He laughed and leaned over toward me. In a whisper he said, "Come by the bakery tonight at 2200 hours and I'll give you some fresh stuff. Right out of the oven, covered in butter." He continued, "It's against regs, but I'll make an exception for a bush man."

"Thanks," I said with another mouthful.

He laughed and sauntered off to his kitchen, screaming at some poor character who was complaining about the meat. "Try it raw," I thought.

Bloated, I forced myself from the mess tent and struck out to walk off the strange feeling of a full stomach. "Burp." I let one fly. "Ah," I said to myself, "Feels good."

Doc Johnston came sauntering up as I stepped from the mess hall.

"Hey!" I said. "What are you doing here? Come to help me celebrate?"

He grinned. "Actually, I had to come in for more medical supplies."

"Got time to grab a beer?"

"Nah, sorry. Got to get back to the bloody bush. Catch you later!"

Spirits up at seeing someone from the bush, I set off with a leisurely pace in search of more of the wonders of the camp. Suddenly gunshots rang out. I tensed up and checked my rifle. It was ready. So was I. The gunfire had come from the direction of the post office but it had sounded like an M-16, not the typical crack of the AK. I relaxed a little and told myself that someone was just having a little target practice. Suddenly MPs appeared to come from nowhere. Screaming and yelling, they converged on the post office like a swarm of bees.

Silence moved in. In a matter of moments, the MPs returned with a prisoner handcuffed in front of them. I caught bits of their conversation. This poor guy had not received any mail from home in months. In retaliation, he had simply walked into the post office and opened up fully automatic with his M-16. One man was dead and many more wounded.

I could easily understand why the man had snapped like that. Letters from home were the only link, the only reminder that there was another place on earth besides the hell in 'Nam. Most men lived for the day—the moment—when a letter would arrive. A simple piece of paper with USA printed on top and three words "I love you" brought tears to the eyes of the meanest man in 'Nam. My heart hurt for him, as well as the men he had killed and wounded.

I watched them march him off to the brig. "He's a dead man now, and all because of no mail from home," I thought. But he was now a war criminal. The wartime situation contributed to his mental state, but because it had broken him, they would destroy him, not for what he had done, but for the blemish he had placed on the Marine Corps's record.

"It don't mean nothing," I said to no one. Placing the shooting on the shelf with my other memories, I cleared my mind and headed for the PX. As I passed through the screen door of the large wooden structure boasting the typical "PX" sign above it, I stopped, awestruck by the contents inside. It was virtually a shopper's paradise, offering all types of food, candy, tobacco products and countless varieties of stereo equipment, jewelry and clothing. A sergeant walked up behind me.

"You coming or going?" he asked.

"Uh . . . oh," I stammered. "Just shocked to see so much stuff."

He laughed as I stepped aside to let him by. "Just out from the bush?"

"Yeah," I nodded.

I set about collecting the various items portrayed on my shopping list. Suddenly, I felt drawn to the stereo section as my eyes fell upon an eight-inch reel-to-reel Akai tape player. I had longed to be able to send tapes home instead of paper. I checked it out. "Yes! It's battery powered," I yelled out. Eyes stared from all directions. I ignored them, adding the tape player and a supply of batteries to the stash I had already created. Then on a whim I picked out a new Seiko "World Time" self-winding watch. With it I could keep up with the date and the time back home. The purchases took all my money but it did not matter. Money no longer held the value it once had. I shouldered my boxes and, leaving the PX behind, sought a safe haven in which to store my goods.

The rest of the afternoon I spent at the NCO Club nursing my one beer. The barkeep kept checking on me to see why I wasn't taking this opportunity to get stone-faced drunk. The truth of the matter was that I wasn't about to break our CAP rule just because some jerk assured me that headquarters was just as secure as any place back home.

"Why, we never even get any incoming," the barkeep said.

"Count your blessings," I returned.

I continued nursing my beer as my eyes began to take in the decor of the bar. The lights were dim, giving the room a cavernous look which was further enhanced by a "camo" parachute suspended from the ceiling and stretched from wall to wall. A pool table, equally lit by a solitary bulb, sat in its own corner awaiting the evening crowd.

The floor was plywood, painted the typical olive drab green, and boasted a wall-to-wall colorful rendition of the CAP emblem. The bar, too, was constructed of plywood with a 2x4 footrest and top rail. Bowls of pretzels were equally spaced and accompanied by ashtrays to complete the ensemble.

The entrance door abruptly swung open, shattering the dark room with the brilliance of the afternoon sun. I shaded my eyes. A couple of early arrivals sauntered into the bar, weaponless, screaming obscenities at the barkeep with orders for "a tall cold one."

I didn't cotton to the idea of watching the two get drunk. I grabbed my M-16 and turned to go.

"Leaving so soon?" the barkeep asked.

"Yeah, one's my limit," I returned. "Y'all keep your heads down." I stepped into the late afternoon sun, thinking what a dangerous place that club could be.

The sun settled into the trees as the afternoon gave way to evening. The sounds of the ocean waves crashing against the coral reefs seemed to increase with the depths of the shadows. Somewhere a generator fired up and penetrated the dusk with a continuous vibrating hum. Dusk faded into night. I sought out the HQ radio tent and tuned into our frequency. Everett was just radioing back his game plan for the night. My heart ached. "I should be out there," I told myself. "Mind if I listen in tonight?" I asked the man on duty.

"No, not at all," he said. "Make yourself at home." He shoved a chair in my direction.

"Is there any way to listen to my squad without staying cooped up like this?" I asked.

"Sure," he answered. "Here, take this radio. We have plenty of spares."

"Appreciate it." I picked up the radio and stepped outside.

I tuned into our frequency. Silence. "Good. Just as it should be," I thought. I could visualize the squad silently moving through the jungle in search of the Cong. I walked across the compound, unable to hold still. Radio on my back, I walked to the north in the direction of my unit. Somehow that made me feel closer to them. Still no radio contact. I sent up a silent prayer for them.

My walk took me down a road that had perimeter wiring and jungle on one side and rows of hooches on the other. The jungle was dark and silent. Suddenly, a movie screen behind one of the hooches lit up. The officers were watching a movie. I snuck up behind them and backed into the shadows. "They have no idea I'm here," I thought. "One grenade would kill them all." I could not get over the false sense of security. No place was that secure, at least not in Vietnam.

Quietly, I moved back to the road. It was shortly after 2100 hours. I could smell the raisin bread baking. "Something good will come out of this trip after all," I thought as I started hunting for that bakery. When I found it, I sat down on a rock and patiently waited outside for 2200 to arrive.

Suddenly, a voice on the radio broke the silence. It was the operator going down his checklist with each CAP unit, as he was supposed to do

every two hours. To minimize noise in the jungle we simply double keyed
our mike to let him know we were okay. A single key meant "standby;
we've got contact." I waited as the radio operator went down his checklist.
There were six units including mine. "CAP One," he whispered. At first,
silence. Then after a few moments one key. A pause, and then a second key.
I sighed with relief.

The bakery door swung wide open. The mess sergeant was momentarily silhouetted in the doorway, reminding me of the night we hit the VC
paymaster. He stepped into the night. "Gotcha some of that bread," he
said. "Are you there?"

I stepped into the light. "Yeah," I answered.

"Wow! Don't startle me like that."

"Sorry, man. I didn't realize you couldn't see me."

"Hey, no problem. Let's find a spot under that palm over there." He
pointed off to his right. He had a plate full of steaming hot bread and a big
slab of butter.

"Okay with me," I said.

We found a dark spot under the tree and watched the bread disappear.
I found out his name was Sergeant Bennett and he came from a little town
outside Toledo, Ohio. He didn't talk much about himself. He just wanted
to know what it was like in the bush. I wasn't used to talking at night. My
answers were polite, but brief. Before we knew it, the plate was empty.

"Want some more?" he asked.

"No thanks," I answered, "but I would like to take some back to my
men."

"Already got you covered," he said. "Hold your position." He returned
to the bakery. I checked my new watch. It was almost 2400 hours. Time for
another check-in. The radio operator went through his routine again. All
CAPs were secure. It looked like it was going to be a quiet night.

I thought back to a night shortly after my initial arrival in CAPs. It
had started out with peace and quiet but before it was over one entire unit
just north of us was wiped out, totally. They never had a chance. They had
walked into an ambush where they were outnumbered drastically. The point
man got it first. He had seen them and tried to fire a buckshot round from
his M-79 grenade launcher, but his round was a dud. Their radio man kept
screaming for help, but to no avail. We were miles away with no way of
reaching them in time. The battle was over in just a matter of minutes. We

could hear the gooks playing with the radio, laughing and taunting us as they pillaged the bodies of our fellow marines. They knew we were listening and were putting on a show for us. "You next, marine." My blood boiled at the memory of it all.

Sergeant Bennett opened the bakery door and peered over at me. Satisfied that I was still there, he trotted over and handed me four loaves of bread neatly wrapped in individual bundles. Regardless of the wrapping job, the aroma still found its way to my nose.

"Mmmmmmmm! Thanks. They'll definitely appreciate it."

He laughed. "I'm gonna hit the rack," he said. "Enjoyed the company."

"Yeah," I said as he disappeared into the night.

I made my way to one of the perimeter towers facing the north and yelled a whisper up to the man on duty. "Hey, mind if I join you?" He peered over the side. I made myself as visible as possible.

"Nah, come on up," he said. "The company will keep me awake."

I climbed up.

The man was using a starlight scope to check the surrounding jungle. "Not a soul moving," he said.

I laid my radio on a sandbag. "May I?" I asked as I reached for his starlight.

"Be my guest."

I felt a little better as I searched the jungle and the nearby village with the starlight. The scope worked on the same principle as an infrared but with more accuracy. Everything was portrayed in a lime green atmosphere You could see a mosquito in flight at 100 meters. Speaking of which, the tower was full of them. "You got any juice?" I asked.

"Sure, help yourself," he answered and handed me a small plastic bottle labeled simply "Insect Repellent." We called it bug juice, but we didn't use it in the bush. You might as well put on cologne or just stand up and put a light over your head. The gooks had an incredible sense of smell, so we let our bodies go natural. As for mosquito repellent, well, we smeared buffalo dung and rice paddy muck onto our exposed skin when we could. This kept away mosquitoes, subdued body odors, and left behind only a natural smell that wouldn't give away our position.

The night passed in silence. "The gooks must be waiting for Tết," I thought. Dawn arrived with a pink glow on the ocean horizon. I thanked the man, climbed down from the tower and returned the radio.

Mission accomplished, I gathered up all the paraphernalia I had bought for everyone back home. My jungle home, that is. Books for the men. The tape recorder for me to send and receive verbal messages from stateside. The rest of my junk included cigarettes, film, candy and other small items. I bought a couple of cases of cigarettes to give to Mamasan Tôu to sell to her fellow Vietnamese as they made their way down the blacktop. As I loaded the junk into the jeep, the CO came walking in my direction followed by two men with sea bags. I popped him a salute.

"Good morning, Corporal," he said as he haphazardly returned my salute. "Got a couple of new recruits here for you. Gentlemen, this is Corporal Goodson. He's your assistant squad leader. He'll show you to your new unit. Good luck." He spun on his heel and headed off.

"Office Pogue,"[6] I muttered to myself. My gaze returned to the men. One was a Puerto Rican about my size and the other was a white guy with a northern look about him. "Howdy," I said to them both.

"I'm Private Elano Mendez," the Puerto Rican offered. Good stance. Good handshake. I liked him instantly.

I reached out to the Yank. "I'm PFC Gary Smith from Jersey," he said.

"Welcome," I said as I grabbed his hand. "You guys are a sight for sore eyes."

We loaded up our gear and climbed into the jeep. I was anxious to get back. The jeep lurched onto the blacktop as the driver headed in the direction of our unit. We were to drop our gear off at the old compound and secure all the "goodies" except for Mamasan Tôu's supplies and the bread. Then we were supposed to meet Everett and the rest of the gang at Mamasan Tôu's.

It was a silent trip back as everyone got caught up in his own thoughts. I was happy to see that we were going to be a stronger unit for Tết. Two more men could make a major difference. During the last Tết, the enemy had struck with surprising force and numbers. I could not help but wonder what was in store for us this time.

We reached our dilapidated old French compound in record time. I studied the two men as we unloaded and stashed away their gear and all of the goodies I had brought back.

"Is this all we have for protection?" Smith asked.

"This place is not for protection," I told him. "It's sort of our home away from home, a place to stash our gear, ammo and a place to rest up."

"You mean . . ." Mendez looked bewildered.

"Yep," I said. "Welcome to the jungle."

They both withdrew into a silent world. I continued in hopes of providing them with some encouragement. "Out here our only hope of survival is to remain extremely mobile. It's worked real fine so far. We haven't lost a single man and our effectiveness is tremendous. We've all had to overcome the 'firebase' mentality.[7] After a while being a bush man will grow on you."

"I don't know!" Mendez stammered. "I sure hope so."

I decided to change the subject in an effort to sidestep their fear. "What are your MOSs?" I asked.

"0331," Mendez offered.

"Nothing special here," Smith said. "I'm just your average 0311 grunt."

"No man in this unit is average," I said. "We all have our special talents and we learn how to handle all weapons. Before the next forty-eight hours are up you will know how to assemble and disassemble every form of weapon in our unit, as well as how to operate each one. Also, we will give you a crash course on the layout of our APR so you will always be able to find your way back to this compound." I read their faces. "There's always a possibility that we could get split up. Especially since Tết is near and a number of NVA units have been spotted in this area. When and if that happens our standing rule is to regroup back here as soon as possible. One last warning," I said. "Our unit rule is no drugs. No marijuana joints, only one beer a day and no one-man recon."

"No problem here," Mendez offered. Smith simply nodded his approval.

I handed them both a couple of belts of M-60 ammo and extra ammo for their M-16s. We split up the cases of cigarettes and miscellaneous goodies, shouldered our load and headed out for Mamasan Tôu's. "You guys are in for a leisurely day," I said. "Mamasan Tôu's place is right off the blacktop."

We reached Mamasan Tôu's in roughly half an hour, close to 0800. "Hey, gang," I hailed. "Come see what I brought back." They all jumped to their feet and shook hands with our new compadres. Mamasan Tôu and Lín accepted their goodies with gracious bowing. In fact, they were so gracious they gave packs of cigarettes to the men who smoked.

"How about some real breakfast?" I asked as everyone gathered around.

"What you got, man?" Jones jumped in. "I'm starved."

I tossed him one of the loaves. The aroma of the wrapped raisin bread filled the air. The rest of the squad caught the scent. I handed one to Everett, one to Ciminski and one to Rodriguez.

"Four loaves is all we have so y'all share with the new guys. I thought about bringing butter but it would have all melted by now."

"No problem, man," Jones said. "This stuff is great!"

The others agreed. I grabbed an end piece and started looking for a place to settle down. Just then Everett walked up next to me. Pulling me aside and waving Taan over to us, he said, "Taan, tell Goodson what you've told me."

Taan's face grew taut as he tried to formulate the words in his mind. "We have trouble, Gooson," he started. He always had trouble with his Ds. I didn't mind; I'd been called worse. He continued, "VC and NVA are moving into area from mountains here." He unfolded a map on the ground.

"The farmers in the School House Valley spotted them," Everett added.

"VC and NVA set up camp in this village," Taan said, pointing to a dot just east of the artillery base Fat City, the one we were supposed to protect.

"What's the count and firepower?" I asked.

"We don't know for sure," Everett said. "All we do know is that there is at least a full company of NVA there plus the neighboring Viet Cong."

I swallowed hard. "A company," I thought, "and there are only a handful of us including our PFs."

"What's our game plan?" I asked.

"Don't know yet. We can't call in artillery on that village until we receive fire from it. I'm not interested in letting them know we're around any sooner than necessary."

I looked out at the blacktop and momentarily studied the hordes of people passing by, wondering how many of them were VC.

"There is one thing," Everett started. He stopped for a moment and studied the ground.

"Yeah?" I answered.

He looked up. "Taan says that every night one of the NVA officers visits a farm on the mountainside directly across from the school house. Taan thinks he has a girlfriend there."

I wanted clarification, "You mean we should capture her?" I asked.

"She may know something that could help us," he suggested. My stomach turned at the very idea. "What do you think?" Everett asked.

It was my turn to study the ground. "I don't see that we have any choice," I answered.

"I agree," Everett said. So did Taan.

We rounded up the rest of the men, filled them in on the situation and ordered them to prepare to move out. Taan picked up half a dozen PFs from the nearby huts and rejoined us. We all struck out into the jungle, heading west towards the distant mountains. Everett and I hung back for a minute. "By the way, happy birthday," he said.

"Thanks," I returned. "At least I made it to twenty." The thought of our little group engaging such a massive force, and NVA on top of that, sent chills down my spine. "Does Fat City know about the gooks?" I asked.

"They should," Everett answered. "I sent word to HQ this morning."

The day was going to be a hot one. It was only 1015 and the air was already thick and sultry. The jungle was engulfed in a steamy haze as moisture rapidly evaporated from the rotting vegetation on the ground.

We reached our side of School House Valley shortly after noon. We had given the valley its name because, on a finger of land jutting out from the

Goodson's 1992 hand-drawn map of CAP Một's APR. Not drawn to scale.

jungle on our side, sat one of the two Quảng Tin Province school houses. The most visible landmark in the entire valley, it was constructed from concrete blocks and boasted the typical palm leaf roof. It was painted all white and was extremely visible in the light of a full moon. The entire valley was renowned for VC activity.

We stopped in the shelter of the jungle just south of the school house about a quarter of a mile. Everett passed the word to stay under cover and chow down if we were a mind to. The farm directly across from our position was the NVA officer's second home. Taan, Everett and I studied the small hut across the valley. It must have been at least 500 yards across. The farmer, his wife and two young boys around five or six were working the paddies. The girl was not in sight.

We waited and watched for about thirty minutes. Still no girl. I looked at Taan. "She is there," he said, reading my mind. A movement inside the hut caught my eye. We all peered into the hut the best we could from our distance.

"I see her," Taan said, pointing to the back of the hut. She had just stepped out and was tossing something to the surrounding chickens. She looked to be in her teens or early twenties.

"Must be a back door," I suggested.

"Highly unusual," Everett stated.

"But a confirmation of VC activity," I offered.

"Yeah, now how do we get over there undetected in broad daylight?"

Taan pointed to his map. The valley took a sharp bend just past the farm, and a tree line was portrayed on the map as crossing the entire valley.

"We better split up the group. This many men couldn't possibly remain undetected in the tree line," Everett ordered.

"Good idea," I said. "In fact, we probably should let the PFs capture her."

"Why?" Everett asked.

"You're short, remember," I said. "And by the way, your replacement is on his way. He's supposed to be in one week early. So, the CO's going to pull you out of the bush one week early." He smiled. "Besides, it will be less obvious if they are detected," I suggested. "We can cover them from here just in case she has any visitors." Everett nodded.

Taan agreed. He picked out four men and showed them the route on the map. "We follow cover of jungle to this place." His finger followed across the map. "Then we use tree line for cover to cross valley. We cross with 100 meters between us to keep cover. Remember, keep watch on both sides of tree line. And watch for booby traps."

That was one thing I was extremely grateful to Taan for. He and his fellow PFs had taught us how to locate and read the signs of a booby trap. Now we knew that every booby trap in Vietnam was marked in some way as a warning of its existence, its exact location and its type. Learning these things made me sick when I thought of all the men in the grunts we had lost to booby traps.

Taan continued, "We slip into jungle cover on other side and enter farmer's hut from rear." He smiled at me. "We capture girl for you." With that, the small group headed off into the jungle and the rest of us found some cover and hunkered down for the wait. It was 1315 hours. After a few minutes you could just pick out movement in the tree line. Taan had chosen his men wisely. They made it across the valley undetected and made their way toward the hut.

Reaching the edge of the clearing surrounding the hut, they hung close to cover for a moment to search for the girl, who was evidently inside again. With catlike ease they leapt from hiding and stormed into the hut. You could just hear a muffled scream. The farmer and his wife stopped momentarily and turned, yelling something toward the hut. The girl appeared in the doorway and waved.

My mind conjured up all sorts of evil situations. We checked our weapons. Suddenly Taan trotted from the back of the hut and faded into the jungle. The three men followed carrying the girl, bound and gagged and struggling like a wild animal. It seemed like eternity before they reached our position again. The girl had hate in her eyes and continually fought her captors, cussing us through her gag.

We moved out towards our old compound. It was impossible to keep the girl a secret so we simply marched her right past the villagers and the blacktop people right into our compound. "Her lover will soon know," I thought.

The compound had an old shack which sat roughly amidships of the south side. It had no windows, only an opening around the top where boards had been removed to enhance ventilation. We rarely took prisoners, but when we did we used the shack for interrogations. We locked the girl inside and sat back to rest. None of us was used to taking prisoners, much less women prisoners, and it showed on our faces. We never personally participated in the torture and questioning conducted by the PFs, but each of us had seen and felt the effects of it. Jones stepped across the blacktop to use the Vietnamese shrine for prayer. I never knew whether he was praying to Buddha or to God, and figured it was none of my business. This night was as good as any for prayer. The girl was in for the worst night of her life and, no doubt, her last. That realization bothered us all.

Taan sent a runner after the head of their PF unit, Sergeant Nyugen Shôu. The sergeant and his interrogation "committee" joined us right at dusk. Being in the compound made me feel uneasy. We were not accustomed to being caged in at night. Nor were we accustomed to being so visible.

Sergeant Shôu and his group entered the shack and closed the door behind them. I just caught a glimpse of the girl as they shut the door. She was still sitting in the chair we had tied her to earlier. Night settled over the compound. You could hear the men in the shack arguing with the girl. An occasional "slap" would resound into the night. The girl held her own. Everett and I set up the men at every opening we could cover in the compound in hopes of detecting possible infiltration.

Suddenly, from the shack came a scream followed by pleading and sobbing. The torture of the girl had started. Evidently she feared the NVA greater than she did us, because she still refused to talk. The shack grew quiet. Moments passed. "Ayyeee." The still of the night was shattered with a bloodcurdling scream. I couldn't stand it anymore, and neither could Everett.

We climbed up the side of the shack and peered down from the ventilation hole at the top. The beaten girl was nude, lying in a pool of water on the floor. Wires, attached to every vital part of her body, led back to a hand-cranked generator. As we watched, the hand on the generator cranked in rapid turns. The girl screamed again as her body jerked around on the floor. I dropped to the ground and simply sat there in a stupor. Tears came to my eyes. "Oh, God," I thought. "What hell are we in? I can't let them do this. I have to . . ." My thought trailed off. I knew that there was nothing I could do. It was their territory. It was their way. No one could interfere.

Then Everett dropped down next to me. "She's dead," he said. "Shock must have killed her. But she did tell them something before she died."

I just stared at him. I couldn't get rid of the mental picture of the girl's body bouncing around on the floor as if under the control of some strange demon. I closed my eyes and tried to push it away, but it wouldn't leave. The bloody face of the dying girl invaded every conscious thought. My mind reeled uncontrollably. "Nothing is worth this," I thought. I looked at Everett. "What have we done?" I asked. Everett simply stared into space, caught up in his own inner battle for justification of the horror.

The door to the shack abruptly swung open. Two men came out carrying the limp body of the dead girl, draped with a bamboo mat. Her arms dangled from her sides. Sergeant Shôu stepped from the torture room out into the night air. His gaze followed the dangling arms as his men and the girl faded into the darkness of the night. He ordered them to drop her body in a remote part of the jungle where the creatures of the night could fight over her remains.

To simply let a body lie was worse, to the Vietnamese people, than death itself. Their belief was firmly planted in reincarnation. However, to enjoy the fullness of the reincarnation, a body had to be buried in a round grave encircled by a ring of earth about eighteen inches high. The "ring" and "mound" simulated returning to the womb of mother earth in preparation for rebirth. Each person was buried with an object they would need in their next life. To simply let the body rot away on the ground meant that the soul would float around in a state of nothingness, lost forever unless some kind person found the remains and returned them to mother earth.

My gaze rested on Sergeant Shôu's face. "He must have a tremendous hate for the Viet Cong," I thought. To commit his fellow countrymen to an eternal state of nothingness, a "floating hell" they called it, had to require an extreme hatred. I envisioned ghosts floating through the remote corners of the jungle or lying in wait somewhere to assist their "live buddies" in their efforts to pinpoint our location.

My mind returned to the real world. Sergeant Shôu was approaching us. "Chào ông," he greeted us with a slight dip of the head. Shôu was short, around five-foot-four, but he boasted a strong stocky body decorated with various ribbons and medals received from previous battles. A scar encircled his neck where a garrote had attempted to complete its evil mission.

Shôu smiled. "Girl no want to talk," he began in broken English. "We make her talk in short time though, huh?" he continued.

"What did you find out?" I asked, trying to shut out the mental image that kept haunting my mind.

Shôu studied my face momentarily and shook his head. "You Americans no like torture of woman?" he asked. He was obviously enjoying this.

I glared at him. "What did you find out?" I repeated sternly.

He returned my gaze briefly. "Woman was Viet Cong with NVA from mountains," he said pointing to the west. He continued, "She say NVA still pay bounty for marine body. Also, she say NVA get ready for Tết. Recruit many Viet Cong to join effort to destroy artillery base and CAP marines and marine base in Chu Lai. They will attack with all men, women and children they can get on night of Tết. Also," Shôu's face suddenly hardened, "VC already in my men and in local villages," he ended his report.

"Do you know who they are?" Everett asked.

"No," he answered, "not yet."

"Tết is just a few days away. That means in just a few nights. . . ." My voice trailed off, lost in the thought of what might await us on the night of Tết.

"Not worry, Corporal," Shôu smiled, "We find Cong first and kill them, okay?"

"Sure," I smiled back.

The next few days and nights were filled with snipers and extremely short contact with the enemy. They would "hit" us simply to test our strength and alertness and, of course, keep tabs on our movement.

Everett and I decided to go one step further with more than just random selection of day sites and nightly patrols. We stayed constantly on the move, never stopping in one place longer than an hour, not even during daylight hours. Hopefully, the NVA and their VC friends would not be able to establish any sort of pattern from our efforts.

The days slid by until we found ourselves watching the rays of the early morning sun filter through the trees on the day of Tết. We all set out to clean our weapons and put new edges on our blades. Tension engulfed us.

Shôu had lined up his entire platoon for a supposed peptalk before releasing them for the day's celebrations. Suddenly a man burst from their ranks, turned and fired an automatic burst before making an attempt to escape into the jungle. The wall of lead from our return fire sent his lifeless body reeling into the rusted remains of the concertina wire bordering our little haven. We all stared in disbelief at the bullet-riddled body, hanging in a grotesque position that only death can bring.

"How bold can you get?" Ciminski asked, breaking the silence. Everett sent Mendez and Rodriguez to check out the body while the rest of us checked out Shôu's unit. Shôu was the only one hit and the wound was not severe—a single bullet to the right thigh.

Tết celebration, 1969, with a speech from a visiting South Vietnamese government official.

Popular Forces participating in the formal ceremony of Tết, 1969. Taan in front row, left end. The Viet Cong assassin is hiding somewhere in the ranks.

Flag of South Vietnam waving above local Chu Lai officials, ranking officiers and visiting dignitaries. Tết, 1969.

"How many more have infiltrated?" I thought as I looked back at the VC's body. Fear took a step inside as I studied the remaining group of Vietnamese men. "Can we trust them? How long have they been moving in on us? Is Taan one of them? No, not Taan, he couldn't be." My thoughts went wild as we attempted to gain control of the situation.

Johnston, our new corpsman, was patching up Sergeant Shôu. The wound was clean and the bullet had passed through without hitting any bone. Shôu would be all right. Ciminski put in a call for a medevac. Within minutes you could hear the chopping thrust of the Huey medevac unit searching for our location. I tossed a smoke grenade and Ciminski asked the pilot to identify our color.

"No problem," the pilot radioed back. "I only see one smoke—it's red and I'm coming in."

"Bring her down," Ciminski radioed back.

Just as the helicopter settled to a hover right at ground lever, Shôu turned the platoon over to Taan. My fears of Taan being VC left with Sergeant Shôu.

The helicopter lifted off with its passenger aboard and disappeared over the horizon, as Taan passed out his orders to the platoon. In no uncertain terms, he assured them that Shôu's absence did not allow them the opportunity to slack off. He planned to be just as tough if not tougher than Shôu ever was. The men winced at his words. Taan ended his sermon with a strong warning to any remaining VC that their death would not be so quick and painless as their comrade's had been. Sermon finished, Taan dismissed his troops and sauntered over to me. "Men are dismissed for day," he informed me. "Today we celebrate new year!"

At the south edge of the compound, just over Taan's right shoulder, I caught a glimpse of movement. "Hit the deck," I ordered. Everyone bit the dust. Silence settled in as I passed the word about the movement. "Probably nothing," I thought. "Just edgy after this morning."

Taan looked over at me, "No VC. They no fight. Today holiday."

"Yeah, right," I snarled. "What about this morning?"

Taan smiled. "That VC beaucoup điên kiện đầu." Taan made a face like a crazy man.

A white flag dangling from an AK rifle barrel suddenly waved back and forth just above the bushes where I had seen movement. Taan and I looked at each other. "A trick?" I asked.

Taan shook his head. "No fight today. I see what he wants." Taan yelled in his best American English, "What you want, you stupid VC?" I cocked an eye in his direction. Taan beamed, "He think I American GI."

The VC yelled back something I could not make out. Neither could Taan. "Lại đây (come here), you stupid VC," Taan yelled back. The man slowly stood, set his rifle on the ground and began to make his way in our direction. Everett ordered the men to set up a perimeter in case of trickery. Somehow I felt safe in Taan's adamant statement that the Cong would not fight today.

The man was dressed in the typical garb of black pajamas with a rope cinch around his waist. Chi Com[8] grenades were shoved underneath the rope. His hat was a typical Vietnamese straw hat but somewhat smaller than normal. His face was drawn and weathered and boasted a scanty goatee beard and mustache. His eyes were coal black. My mind flashed back over the past few weeks. I had seen this man before. He had been working the fields in School House Valley the day we captured the girl. This morning he had been selling odds and ends just outside our perimeter. My blood boiled.

At approximately twenty feet away, I ordered him to stop. "Dừng lại," I yelled. He stopped abruptly. I circled around him watching his every move and searching his body for trip wires, detonators or satchel charges. There was nothing, just the grenades. I motioned him forward. Taan leered at him, an obvious hate and disgust building up in his eyes.

"Ask him what he wants," I suggested.

As Taan and the VC carried on their conversation, I noticed that I had missed a very important part of the VC's attire. His shoulders boasted the red, yellow and green insignia of the NVA. This man was no Viet Cong. He was Regular North Vietnamese Army. "Probably the girl's boyfriend," I thought.

Taan ordered the man to stay put as he pulled me to one side. "Man no VC," Taan stated.

"I know. He's NVA," I answered.

Taan nodded, his face tense. The South Vietnamese soldiers were in constant fear of their ruthless enemy. VC were simple local folks paid by the NVA to create havoc and death wherever possible. NVA were highly trained, ruthless killers and masters at torture.

Taan forced a smile. "He say they have hundred of men that will destroy all of us and the artillery base tonight. He say that today they want to honor us as good warriors. They want us to lay down our weapons as they will do and join them in the celebration of the Vietnamese New Year."

"They want to *honor* us?" I asked. It smelled like a trap to me. I looked at the NVA. His face provided no reassurance.

Everett joined us. "What's going on?" he asked.

I repeated what Taan had told me.

"I've heard of such things," Everett said, "but I doubted they were true. What do you think?" he asked. I looked at Taan.

He smiled weakly. "VC no fight today," he repeated. He obviously was not at ease with the NVA soldier, but he trusted his word implicitly.

I looked back at Everett. "I think we should do it," I said. "After all, if we can show such courage face to face, it may strike a little fear into their worthless hearts."

Everett smiled, "What can we lose? They're going to hit from inside and out tonight anyway. So we may as well fill up our bellies." We all laughed. Except the NVA, who simply stood there waiting for our answer.

"Tell him okay, Taan," I ordered. As Taan told the NVA soldier we would honor him as he honored us, Everett called the rest of the men over and explained the situation to them. No one was too excited about the idea, but they all agreed, with the exception of the new guy Smith. He wanted it on record that he was against the whole thing, but he was not about to be left alone all day.

The NVA waited patiently as we stacked our rifles, grenades, M-60's and other weapons in a neat stack in the back of one of the buildings in the compound. Taan went to the NVA's previous hiding place and retrieved his AK and placed it in storage with ours. In addition, the NVA handed the Chi Com grenades to Taan for storage.

We all felt naked without any weapons. "We leave now," Taan interrupted my thoughts. "NVA will lead us to camp and bring us back before sundown."

"Okay," I nodded, "Lead on." The NVA smiled. "God, don't let this be a trap," I thought.

We left the old French compound and our weapons behind as we entered the jungle leading back to School House Valley. After an hour of walking, we came upon a village in the western sector of the valley, about halfway up the slopes of the mountain range. There were black PJs everywhere, mingling with just as many NVA uniforms.

We felt like lost sheep that had just stumbled into a den of lions.

"Look at 'em," Jones growled. "Wish I had an M-60."

I smiled at his courage. "I'd settle for a radio and a full battery of 105s or, better yet, a squadron of Huey Cobras."

"Dream on," Mendez piped in. "We're sitting ducks, guys, being fattened for the kill."

Silence settled among us as we entered the village. No guards were posted, at least none that we could see. The village, although somewhat larger than most, still boasted the typical "village atmosphere." Small yapping dogs with tucked tails darted to and fro like bees on a patch of flowers.

The more numerous chickens were in constant combat over a stolen morsel of food. Off to our left we passed a small group of VC huddled around some sort of activity we could only catch glimpses of, but glimpses were enough. A mongoose lunged viciously at a large gray snake, a king cobra. A game for the VC. A mortal combat for the cobra and the mongoose.

Every man in black PJs and NVA uniforms nodded respectfully as we passed, giving us forced smiles that made no attempt at camouflaging the contempt and hatred they held for us. Yet even past the hatred you could sense a fear and reverence for our presence. To most, if not all of them, we were no doubt the first Americans they had seen up close, much less walking boldly into their camp to celebrate their day with them, to eat their food with them. Countless numbers of them; eight marines and one PF of us.

Taan was enjoying it, primarily because it was a great honor to be recognized in such a manner by your enemy, but secondly because he was picking up bits and pieces of their conversation as we passed by.

"They see the men who have caused so much trouble," Taan reported. "Another said, 'They killed my brother last month.'" Taan smiled at me and said, "It is good that we come. VC more scared now that we walk into their camp." I could only nod and smile back. If I talked, I would reveal my fear. I straightened my back to make sure all six-foot-three inches of me was showing.

Our little jaunt in the country ended at a concrete-block hut in the center of the village. The front was open. Smoke curled upward from a small opening in the roof. Pigs squealed in the adjoining pen as they fought for a morsel of food someone had just tossed their way. We stepped inside. Brass was everywhere. Colonels, majors, captains; you name it, they were there. At least a dozen men gathered around a floor-level table constructed of bamboo and covered with a variety of dishes. I had never seen so much cooked rice, fish and pork at one time. In addition, there were various concoctions of sugar-coated potato slices, rice cakes, bananas, coconuts, dates, and many items I did not recognize.

"Eat what they give you," Everett reminded the rest of us. We nodded, greeted our "friends for the day," and dug in. Some of the food was quite tasty. What was not required total concentration to keep it down. Women darted among us with their heads hung low, never allowing their eyes to meet ours. Like mother birds feeding their young they returned time and again to replace an opening in our bowls with a fresh morsel. The hot tea was fantastic, and helped wash down the morsels that refused to stay down on their own.

Reaching my limit, I left a small portion in my bowl and assured them with a motion to my belly that I was full. Thank God, a Mamasan brought more hot tea. One man, obviously the one in charge, stood up and rubbed his stomach in mimic of my gesture. Everyone laughed. He nodded in our direction and began in rather fluent English. "Welcome, Gentlemen," he said. "I hope you have enjoyed your meal." He continued, "You honor us with your presence as warrior honors warrior."

"Must be an officer," I thought. "He loves flowery speech."

We settled back to listen to him rave. His speech reminded us that we were invaders of their country and that they were determined to put a stop to our incessant burning of villages, raping of women, killing of children, and general abuse of the villages in our area. The General, or whatever he was, assured us that his army would annihilate us and our friends—at Fat City, in surrounding CAP units, and eventually our command post in Chu Lai itself. "You will all die tonight, just as your friends died last month," he said, reminding us of the CAP unit they had just wiped out. An evil grin came to his face. "Tonight, marines, some of our men will collect the bounty we have placed on your heads," he smiled. He spread his hands before him. "Tomorrow we celebrate with same meal over our victory!"

My blood boiled. So did everyone else's. Perhaps sensing this, he changed from his boasting mood back to his mock-jovial self. "But today, enjoy yourselves," he said. "Please visit all of our huts and all of our men and eat as much as you like." With that he sat down and dug his greasy fingers into another bowl of rice, fish and Nước Mặn sauce.

"Hope we see you personally tonight," I thought.

"Let's go to other huts now," Taan suggested. He received no argument from any of us. We had had about all we could stomach in many ways. My appetite was totally gone, as was everyone else's. That is, except for Jones. He ate at least one full bowl at every hut. "Must have a cast iron gut," I thought.

We briefly stopped at each hut and accepted a tidbit from the Mamasan serving that hut. Our eyes never left our enemy. The day dragged on until finally the sun was approaching the tops of the trees. I checked my watch. "1612 hours," I said.

"Just enough time to get back and get ready for our visit tonight," Everett said.

"Yeah," I said. "Let's find our 'friend' and get out of here."

Our "friend" was ready, too, obviously not too anxious to risk nightfall before his return to his camp. Nothing was said to us as we left and we offered nothing in return. The day had been too much already and, coupled with the overwhelming thought of the rapidly approaching night, left no room for worthless salutations.

We left, following our VC guide back to our own territory. As we reached the top of the hill, I turned and looked down at the village one more time, trying to lock its size, layout and location into my memory. Sensing my motive, the NVA scout urged us into the jungle. The village disappeared. It would have been a futile effort anyway. By the time we made it back to the radio to call in an Arty drop, our enemy would already have either gone back into the tunnel network or be en route to their target for Tét. Either way, they would no longer be in the "vil," so the destruction of our Arty would fall upon the families rather than our enemy.

We broke into a fast paced march which accelerated into a near run the farther we got from the village. Time was of the essence and we knew it. We had only a couple of hours before dark to rehash our ambush plans and make what changes we felt the day's activities deemed necessary.

Once inside our old compound, the VC collected his rifle and grenades and then trotted back in the direction of his waiting buddies. No order needed, we systematically began to check our weapons, ammo and gear.

"Tonight we better load down with ammo," Everett ordered. Everyone strapped on as much as they thought they could possibly carry and then strapped on some more. Everett radioed back to Command and filled them in on the day's activities and advised them to inform all bases to prepare for a major offensive for the night, and in all probability, the next day.

Silently we completed our preparations. As we left the compound, we stopped at a nearby buffalo shed and covered our exposed skin with buffalo dung. Darkness settled in. The stars were so bright they seemed close enough to touch. There was no moon. "Good and bad," I thought. "We can't see them and they can't see us."

Just as a precaution Everett and I decided to change our ambush site at the last minute. We were maintaining radio silence so we could not inform command of our new position. "Say a prayer," I thought.

Our new site was farther away from the VC village and placed our backs close to the ocean. It was a trench about five feet deep and bordered on both sides with a variety of trees and prickly pear cactus. As long as we hugged the walls of the trench, we would offer very little target to the enemy. Our only vulnerable spots were at each end of the trench which opened up into the jungle. We placed two men at each opening in hopes that both would keep each other awake and that two sets of ears and eyes would possibly aid in early detection of the enemy. From experience, we knew the Cong would not seek us out until around 2200 or 2300 hours. Their strategy was to give weariness a chance to take over and utilize complacency—and hopefully sleep—to aid their surprise attack. I doubted tonight that weariness had a chance. "Tonight you die," the NVA officer's voice echoed in our brains.

With painstaking care we set up claymores[9] in a deadly perimeter around our position, making sure that they were sufficiently hidden to prevent the Cong from discovering them. A favorite trick they liked to play was turning the mine around and making a noise to let you know they were there, prompting you to set off the mine. In seconds you were blown apart by your own trap. Consequently, even when we did set the mines off we always took cover just in case the VC had outsmarted us.

I set up the M-60 dead center of the trench, replacing Rodriguez on the trigger. Jones, Ciminski, and Smith flanked me on the right. On the left flank, we positioned Johnston, Mendez, Rodriguez, and Everett, with his M-79 grenade launcher and his M-16. Tonight, even Johnston was loaded down with ammo in addition to his M-16.[10] In between each one of us was a Vietnamese PF, including Taan at my side. Altogether we had thirteen men. Mines in hiding, men in position, we settled back to wait silently. I checked my watch. It was 2150 hours.

We had been extremely careful to avoid contact with any Vietnamese en route to our ambush site. No one knew of our position—we hoped. It was a pitch-black night and, unless we allowed some noise to give us away, no one would know we were there. Tonight we weren't looking for them; we had their promise they would hunt for us. We watched. We waited. As usual, the time dragged by. 2200 hours snuck up on us and silently slipped into the past. You could feel the tension in the air as we each strained our eyes and ears in every direction hoping to hear a sound of warning, yet praying for continued silence.

The VC kept their promise. Just before 2300 hours, the night erupted with an initial scream followed by a simultaneous burst from AKs and M-

16s. The gooks had hit us on our right flank. Green tracers were flying in all directions.

Everett let fly with an M-79 flare grenade in hope of illuminating the oncoming VC. Just as he fired, the initial assault stopped. Word passed down that Smith was dead and Ciminski had gotten it in the leg. Johnston made his way to Ciminski to patch him up and to verify that Smith was dead. My gut tightened up. "This is it," I thought. "Tonight you die." But I answered myself: "Not without one hell of a fight."

"Get ready," I passed the word, "and don't waste ammo!"

The flare reached its peak, popped its tiny chute and instantaneously illuminated the jungle for 100 yards. At first nothing. Then as the flare floated down to just above the tree tops, the Cong slid out from behind their cover. It seemed like every tree and bush was alive with NVA and VC. Brazenly they stepped into the light and opened fire with their AKs and machine guns. Green tracers and their deadly partners sliced away at the trees around us. So far, they were only attacking from directly in front and our right flank. Lying prone with the M-60 in my grips, I selected a group of Cong and squeezed the trigger. "Short bursts will keep you alive," a command from the past echoed in my brain. A dozen or so rounds left the barrel as I released the pressure on the trigger. An RPG round exploded against the mound protecting us. Dirt and debris showered down on us, but the mound's thick body absorbed the impact of the explosion and left it virtually ineffectual. Another burst in the trees behind us, again with no effect, except for the destruction of some of our cover. Our plan was working, at least as far as protection—that is for everyone but Smith.

Gooks were coming steadily, passing a hail of lead and shrapnel in front of them. We returned with our own steadily controlled barrage. The Cong were dropping like flies as Everett's M-79 sent bodies flying all directions.

Abruptly the attack stopped. The Cong retreated back into hiding as the last flare sizzled on the ground, popped and gave up to allow darkness to settle back in place.

"Ammo check," Everett whispered. The order traveled silently down the line. Everett crawled close to my position. "Only got three flares left," he said. "Why don't we try to slip out in the cover of darkness?"

"Could be a good idea," I agreed. "Let's test the waters." Without a word Everett groped on the ground until he found a rock and then heaved it in the direction of our open left flank. The rock bounced through a clump of bamboo, creating a rapid clattering sound. Without hesitation, green tracers and Chi Com grenades annihilated the area around the poor rock.

"They're trying to flank us!" Everett yelled.

"No sense whispering now," I thought. Anticipating his decision, I ordered every other man to take the opposite side of the trench. Everett fired off two of his three remaining flares, one on each side. The flares burst within seconds of each other, illuminating the jungle with a white phosphorous glow. The timing was good. The gooks indeed had flanked us and were crawling on bellies from all directions like cats stalking their prey. The flares startled them and they all jumped up in a wild yell and starting charging and firing.

"Get down and hold your fire!" Everett yelled. "And prepare your claymores. They're almost in range!" Like raging animals the Cong stampeded in our direction. Sixty meters, forty, twenty. "Fire!" Everett yelled.

We hunkered behind the mounds as we each activated our own set of claymores. Explosions and screams resounded from all directions. Grabbing our weapons we jumped up, ready for the onslaught of maddened gooks, but the mines had taken their toll. Dismembered bodies lay everywhere. A few Cong were trying to drag themselves into cover while their remaining buddies faded back into the jungle away from the illuminated area.

"Ammo check!" Everett yelled.

"Bad news," I said. "Only five belts of 60 ammo left."

"Same problem down here," Jones agreed. The others piped in identical situations. Between all of us we had only a few hundred rounds of ammo and a dozen or so grenades.

Darkness had returned. I passed word for Rodriguez to join me. Quickly and quietly he slid next to me and handed me the transmitter. I rapidly cleared the channel: "CAP One to Base. We have contact. I repeat. CAP One to Base. We have contact." A momentary silence and then a crackling metallic sound echoed into the night. "Hurry up," I thought.

"Clear the channel. Clear the channel. Go ahead, One."

"Contact since approximately 2300 hours." It was already 0025. We had been fighting for almost an hour and a half and the gooks weren't about to give up. "Ammo low, one man dead, one wounded. We need reinforcements ASAP along with fire support."

"No dice on fire support. Hold for CO."

"CAP One, this is CO. Over."

"Go ahead," I returned.

"Be advised that the artillery battalion is under heavy fire and unable to render assistance."

The gooks were back into their sneak position. Everett let fly his last flare with a yell. "This is it, guys. Give 'em hell." The flare revealed the already too familiar scene of countless gooks, about fifty meters away, converging on us from all directions, but this time approaching in a slow crawl.

"You're on your own," the radio advised.

"Hold your fire until they are close in!" Everett yelled. "Grenades first, then let 'em have it. And for God's sake, make your shots count! Switch your 16s to single shot to conserve ammo."

Then it happened. Just as the gooks were closing in for the kill—"CAP One, this is CAP Base. Over." The CO was radioing back. "Be advised that we are on to your little scheme and will not fall victim to your masquerade."

"Come again?" I was startled at the response.

The CO raved on. "We have checked with the other CAP units and have found no contact with VC. It's the night of Tết and you are faking a fire fight for glory and medals, so we're resuming normal status to thwart your deceptive efforts."

Shocked, I looked at the transmitter in disbelief. Hatred and bitterness boiled inside of me. The gooks were less than fifty meters away. "Everett," I stammered.

"I heard," he said. "Let's pray at least one of us survives to pay that CO a visit."

I fought back the tears of fear and hatred. "God! This can't be happening," I thought. Yet in my heart I had always thought that death awaited me in this hell hole. I'd seen too many guys blown apart right beside me to begin to think that I was invincible. I looked at the transmitter once again, wishing I could reach through it to the CO's neck. A quick glance at Rodriguez. A single tear reflected on his cheek as he watched the VC crawling toward our position.

I squeezed the transmitter. "CO, this is CAP One. Be advised that I have one man dead, one wounded, and gooks advancing in all directions. We need reinforcements and ammo now!" I screamed.

"Go to hell," the radio answered.

"Look, you lousy. . . ." Words wouldn't form. Hatred took over. I squeezed the transmitter with all my strength hoping it would somehow communicate our situation to the CO. Gritting my teeth I made one final effort. "CO, either you get off your tail and get us help or I guarantee you that I will survive and will make you suffer a death for each one of my men. That's a promise." I breathed my threat into the mike.

"I have witnesses to that threat, Corporal," the CO radioed back, "and I'll haul your little carcass in here in the morning for court martial."

"You better hope I'm just a carcass!"

"Shut up," came flying back at me over the radio.

"What?" was all I could answer back.

"This is Colonel Andrews," the radio advised. "CO, get off the air. CAP One, be advised that two Cobras are on their way to your position. They'll be on your frequency. I'm bringing out a full platoon and my entire arsenal." The radio went silent.

As if on cue from the ending of our radio conversation, the gooks jumped up in a mass yell and started raking our position with gunfire. They were coming from all directions like a pack of wolves moving in for the kill. "Help is on the way!" I screamed. "Let's make their trip worthwhile."

We watched the gooks move in on us and prayed that the ricocheting lead would miss its mark until help could get there. They were only fifteen or twenty feet away.

"Grenades and fire!" Everett yelled. Single shots echoed against the volley of automatic gunfire coming from the gooks. They let out another yell and began running at us with full fury as they realized what our single shots were telling them. The grenades exploded in rapid succession and momentarily stopped them, but within moments they were back on their feet and sending their deadly barrage of lead at us again.

Jones yelled, "I'm out of ammo!"

"Take charge of the 60," I ordered, "but quick squeezes only. That's our last belt."

Jones nodded as he grabbed the machine gun and zeroed in on a victim. I pulled out my .45 pistol. Only three magazines. Twenty-two rounds. I faced my enemy.

"Grab rocks and throw if you run out of ammo!" I shouted. "Yell 'grenade' when you throw 'em and maybe we'll keep 'em from over running us." The VC opened fire again, growing bolder with each step. They were ready to collect their bounty. Rocks and screams flew out at the gooks.

They hit the deck, but we knew it would only work once. Mechanically, we prepared for the inevitable hand-to-hand.

Suddenly God answered our prayers. A telltale "chop" let us know that help was on the way. The Cong heard it too, and jumped up for a last ditch effort to move in for the kill.

The silent radio crackled. "CAP One, this is Cobra One. We're approaching you from the south and can see gunfire. Please advise of your exact location."

I grabbed the transmitter. "Don't fail me now, baby," I told the radio. "Cobra One. We're in a bamboo-lined trench lined with palms and banana trees. We're surrounded by gooks to within twenty feet. We'll send up a pencil flare to mark our position."

"Everett!" I yelled.

"I'm already with you," he said as he pointed the tiny pencil flare towards the sky. The choppers were still about a hundred yards to our south.

"Pop!" The tiny red light streaked towards the stars and then arced towards the ground as it reached its peak about twenty feet above the trees. I clenched my fist, hoping against hope that our friends in the sky would be able to see the small light and mark our position.

"Roger," Cobra One answered. "I copy your position. You guys hug that trench and we'll tail up and give your friends something to think about."

"Get down," I yelled, "but keep firing!"

The two beautiful choppers hovered directly over our heads tail to tail and with noses searching toward the ground. Suddenly flares filled the night sky, lighting up the darkness. Everywhere you looked, there were Viet Cong and NVA. Within moments of the flares the Cobras opened up with every weapon they had. I was familiar with their tactics. The flares served two purposes. One, they lit up the area, thus revealing the gooks. Second, they blinded anyone looking up in an attempt to shoot at the choppers. The Cobras would then rotate, as if on a fixed pivot, and rake the area below them. This was only a pitch black night tactic and only for an initial assault. To hover indefinitely was sure death from an RPG.

The Cobras let it fly—rockets, M-79 grenades from their turrets, mini-guns blazing from the same turrets. Trees and gooks were falling everywhere. Minutes passed as we picked out targets in a minute effort to do our part in the battle. Everyone was out of ammo, except for my .45 and a couple of 16s. The machine gun was silent. The barrel had warped from overheating. Jones and the others, out of ammo, simply stared into the oncoming enemy, helplessly waiting for the battle to end in a hand-to-hand struggle.

The Cobras broke formation and began their criss-cross darting to and fro, sending their hail of lead and shrapnel in all directions.

The radio joined us once again. "CAP One, this is Full Bird. Over."

"Go ahead, Bird," I answered.

"Be advised we are on your position ready to drop our load. Pop a flare for us in the landing zone."

"None available," I returned. "There's a clearing just north of our position. Maybe your friends could bring you in there." Everett's pencil flare had been the last one.

"Roger," was all he answered.

Suddenly the gunships dropped from the sky into the clearing. I grabbed Jones and Mendez and headed for the choppers. Men were pouring out of both sides firing into the jungles as they headed in our direction.

We reached the choppers and grabbed the crates of ammo the men had dropped onto the ground. The Cobras were continuing their flirting battle in an effort to keep the gooks pinned down, while we unloaded the ammo.

A man about six feet tall, burly looking and boasting an unlit cigar between his teeth, jumped out of the chopper. "Where do you need us?"

"First take off those birds," I yelled frantically as I pointed to his cover and collars.

He hit the deck, jerking off the insignia. He grinned over at me. "Been in the rear too long—thanks."

I nodded. "Let's go," I yelled. We each grabbed an ammo crate and started running back to our haven. One of the Colonel's men screamed and rolled onto the ground. The Huey gunships completed their delivery and were joining their compatriots in the sky with machine guns blazing. Two other men grabbed the wounded man and helped him toward the trench. The ground around us was alive with ricochets and exploding rounds.

"Thank God those gooks are lousy shots," I thought as we zigzagged our way back and flung the ammo and ourselves into the trench. My men dug into the ammo and grenades like chickens at feeding time.

"Give 'em hell!" the Colonel yelled. We did.

The gooks didn't want to give up. They started moving in on us again, seemingly impervious to the barrage of lead and shrapnel from ground and air. Jones still had the 60, which now had a new barrel we had found in one of the ammo crates. I was using the M-16 that had belonged to Smith. Jones yelled for more ammo. "Slow down, man, you'll melt that barrel, too!" I yelled as I reached for a box of ammo right beside my head. The box felt funny, so I checked it. Three bullet holes clean through. Sweat trickled down my back. I jerked the box open and fed a new belt into the 60. With a pat on the back, I told Jones, "Kill those little . . ." words failed me. I turned and rejoined the battle.

Daylight slowly drove away the night as the battle dissolved into sporadic gunfire. The gooks had lost their steam. As the sun broke the horizon, all gunfire had stopped, giving a new meaning to the rising sun. As far as the eye could see smoke hovered over the ground like some sort of eerie fog.

We all sat back and relaxed a little, waiting to make sure the assault was over. The Colonel lit up his cigar. "Feels good to be alive," he said.

I simply nodded and forced a weak smile. "Good for some of us," I said as my thoughts returned to our CO, safe back at the rear. I motioned Rodriguez over and squeezed the transmitter one more time. "CAP One to Base. Over." I had visions of the CO lying still asleep in his cot, safe in the rear. "I want that man dead," I thought. I wanted him to feel the dry taste of death in his mouth as his enemy converged on him from all sides. Somehow I felt a responsibility to my men to see to it that the man paid for the stupidity of his actions.

Sensing my thoughts, Everett patted me on the back. "Blow it off, man," he said. "The man will get what he deserves, sooner or later."

"Sooner won't be soon enough," I growled.

Colonel Andrews joined in. "Now look, Corporal," he started, "what your CO did does deserve punishment, but let's keep it legal, okay?"

I just stared at him.

He continued. "I know you feel like nothing will really happen other than an official handslapping and you're probably right. But if you try to kill him, it's definitely the brig or even execution for you. He's not worth the effort. He'll get his. Men like him always do. So let the good Lord take care of him."

I knew he was right. Besides, the chance of even making it the thirty or so miles back to the rear was slim to none. The CO would wait. The Cong wouldn't.

Everett sent Mendez, Jones and Taan along with a couple of PFs to finish off the wounded Cong that should be lying out there.

The radio crackled. "Base to CAP One, go ahead."

Bitterness in my voice, I relayed my report. "The firefight is over except for clean up operations. Send medevac for two wounded and one dead."

"Roger. Medevac on its way. Over."

"Tell the CO . . . aw, tell him *nothing*! This is CAP One. Over and out."

Suddenly it dawned on me—no gunfire. Our standing order was to "not mess with the gook bodies" for fear of booby traps. We were to simply plant more rounds in them to make sure they were dead. I checked the jungle. Our men were systematically searching, weapons at ready. Jones made his way back to us.

"They've done it to us again," he said. The look on his face told the story. Mendez and the PFs slowly returned to our trench with the same reports.

"What's the body count?"[11] asked Colonel Andrews.

"A big, fat zero," Everett snapped.

"What?" The colonel was startled. "But we saw bodies lying everywhere when we landed plus the dozens of bodies we saw fall after we arrived."

"Yeah," I agreed. "But the Cong's old trick is to haul off every piece of evidence so that we can't confirm a single kill."

"Well, we'll simply ignore the confirmed body rule," the Colonel answered. "I saw what I saw and I'm going to credit y'all with at least seventy-five kills even though I know there must have been many more. That's what will go into my report and you do the same—that's an order."

"Thanks," Everett said. "Maybe that will help some, but I'd still like to stand over my dead enemies and confirm that the battle wasn't for nothing."

"Yeah," I agreed. "Especially since we haven't taken a hill, village or compound as evidence of victory."

"Well, in my book you guys fought one tough battle and with one fantastic kill ratio. And no one is going to refute what I put in the records," Colonel Andrews concluded.

We watched as the choppers began their descent. Everett sent the remaining PFs along with Mendez and Jones to secure the perimeter as the Hueys chopped down between the trees. One helicopter remained aloft, a Cobra. It circled erratically above, searching the jungle for remaining gooks.

No tracers, no gunfire. The jungle had returned to normal, except for the helicopters. We loaded Ciminski and the Colonel's man onto the chopper with a blessing that they would be sent home.

I grabbed Ciminski's hand in a firm grip. He looked pale and hollow, obviously drained from his brush with death.

"You've got a million-dollar wound there," I yelled out above the noise of the choppers.

"Yeah, I hope so," he agreed. "I'm ready to go home."

"You deserve it man. You fought a good battle."

I stepped back as the medevac prepared to lift off and waved my last farewell to a friend . . . a very good friend. I turned and looked at Smith as they slipped him into a body bag. His body was riddled with bullet holes from the AK. I fought back the tears of bitterness and hatred for the enemy, whoever he was . . . .wherever he was. My thoughts returned to our Commanding Officer. "Someday," I thought, "someday."

We shook hands with the Colonel and his men, thanking them for saving our lives.

"I'll go into battle with you guys anytime—just call," the Colonel said as he climbed into the chopper.

The medevacs reached for more air and quickly rose above the treetops and disappeared to the south. The Cobra followed them. The quiet of the morning settled in around us. Each man, engulfed in his own thoughts, settled down to clean his weapons and to prepare for the day. The battle had taken its toll. Everyone was mentally and physically drained. No doubt our bodies could have slept for a week, had we been able to separate them from our minds. Battles such as this one simply do not end with the last bullet. They are lived time and again in your mind as your senses attempt to cope with the horrors and the highs. "To really live, you must nearly die," was our usual way of explaining the mental high that comes with living through the hell of a battle. In addition, we had to cope with "survival guilt," wondering why we had been chosen to live while others had to die. Both feelings bombarded us simultaneously, hence sleep became elusive, sometimes for days.

Each of us was silently trying to deal with Smith's death. We had not known him long, but in a way, that made it even tougher to deal with. We had not lost a man in the previous time I had been with the unit. We had almost believed that we were invincible. Smith's death brought reality back.

As my mind returned to semi-normal, I began to feel a tingling from head to toe—no, more of a stinging and itching. I began to check out my body. Had I been hit? Suddenly aware of the source of the problem, I broke out into hysterical, uncontrollable laughter.

"What is it?" Everett asked.

I showed him my arms and legs. "Evidently, I picked the best place to hide during the battle," I said, "a prickly pear." My body was covered in countless tiny thorns. My involvement in the battle had made me oblivious to the little devils. The Doc and I spent the rest of the morning coaxing the spiny critters to "let my body go."

"Reckon I can file for a purple heart," I prodded Everett.

He laughed. "It ought to look good on your record."

"Yeah, I can see the headlines back home," Doc piped in. "Marine wins battle with prickly pear." We all laughed.

"Only a Texan would do that," Mendez added.

The sun was high in the sky as we gathered our gear and our thoughts and set out for our French compound to prepare for the oncoming night and another meeting with our illustrious enemy. Smith was dead, but the Viet Cong were unable to claim his body for their filthy reward, thanks to our Colonel who happened to choose that night to check out the radio transmissions. Our little troop was still intact. Instead of destroying an enemy, the North Vietnamese and their local buddies had only awakened a monster inside each one of us. Our common resolve was to inflict as much pain and death amongst their ranks as CAP Một could possibly do. They would pay for the death and pain of our friends.

---

[1] "Short" or "Short-timer" is in reference to the U.S. military practice during the war of maintaining troops in Vietnam for one year (thirteen months for marines) before being transferred elsewhere or sent home. If a marine was "short," he was getting close to meeting his thirteen-month tour of duty in Vietnam. Both soldiers and marines often kept "short-timer" calendars.

[2] Tết is the lunar new year and Vietnam's most important holiday. The previous year (January 30, 1968) during a holiday cease-fire the Viet Cong and North Vietnamese Army launched a spectacular offensive directed mainly against urban areas. In all, they attacked Saigon, the six largest cities, and numerous provincial and district capitals. American and South Vietnamese forces smashed the so-called Tết Offensive, but the attacks had a profound impact on the political climate in the U.S. Most historians believe that the 1968 offensive was the turning point of the war in that it

led to a gradual withdrawal of U.S. forces from Vietnam. Don Oberdorfer, *Tet! The Turning Point in the Vietnam War* (Garden City, New York: Doubleday, 1971); Bernard Brodie, "The Tét Offensive," in Noble Frankland and Christopher Dowling, eds., *Decisive Battles of the Twentieth Century* (London: Sidgwick & Jackson, 1976), 321–34.

3   Large rolls of barbed wire used in this configuration.

4   A .50-caliber standard U.S. heavy machine gun.

5   A 106-millimeter recoilless rifle used by U. S. forces.

6   A bush term for someone who never saw combat.

7   "Firebase" mentality, or "firebase psychosis," as General Westmoreland would call it, refers to the relative lack of mobility of U.S. combat troops in Vietnam despite the obvious advantages which U.S. forces had with regard to transport, especially the helicopter. Often, however, once U.S. forces established a powerful firebase to support their ground operations, they remained anchored to it and its heavy firepower while enemy forces, without such resources, were more mobile and often eluded U.S. forces. Dave Richard Palmer, *Summons of the Trumpet: U.S.-Vietnam in Perspective* (San Rafael, California: Presidio, 1978), 91–103; Andrew F. Krepinevich, *The Army in Vietnam* (Baltimore: Johns Hopkins, 1986), 196–205.

8   Chi Com grenades refer to Chinese Communist grenades. The North Vietnamese Army and the Viet Cong received a good deal of military aid from the People's Republic of China and the Soviet Union. Robert F. Turner, "Red China's Role in Vietnam," *Washington Report* 69 (March 3, 1969), entire issue.

9   Directional command-detonated antipersonnel mines.

10  Normally the corpsman's ammo load was kept as light as possible, allowing him more room for bandages and such.

11  The body count was the most famous statistic in a war in which just about every imaginable thing was tabulated by U.S. authorities. Because the enemy made every effort to recover its dead and wounded and because of the difficulty of determining the impact of aerial bombardment or long range artillery fire on the enemy, it was usually difficult to determine a precise body count. Given the strategy of attrition set forth by General Westmoreland, however, it was an important statistic in determining how well the war was progressing. Therefore, the body count was often inflated (especially by or at the behest of officers) to reflect a favorable kill ratio (U.S. combat deaths as compared to the enemy), which indicated the U.S. was succeeding in its mission. Douglas Kinnard, *The War Managers* (New York: Da Capo, 1991), 68–70; James William Gibson, *The Perfect War: Technowar in Vietnam* (Boston: Atlantic Monthly, 1986), 110–21.

## Chapter 6

# Viet Cong Village

**T**ết had taken its toll. We were all mentally and physically drained . . . but alive. The loss of Smith gnawed at us with an intensity that left an edginess in the air. We all jumped at the slightest noise. I suppose, down deep, we each blamed ourselves for Smith's death. Our battles had been completely successful for months. None of us had received even a scratch. We had become too cocky for our own good. It was ludicrous to think that we were impervious to death. I mentally pictured the helicopter that hauled away Ciminski and Smith to God knows where. Smith was dead. His worries were over. But Ciminski had been shot up pretty bad. None of us knew whether or not he would be able to keep his leg.

After receiving sporadic reports of "the night of Tết," we realized just how fortunate we had been . . . and also how close death actually came. The Army artillery base, Fat City, had been caught off guard and was overrun by an untold number of VC. The story that reached us through the locals portrayed the VC as undaunted conquerors who captured the watchtower bunkers with ridiculous ease and then opened fire on the soldiers as they ran from their barracks. They used the Army's own LAWs and a watchtower recoilless rifle to blow up the havens the Army had so proudly built. We heard that the NVA Forces and the VC simply walked through the row after row of concertina wire, barbed wire and mined areas that were supposed to thwart the attack of any enemy on foot.

It was not hard to imagine what had happened. The signs were all too obvious. The Cong had a specialty squad referred to as "sappers," who were deadly and unquestionably devoted to destroying their enemy. Utilizing local women and children, they would infiltrate a base by posing as workers of some sort and live among their enemy for weeks, sneaking around, locating every vital section, bunker, command post and storage site that would enable them to launch an effective attack.

Once the sappers had mapped out the entire base, they would return to their unit and formulate a plan of attack. Normally, for a week or two prior to a major offensive they would launch a continual, daily attack with harassment rifle fire and mortar or rocket fire, enabling them to study reaction times, patterns, and weaknesses. Unfortunately, military success is normally based on specific patterns, every soldier reacting like a well oiled machine. You are told to take a certain path to a bunker or your post. Every man is trained to react in robotic manner. It definitely got you to your post in the fastest, most efficient manner, but it also allowed the sappers to accurately predict your every move, and plan your death accordingly.

After a few weeks of harassment fire, the gooks knew exactly when and how the Army was going to react. They had every position and every reaction pinpointed with extreme accuracy. As the week preceding Tết arrived the sappers had, under cover of darkness, crawled for hundreds of yards to the perimeter wire surrounding Fat City. The undetected Cong then cut the wire and slid it back to allow enough room for a man to run through. They continued this process until all the wire was cut, clear up to the trenches and bunkers of the unsuspecting soldiers. As they reached the mines or claymores that had been mapped out during their earlier visit, they would relocate them so that, when activated, the explosion and shrapnel would not harm them. Instead, Army personnel would be annihilated by their own traps. Once every explosive device had been relocated and reset, the sappers crawled back out the way they came, tying the cut strands of wire back together with bits of bamboo or hemp that could be easily cut with a knife. When daylight came, the perimeter, from casual observation, looked unchanged. The soldiers would have no warning when the Cong moved in for the kill.

On the night of Tết, the sappers had simply crawled up to the already cut wire, snipped loose the bamboo, and infiltrated the base with speed that would have completely bewildered, confused and disarmed their enemy. Once inside the base perimeter, each sapper headed for his pre-assigned task to either open fire on the trenches hiding the soldiers, toss satchel charges into their assigned bunkers, or fire RPG rounds into a specified, predetermined target. Within minutes they could wipe out the entire base and slip back into the jungle before reinforcements could arrive.

We knew sappers had hit the base and that the mortar for which we had searched for so long belonged to them. We had to locate them somehow and turn the tables on them.

The days that followed were mild compared to Tết, but not uneventful. We continued the daily exercise of working in the fields and villages,

Goodson in the village with one of Taan's children.

helping the villagers in whatever way we could. Doc treated the sick, we
built huts, cut rice and played with the kids and catnapped whenever we
could. Every night we had sporadic contact with one or two VC we caught
trying to infiltrate our area. Yet still no Mortar Gang.

It only took a few days for the Army Engineering Corps to rebuild the
devastated firebase. Soon memories were all that were left to remind everyone of the horrors that had fallen upon our friends that night. The bodies

Goodson in the village with one of Taan's wives and children.

had been replaced with a fresh new company of troops along with new commanders.

I suppose that was one of the benefits of being a CAP Marine. Since we never fought in the security of a compound or firebase, we had no worries about reconstruction after the battle. Our unit simply packed up the remaining gear and left the smoldering jungle for Mother Nature to repair. The only restructuring we were faced with was to somehow deal with the horrors of the firefight in a manner that would least affect our ability to continue the fight. We had to somehow put the destruction and deaths behind us. It was the only way to remain sane through it all. The memories and the pain had to be controlled, so night after night, day after day, we dealt with it; each in our own way. No one dared to express his feelings for fear of losing control and allowing the torment to overwhelm him.

Goodson in a hut with Taan's mother or mother-in-law.

On one particular pitch black night, with nerves still on edge, we decided to revisit the area where we had spent the night of Têt. The PFs had established a standing rule of curfew with all the villagers in our area of prime responsibility: there was to be no activity after sundown. Anyone seen or heard moving around in the dark of night was considered to be VC and shot without hesitation.

It was around 2100 hours. We were approaching the trench in which we had spent that dreaded night, placing one foot down at a time, checking the ground with a light touch of our boots before placing our full weight down, to ensure no sudden noise would give us away. Suddenly off to our left flank we heard a rustling of leaves. There was no breeze, so it had to have been movement. Instantly we turned and opened fire. . . . Nothing! Everett let fly one of his infamous M-79 grenade launcher flares. We faded into a nearby tree line and attempted to blend in with the jungle growth. The flare popped and started its illuminated descent. Our eyes searched the area into which we had fired. The dancing light of the flare revealed nothing but disfigured trees and plants riddled by our gunfire.

Suddenly a rapid burst of unintelligible uttering and jabbering broke the silence. Taan broke into convulsive laughter. He pointed to a small figure peeking from behind a palm tree. Our vicious VC turned out to be a fiftyish mamasan who was simply outside to answer the call of nature. She had the proof of it all over her black pajamas. The laughter was contagious, spreading through the squad like wildfire. Then silence moved in just as quickly as we realized how close we had come to murdering an innocent old woman.

Taan called her over as darkness quietly overtook the sputtering flare now lying harmlessly on the jungle floor. Taan gave the old lady a sufficient chewing out along with a stern order to relieve herself closer to home. She didn't argue. She was one villager we knew would obey the curfew in the future.

The next few nights were uneventful and grew brighter as the moon completed its metamorphosis into a full glowing ball. The moon in Vietnam sometimes seemed to close in on you, it was so overwhelming. The massive ball covered the horizon with its glow.

Just as the moon reached it fullest, we opted to change our battle plan and split up the group. We sensed that somehow the Cong were slipping past us and figured that we could double our chances of picking up some contact if we split up.

Everett took Rodriguez, Johnston and Lackey (Smith's replacement), the latter a stocky man with an impressive combat record and a disarming smile that seemed to melt away the foreboding feelings that came when we thought of Smith. I kept Jones, Mendez and Taan. We each took four PFs and struck out in different directions. Everett was on his last day before his early week short-time arrived, so I talked him into heading back toward the old French compound we laughingly called home. I took my group and headed off to the north, braving the blacktop to hopefully reach our ambush site before the Cong started moving.

"Call if you get any contact," Everett said as he gathered his brood to head off toward the compound.

"You, too," I returned. "In fact, avoid contact if possible. Just call us if you run across any gooks and we'll do the fighting. I want you out of the bush."

"You know me," he said grinning.

I did, too. I knew that he had a stubborn streak a mile long. That, coupled with his love for the people he had been assigned to protect, would encourage him to go after any gook he laid his eyes on.

It was going to be a full-moon night, which usually meant that the possibility of VC movement was slim. Any activity would be restricted to the shadows of the jungle and the villages themselves. The blacktop would soon be a dangerous place to be, but since the moon didn't come out until about 2200 hours, it was relatively safe for the moment and without doubt the fastest route to our objective for the night, a known Viet Cong village located about ten miles north and half a mile west of the blacktop. The dozen or so farms just east of the village on the east side of the blacktop were also VC sympathizers. Next to School House Valley, this was the most probable area of activity.

As we rapidly made our way north under the temporary cover of darkness, my thoughts turned to the events of the day. The supplies of ammo and explosives left with us at Tết were getting pitifully low. In fact, a night even half as severe as Tết would completely exhaust our supplies. Rear supply said it could only provide us with "practice rounds" which, although they consisted of live ammo, were all "tracers," —fire trailing bullets. Every time you pulled the trigger you let the enemy know where you were, not from the muzzle flash, but from the solid red line that came streaking from the barrel of your weapon. We didn't like it one bit, but it was our only choice.

My thoughts also turned to another discouraging bit of knowledge I had received that morning from rear supply. Not one ounce of cleaning fluid was available, and none was on the way because the American company that manufactured it was on strike. In the bush your weapons would begin to develop rust within twenty-four hours if you didn't clean them. The M-16 had an aluminum bolt but every other piece was steel. A neglected bit of rust would make your rifle jam, never to fire again. I had sent a letter off to my parents with an urgent request to send all the cleaning gear they could get their hands on, "pronto." I felt sure my dad would come through with the gear we needed, even though time was not in our favor.

We covered the ten miles separating us from the VC area in record time. It was 2115 hours and you could just make out the outline of the enemy-occupied village on our left. It was completely dark, lacking the flickering of candlelight and dancing shadows you would normally see through the cracks and window openings of the huts.

They knew we were there. I felt it. I don't know how, but I knew that they knew. I passed the word for "silence." Since we still had about thirty more minutes of darkness before the moon lit up the area, I decided to set up our initial ambush to the east of the blacktop along a trail that connected the farmers with the VC village. It put us in a vulnerable position but it divided the forces against us. I couldn't shake the chill that kept crawling up my back, even though the night was warm. I knew the feeling well. It was my early warning system and it had never failed me.

We settled in for the wait scattered in the cover of a tree line bordering a dried up, abandoned rice paddy. The trees would produce plenty of shadow cover against the flare of the moon and provide us with an excellent line of sight with the nearby huts as well as the VC village, now invisible, just over half a mile away.

We waited in silence as the eastern horizon took on an eerie golden glow which I realized suddenly I had been staring at. I quickly closed my eyes to regain my night vision and passed the word for the others to do the same. It was always a temptation to watch that big white ball rise above the trees, but to do so meant a guaranteed loss of night vision for a good thirty seconds to a minute. A firefight could be over in that time.

We concentrated our gaze on the shadows of the nearby huts with an occasional glance back down the trail to the village. Something was wrong. The chill returned. Somehow I felt like they knew we were there. "But how?" I thought. "A leak, but where?" The moon reached the treetops, turning the golden glow into a brilliant white that seem to penetrate the shadows of our tree line. Fear made an attempt to raise its ugly head. I swallowed hard and prepared myself for the inevitable. Tết was still too fresh a memory to allow us to loosen up, even a little.

The moonlit jungle seemed to come alive with movement as the slightest breeze created a dancing shadow. "Get ahold of yourself," I thought as I realized the tenseness of my trigger finger.

The silence was interrupted by a quick "plop" down toward Jones. "What the——?" I thought. Then another followed directly in front of my position. "Grenades!" I yelled. We all hugged the ground. Simultaneously with my warning came a popping sound as the "grenades" released their deadly contents. "We're being gassed!" I yelled this time. Someone wanted us out of that tree line, out into the open. No order was needed. We had all been gassed before. "Don't touch your face. Breathe short controlled breaths. Don't hold your breath." The orders echoed in my brain.

I passed the word. "Let's crawl out the left flank," I ordered. The men didn't hesitate; even Taan and his men were under control. My eyes caught movement through the stream of tears flowing down my cheeks. I could just make out silhouettes as the Cong lobbed more gas grenades toward us. "Why don't they rush us?" I wondered as I called our crawl to a halt.

"Ready grenades and toss them hard to your right," I passed the word.

Grenades flew in the direction of the movement. We hugged the dirt. "Boom. Boom. Boom." The grenades exploded in rapid succession. The night echoed with a scream as a figure came running toward us out of the jungle. We opened fire. I passed word to gather up everything and charge on my command.

"Charge!" I screamed. We erupted from the tree line like raging bulls, tears reflecting on our cheeks and guns blazing toward the nearby huts. Fortunately, a breeze off the ocean had rapidly cleared the gas from around us, allowing our tears to clear our burning eyes. Our attacker lay dead before us. I ordered Jones, Mendez and the PFs to seek the cover of nearby shadows and cover us. Taan and I quickly made our way over to the dead VC.

I felt Taan tense as I squatted down by the body. There was no worry that it might be booby trapped. The bullet-riddled body and half blown-off arm assured me that he had not had time. He was a small man, barely five feet tall. I reached out and turned him on his back. My stomach turned. The "man" was a boy, barely twelve or thirteen years old. We had killed a boy. My head hung low as I inwardly cursed myself for killing him. I looked up at Taan. "He was only a child," I said.

Taan laid his hand on my shoulder. "We go now," he said. "Not worry, Corporal, he still VC."

New tears welled up in the corners of my eyes, this time not from the gas. What kind of country would send boys into battle? What kind of men would condone or even allow their sons to be used in a war? I knew the answer, but it didn't make me feel any better. The VC recruited boys for service, just like our own country drafted boys out of high school to do their part in this war. The average age of the American soldier in Vietnam must have been nineteen.

The Viet Cong, with their drafting techniques, were looked upon as common criminals, as kidnappers and brainwashers of children. They would go into a village and demand food, storage of weapons and explosives and a place to hide. They would set up booby traps in the surrounding jungles, marked to protect the villagers but a constant threat to the children. Last but not least, they would draft or kidnap every male old enough to carry a satchel charge or strong enough to squeeze a trigger, which gave them a broad age range from four years old or so to old men. The village males, like the drafted American soldier, had no choice. In the U.S., if you refused the draft you risked the possibility of jail. Therein lay the difference between a civilized nation and an uncivilized one. The Vietnamese male had three choices: join up, die, or watch your family die. At least we were civil with our coercion techniques.

We turned away from the boy and left him to be buried by his recruiters, then we made our way to the tree line where Mendez and the others were waiting. "Did we get him?" Jones asked.

"Yeah," I returned without volunteering any details.

Before I could say another word the opposite side of the blacktop came alive with the fire from a dozen AKs. It looked as if the boy's "friends" had been awakened by our gunfire, or worse, the purpose of the gas had been to drive us back into their deadly trap. Fortunately, the firefight with the kid had lasted only minutes and the gooks weren't exactly sure where we were. In fact, their shots were actually aimed far off to our right flank.

"Hold your fire." I quietly passed the word. Turning to Taan, I said, "We have to find a quick way to get within grenade range of those VC."

Taan understood. If we could keep under cover long enough to lob grenades into the pack of VC on the blacktop, then their buddies, with any luck, would be unable to sneak up on us.

Taan pointed to the end of the tree line we were sheltered in. It joined with an even denser tree line that emptied out within fifty feet or so of our side of the blacktop. Taan in the lead, we quickly and quietly made our way toward that tree line. Just as we turned onto the trail of the second tree line, an RPG projectile exploded in the place we had just left. The explosion was followed by AK fire. I risked a look over the berm of the tree line to study the situation. The moon was at its brightest. The Cong were still hunkered down on their side of the road unwilling to move until we made contact. I could sense their fear as our whereabouts remained hidden from them.

I rejoined the others who were still making their way toward the black-top. Luckily, the full moon provided sufficient light that we could locate telltale marks of booby traps and pass by them without fear of harm or detection.

Suddenly the tree line opened into a small clearing that bordered the road. My cocky thoughts faded as the reality of the battle began to take its rightful place. Sweat trickled down the side of my face, making my cheeks burn from the effects of the tear gas.

With Taan at point, we began our crawl to cover the short distance to the blacktop. "Boom. Boom." The gooks were still searching, hoping to draw our fire and then slip away unharmed. They were so caught up in their search that we covered the open area virtually undetected. They were oblivious to the death that approached them.

We waited for another volley of gunfire and explosives. It came. We each tossed our grenades across the blacktop into the unsuspecting group of Cong. The grenades exploded in rapid succession. "Boom. Boom. Boom." They illuminated the already well lit night, interrupting the harmless bar-rage of gunfire from the Cong's AKs. Screams mingled with the explosions as bodies and parts of bodies flew in every direction.

About half the distance back to the VC village, the ground suddenly came alive with VC as they tossed aside their spider trap covers and searched in vain to locate their enemy. There were at least fifteen or twenty of them.

The radio crackled. "Black One to Black Two. Over." It was Everett.

"We have contact," I answered anticipating his question.

"We're on our way," he returned.

"Roger, Black One. We'll probably need the help. We're due east of VC Villa. Watch for contact on your way."

"Roger," he answered.

The radio went silent once more. I passed the word, "Move out on line low and fast." They did. The gooks were coming at us but their pace was slow, even somewhat checked. It seemed as if they were still unsure of our position. "We *have* to be visible," I thought. Then it struck me. "They must think we're their fellow VC. Good, let 'em come."

We reached the trench the first group of VC had occupied. All of them were dead or dying. We quietly finished them off and hunkered down to wait for their friends to walk into range. The expanse stretching between our position and the VC village was nothing but wide open sand dunes, difficult to move in, yet easy to hide in.

The Cong sensed trouble. Their leader yelled out at about 100 yards. Taan looked at me. I tapped Jones on the shoulder. "Let 'em have it," I whispered. The 60 opened up with a growl. Jones did it right. One long burst to instill fear followed by short, rapid, five-round bursts.

Everyone else opened up simultaneously with the 60, and as we did so, deadly red lines streaked out of our weapons searching for their prey. I had forgotten about the "all tracer" situation. "Oh, my God," I thought. "They know exactly where we are now." I silently cursed the rear for having nothing but tracer rounds available.

The Congs' reaction to the red lines of death was wild. I couldn't believe it. They suddenly lost their motivation to assault, instead scattering like scared rabbits—running into each other, tripping, falling and, in some cases, just throwing down their weapons and hightailing it away. They must have felt that a red monster had been unleashed on them.

Ricochets helped with the confusion. Every direction the Cong turned, a wild barrage of tumbling, ricocheting bullets would bounce around them like a burst of sparks from a campfire.

Everett and his gang showed up, out of breath. "Ran all the way. Where's the gooks?" he asked.

I smiled and pointed at the group running and falling in front of our deadly hail of "red lead."

"The tracers have them confused," I shouted. "Set the other 60[1] at the opposite end and we'll set out on line and catch 'em in a crisscross fire."

"Good idea," he agreed. Everett rapidly set up his men and we left our little trench, on line, following our "red lead" toward the VC. The extra 60 was the icing on the cake. The rest of the VC turned and ran as fast as their legs would carry them and disappeared behind a line of tall sand dunes just shy of the village. We continued our "on line" sweep, but ceased fire. The Cong were evidently in morbid fear. Even with our cease fire, they didn't risk a single shot in our direction.

We reached the dunes and settled in behind them. Everett lobbed a couple of M-79 grenades into the depths of the dunes. Nothing. Suddenly back at the edge of the village, we caught a glimpse of movement between the huts.

"There they are," Jones pointed.

"Let's go get 'em," Mendez yelled.

Everett looked uneasy. Village contact was never easy and, without fail, women and children always seemed to get caught up in the worst of it.

"We've got to check with the rear first," I stated.

"Go ahead," Everett agreed. He deployed the men into temporary positions to wait until CAP Command radioed back their decision.

"CAP One to Command. Over." I keyed the mike. After the typical fifteen-second delay the radio crackled back with a voice we'd never met.

"Command. Go head, CAP One. Over."

"Completed firefight with Victor Charlie with remainder hiding in Diêm Phò Hai village at grid 403133," I radioed back.

"Checking," the radio answered. We waited, watching every shadow of the village. The radio crackled again. "Negative. The CO will not allow village entry at night. Too risky," the radio said.

I couldn't argue but I didn't want the gooks to return with their buddies and catch us in the middle of the desert dunes. "What do you think, Everett?" I asked.

"Let's give 'em this one," he suggested.

"Okay," I agreed. "But let's call in a fire mission to cover our exit. We're like sitting ducks out here."

"Agreed," Everett said.

"Command, this is CAP One. Over."

"Go ahead, CAP One."

"Roger on the 'no attack.' Request full battery of HE (High Explosive) fifty meters due east of Diêm Phò Hai five minutes from now," I radioed back, checking my watch. 0115 hours.

"Roger, CAP One. HE rounds will drop at 0120 hours. Get out of there."

We turned and ran as fast, probably faster, than the VC had run from us. I had already had one encounter with our renowned artillery barrages when a battery of short rounds landed on my patrol with the grunts in Elephant Valley. My thoughts returned to that day as we covered the half mile of desert sand dunes.

*It had been an uneventful day except for the volley of 105 harassment fire from the rear which was supposed to pass over our heads and land 1000 meters past us to clear the way for our patrol. We had just started to cross some old concertina wire left by the French when a short round exploded about 100 yards down the mountain from us. I was right in the middle of the wire when it went off. The blast loosened my grip and I slipped and fell to the opposite side with my legs still entangled in the grip of the barbs. The others helped free my legs and we rapidly took cover. Thinking it might have been an attack by the VC we waited in the bush. Nothing happened. We radioed back to confirm the short round.*

*We continued our trek through the jungle. I felt a stinging in my left arm and chanced a quick check. Blood was oozing from a wound in the back of my upper right arm. At first it looked like I had picked up a small piece of shrapnel, but we agreed that it was probably a cut from the fall and simply dismissed it. That night we ambushed a patrol of VC and my 60 jammed. Without hesitation, I reached down to grab my .45 pistol. Pain jabbed through my hand as it tightened around the grip. I jerked away, blood pouring from my palm. Startled, I risked a look at the weapon and discovered a piece of shrapnel about two inches in size that had passed through one side of the handle, through one of the bullets and was protruding out the other side. Had the shrapnel missed the pistol, it would have entered my left side and, no doubt, ripped me apart.*

"Another of God's little miracles," I thought as we burst out onto the blacktop once again, bringing me back to the present.

"Hit the opposite side," Everett yelled. "It's 0120 hours."

We didn't check our watches. Just as we bit the dirt you could hear the soft boom of the 105 howitzers in the distance. That meant the shells were on their way. Within seconds a dozen HE projectiles turned the dunes into craters of sand. I grabbed the transmitter. "On target. Wait five and give us one more battery."

"Roger," came the reply.

We gathered ourselves together and set off down the road hugging the shadows as we went and keeping a sharp eye out for VC ambushes and booby traps. The second volley lit up the dunes as we checked their accuracy once again. "Right on," I thought. "That will make the VC think twice about trying to follow us."

We traveled about a mile south along the blacktop and then melted into the jungle in hopes of finding a sheltered, fairly safe area where we could unwind and wait for daylight. It was 0325 when we settled into a sheltered tree line similar to the one we had used on the night of Tết. Our visibility was clear in all directions across the rice paddies for about a hundred yards, making us virtually unapproachable unless sleep overtook us. No worry there. Our adrenaline was racing.

About an hour passed and we had all moved into the shadows waiting and watching and wishing the sun would be early for once. We knew they were hunting for us but hoped the artillery had kept them from watching our escape.

Suddenly, around 0430, a loudspeaker broke the silence of the early morning hour. "Marines, we know you are there. Why not surrender? We will send you home to your families." The speaker sounded like a Harvard grad. He continued. "Why do you continue to invade our country, rape our women and murder our poor children? You are a disgrace to mankind. Come, surrender to us before we have to kill you."

"That's it," I said. "Give me that map."

Everett tossed it to me. I called Taan over and we studied the surrounding area due north of our position. The sound seemed to be coming from a palm grove just north of us about 150 to 200 yards. Taan and I agreed. "Everett, let me call in artillery on those bums," I requested.

"Go ahead," he said. "We can't get any sleep anyway."

"Command, this is CAP One. Contact again. Over."

Response was immediate this time. "Go ahead, CAP One," the radio answered.

"Fire mission at 428116," I requested. "Give me one battery HE with follow-up battery of $VT^2$ set for 20 feet."

"Roger," the radio replied. "It's on its way."

The loud speaker continued to taunt us as we faintly heard the artillery boom away in the distance. With rapid succession the HE ripped into the palm grove. Seconds passed as the VC continued speaking. I had asked for detonation at twenty feet. We hugged the ground. VT had a range of up to 1000 yards, and we definitely did not want to risk being mangled by our own artillery. When it hit, the explosions resounded into the night.

The voice on the loudspeaker abruptly stopped. The speaker, our tor-
mentor, was silenced. Forever.

---

[1] Two weeks before, we had run across a downed Huey gunship covered in a month's
growth of vegetation. Every usable piece of material and hardware had been stripped
from it by the local farmers. Evidently, the VC and NVA had never located it because
still attached to its turret was the M-60 the gunner had used. Empty shells were
everywhere and the gun was empty, which told us that the gunner had exhausted all
of his ammo. There were no bodies, so we figured that the men had been medevac'd
or captured. We let Command know about the chopper and its location. The 60
became ours.

[2] VT stood for Variable Time explosive, which was preset to explode by request at a
certain height above the ground.

## Chapter 7

# Killer Team

The artillery barrage had served its purpose well, not so much because of the destruction it created but simply because of the healing it caused. War was already hell on earth, and to blatantly accuse battle-worn soldiers of rape, mayhem and child-murder was rubbing salt into our wounds.

Deep in our hearts, we knew we were fighting not simply because our country's politicians told us we were protecting our own shores from Communist invasion. In fact, I doubt any of us truly believed Communism to be a threat. But because of the reports that kept trickling in from home—that our own country was calling us rapists and baby-killers—we all were developing second thoughts about returning home even if we did survive.

So it wasn't that the words were being used by Viet Cong that bothered us so much. The VC were simply repeating the propaganda that was already being broadcast by our own news media. What we could not understand or accept was that our fellow Americans hated us. Were it not for the little bits of encouragement we received from relatives and friends, I doubt that any of us would have cared to return "home."[1]

At this point, Vietnam was our home. Our goal of protecting an abstract, faraway country—especially one that hated us—had been traded in for a goal that seemed more physical and real. The people of Quảng Tin Province, Vietnam, loved us and knew we were not rapists and baby-killers. They knew that we were foreigners, but they readily took us into their homes, fed us and encouraged us to help protect them, not from an abstract "Communist invasion," but from the daily oppression and threat of death

Vietnamese villagers
standing in front of
the one school house
in the Quảng Tin
Province that the PFs
had been able to
protect from VC
influence.

Goodson and one of
the PFs in front of the
Quảng Tin Province
school.

they faced at the hands of Vietnam's infamous VC and NVA soldiers. The Vietnamese were aware of the accusations against us, yet they still wanted and accepted our offer to help them survive.

As marines, we traded an abstract for an absolute. We were Quảng Tin Province's resident police force, helping the people of the province live their daily lives without constant fear of harm or death. We were there to help the people in whatever way we could. We taught them simple things like how to brush their teeth, how to best cultivate their fields or to rotate crops and, last but not least, how to care for the educational needs of their children. The people were eager to learn, and in return they offered us the sense of "home" that America had taken away.

As dawn rapidly forced the jungle darkness to retreat, we checked our weapons and our gear, risked a momentary stretch of our limbs, and set off in the direction of the palm grove. The artillery had definitely done its job. Everywhere you looked for roughly a hundred yards, palm trees were ripped, shredded and uprooted. Leaves boasted telltale holes created by pieces of shrapnel in search of someone or something it could harm. It was not a pretty sight. Destruction was everywhere, but the men were elated.

Jones yelled out, "Goodson, Everett, everybody, over here!"

We hurried over to his position and followed his pointing finger. Suddenly we all broke out in hysterical laughter. A small palm tree, completely mangled by the artillery, was still standing. Dangling from its battered trunk were the remains of the loudspeaker. The men cheered and began marching around in circles chanting, "Corporal Goodson—VT Man," like a cheering squad at a football game.

Everett sauntered over to me. "Looks like you've made some friends." He smiled and waved his hand in the direction of the men.

"Yeah," I smiled weakly. "I just hope I never lead them into trouble."

"Just always leave yourself an out, man," Everett said. "Don't plan an ambush or even a trek through the jungle without preplanning artillery drops, escape plans, and hideouts. And keep the villagers on your side. They're our biggest asset."

"They're the reason we're here," I said.

Everett smiled. "You'll do good. Respect the men and they'll respect you, and the same goes for the Vietnamese people. Respect is what's going to keep you alive out here."

"Yeah," I looked at Everett sternly. "Speaking of alive, let's get you out of the bush. This is your 'D' day."

"Don't think that's not on my list of things to do today," Everett said. "Why I even thought about chancing a bath before I head for the rear."

"Bad idea," I snapped. "You'll get on that chopper, leeches, muck and all. Let the rear take care of cleaning you up. They probably need a challenge anyway."

We smiled, shook hands and simultaneously yelled, "Let's move out." The men laughed at our "mutual command" and began marching in line in our direction with a new chant: "Stateside Everett and VT Man." With a half-hearted order and stifled grin, Everett commanded the men to "cease the noise."

"I agree," I chimed in. "You're going to ruin our reputations."

We struck off in the direction of our dear old French compound. Everett would collect his gear and keepsakes, board a chopper at 0800 and leave the jungles of Vietnam forever. That would make two, counting Ciminski, who made it out of the jungle alive.

We reached the compound around 0700 with ample time for Everett to round up his belongings. Good-byes are always difficult, but this one was more so. We knew Everett longed to return to his family, but we also had an idea of what he had to face back in the states. We prayed he could withstand the ridicule and rejection waiting for him stateside. We also figured that Everett knew he was saying good-bye to dead men. Men with a bounty on their heads. In fact, our conversation had bounced along those lines a number of times. There was a good chance all of us would be dead or wounded before Everett even reached stateside.

"Give 'em hell," Jones encouraged as he grabbed Everett with a breath-taking hug.

"Don't forget us back here in the bush," Mendez chided, trying to duplicate Jones's hug.

"Give my ma and pa a call, will you?" Lackey asked, giving Everett a quick handshake.

Johnston stepped up. "Say, chap, you wouldn't be going by way of Australia, would you?" he asked. We all laughed.

It was my turn. Everett didn't know it, but he had been my rock, my strength, in our little hellhole. I felt like a part of me was being ripped away. I was happy for him, yet I felt inadequate to fill his shoes. He knew so much more than I did about the VC and their jungle. I wanted to ask him a thousand different questions I'd never thought to ask before, but all I could do was grab his hand with a vice lock and smile while a tear fought its way down my cheek. He was having the same problem. We just stood, staring at each other, all four hands locked in a unified grip as the chopper began its descent above us.

As the chopper dropped to the ground, Everett and I hugged and slapped each other on the back. He turned to go as I said, "Keep a pot boiling for us." He turned, smiled, waved and leaped into the waiting helicopter. Immediately, the Huey Gunship lifted off the ground and streaked to the south carrying its precious cargo, a live soldier heading home. As the dust settled around us, we watched and waved until the chopper was a faint spot on the horizon. "God bless you, Everett," I thought.

I returned my thoughts to the present, turned and started to gather the men together for a debriefing of the coming day's activities, when I noticed a new hat in the outfit. The gunship had dropped off Everett's replacement while we were watching our old leader hop on board.

The new man was a Puerto Rican whom I judged to be about twenty-two years old, about five-foot-nine and kind of stocky. We found out later that he had been transferred from another CAP unit located somewhere near Saigon. "No one can replace Everett," I thought, instantly disliking him. Regardless, he was our new Sergeant. I extended my hand and forced a smile. "Corporal Goodson, your assistant with this bunch of rebels."

"Rivera," he stated simply, extending his hand.

He didn't even bother closing his fingers around my hand as we shook. In an attempt to get him to respond I squeezed extra hard. No response. "Great," I thought, "just great."

He turned away from me and started shaking hands with the other men. He and Rodriguez took an instant liking to each other, but the other men—even Johnston, our always jovial Australian—seemed as leery as I was.

"I hope my instincts are wrong," I thought. "We don't need another Sergeant Rogers in this unit."

Introductions complete, Rivera turned back to me. "Where do I stash my gear?" he asked.

"He'll show you," I answered as I nodded in Rodriguez's direction. "Get your gear stashed and I'll bring you up to speed on our unit and our plans for the day," I yelled after him as he and Rodriguez headed toward our storage shack. Turning to the men, I ordered: "You guys clean your weapons, and be sparing."

"Sparing?" Jones asked.

"Yeah," I hesitated. "Y'all may as well know. Supply has dropped another goody in our lap. They can't get anymore cleaning gear for now and probably won't for another thirty days."

"Stateside strikes again," Mendez mused.

"We need to clean our weapons every day regardless of whether we've had any contact or not. That way we can minimize the major cleaning required after a firefight or from a week's neglect. So use only a drop or two for each cleaning instead of the typical method. If anyone runs out before a shipment arrives we'll all need to share to ensure that every weapon is in tiptop working order."

"No problem here," Jones offered. "I've got enough to last thirty days unless we have contact every day."

"Me, too," Mendez chimed in.

"Yeah," Johnston said. "Don't worry, Corporal, we'll make it all right."

Rivera and Rodriguez returned.

"All stashed away?" I asked.

"Yeah," Rivera nodded.

"Well, grab a hunk of dirt there and I'll fill you in on what's happened up to now."

"No need," he said. "The CO has already debriefed me on all the contact and the supposed bounty on your heads." He sneered sarcastically and continued. "The CO and I feel like you guys may be letting a few gooks through in spite of all the damage you've done. But we like your idea of killer teams and plan to make that the SOP from now on." He continued, this time addressing everyone. "There have been far too many mortar, RPG and B-122[2] attacks on the Chu Lai rear area, as well as the artillery base you guys allowed to get overrun during Tết."

"Blood can boil," I thought as I recalled our own narrow escape from death that infamous night. "No problem. He'll soon find out how much ground seven men can cover." I muttered to myself. I checked the faces of all the men. They all had stopped cleaning their weapons and sat simply staring at their new sergeant. "Hang in there, guys," I thought. "Give him a week and he'll change his tune."

Rivera continued, "My plan is to set up a base operation in this compound and we'll run all of our killer team patrols out of it. I'll remain here with three other men as backup, along with the second radio. You, Goodson, will lead every patrol."

"Now, *that* I have no problem with," I thought. "There is no way I want to get trapped in this old compound."

Rivera concluded, "This order is effective immediately."

The men glanced over at me, shrugged and returned their attention to their weapons. Since I wasn't protesting, they figured it was an okay idea. The killer team approach had already proven effective—but only with the help of a decoy group. To gain the same advantage from a command post was more than questionable.

"Oh, yes," Rivera interrupted my thoughts. "There have been reports that a black man and a white blond-headed dude surrendered to the VC in this area. When they surrendered they took with them one M-60 and a radio. The VC are using them as decoys to wipe out patrols and also to help locate ambushes through the use of the radio. So each team must maintain radio silence until actual contact is made. There is a reward for the capture of these two gentlemen, by the way, dead or alive."

We had heard this same rumor from a couple of Army convoys passing through our area right before Tết. However, we had seen nothing that lent credence to the story. The very thought of our own kind fighting against us was hard to swallow.

Rivera walked over to me. "I want to keep Rodriguez here at the command post with me," he said. "Who else do you recommend?"

I was not about to volunteer anyone else to remain with him, much less confined to the base at night. "Our approach so far has been strictly on the volunteer basis," I offered. "Whether you stay or go, it can be equally dangerous both ways." You could see he deemed it an honor to remain with him in his command post, and wanted only the "elite" to stay with him.

"Who is your best man?" he asked.

"They are all equally important and each possesses his own special attributes."

Disgusted with my answer, he spun on his heel and studied the men. "Rodriguez is going to help set up my command post," he told them. "Which one of you feels qualified to assist us with our task?" he asked. Everyone momentarily stopped cleaning their weapons, glanced at him and then over to me. They were waiting for me to say something.

"Sergeant, may I talk to you for a minute?" I asked. I didn't want to get into a verbal battle in front of the men.

He nodded and joined me a short distance away. I hoped the men weren't concerned about my act of secrecy.

"Respectfully, sergeant, I really could care less about your preconceived opinions of me or our unit. Our performance record stands on its own."

"Corporal, you can . . . " he started.

"Hold it," I said. "Arguing is not going to solve anything, and I don't want personal feelings to take command of this unit. So just listen to what I have to say, then I'll shut up and you can speak your piece." I paused and looked around. "This compound is in total disrepair. We've toyed with the idea of rebuilding all the bunkers, planting mines and stringing new wire. But even with that, our numbers are far too few to even hope to withstand any sizable assault. Besides, there is a sapper unit operating in this area. We are positive they are the ones who overran Fat City firebase during Têt.

"The past three months have proven highly effective only because we used a totally mobile approach. Our hit-and-run tactics have left the VC and the NVA confused and devastated. Being unpredictable has kept us alive and the men know that. If you set up a base operation you are going to give the VC exactly what they have longed for—a stationary target."

"Are you finished?" he asked.

"Yep," I answered.

"Good," he snapped. "Now you listen to me! What you and your previous squad leader felt comfortable with does not interest me in the least. I'm in charge now and in my last unit we worked with a command post and it worked well. We lost a few men, but that's the risk in this type of unit."

My tongue was starting to bleed.

He continued, "We will set up this base as a command base, but to throw off the enemy you're so afraid of, we'll vanish into the jungle every morning and sneak back in every night. That way I can stay in direct contact with my Vietnamese counterpart, Sergeant Shôu. I also will have immediate radio contact with Command Headquarters and the CO." Rivera stopped, stared at me, and then continued. "It worked in my last unit and it will work here. Oh, and I've decided to keep the corpsman and Mendez with me."

"Let's get out of here," was all I had to say. "I'm getting edgy spending so much time in one spot."

"Okay," he said. "Round up the men and let's head up the blacktop."

That was fine with me. I wanted to check in with Mamasan Tôu and see what report she had on Viet Cong activity.

The men were edgy and distrusting of their new commander. As we readied to leave they were all muttering. I stepped in among them. "Can the small talk," I ordered. "Mutiny is not in my vocabulary."

Mendez was the first to react. "Come on, Goodson," he stated. "If we do what he says, we'll all end up dead."

"Hey, trust me. I've got a plan that will minimize the danger."

"Oh, yeah?" Jones joined in. "What?"

"Not now," I answered. "You'll just have to trust me," I smiled at him.

Rodriguez was hanging on every word. I had a feeling he was going to be Rivera's stoolie. I'd warn each man individually as the opportunity presented itself. Right now, our new sergeant was ready. "Let's move out," he yelled.

Lackey took point, not that it made any difference. The blacktop was crowded with Vietnamese coming and going in both directions. Any one of them could have been a VC. I followed behind Lackey, with Jones, Mendez and Johnston closing up the middle. Rodriguez lagged back with our new sergeant.

The road was unusually crowded for midday, which sometimes meant the villagers were moving out of the VC's way. I checked their gear, though, and saw no signs of belongings—just the typical fruit, fish and numerous baskets of assorted items. No warning signs to worry over.

We stopped off at Mamasan Tôu's house to check on her needs, give the men a chance to cool down, and introduce the new sergeant. Mamasan had seen so many soldiers come and go that a new man meant very little to her. Her main concern was to keep us happy and content.

Mamasan was glad to see us and seemed overly anxious to cater to our needs that day. "De first Coke, no pay," she offered in her broken English.

"Cám ơn u la," I smiled back at her, to offer thanks. She smiled at my equally broken Vietnamese. She had on her typical "pajamas," a loose-fitting black silk outfit. Her smile was constant, revealing the beetle-nut-stained and opium-rotted teeth common to all the old people in the village.[3]

Mamasan Tôu pulled Taan aside and began jabbering away at him. They both laughed, took a quick sideways glance at me, laughed again and then continued. I ignored them, shed my gear next to my favorite palm, and settled down to rest my body and mind in preparation for the night to come. Weapons already clean, most of the men settled down for a nap.

Mamasan Tôu had sent her runners to establish a security net around us. We appreciated that more than anything else because it gave us a chance to lower our guard and relax, if only for a few hours. I was somewhat leery of establishing a pattern so we never frequented her place on a regular basis and never announced our arrival. We also approached her hut from a different direction every time we came.

I was tired, but I had to get a couple of things off of my mind before I could allow myself the pleasure of a nap. I dug into the depths of my pockets and came out with a stubby little pencil and a blank piece of paper. It was time to send a letter home. My poor mom always ended up a sounding post for my frustrations. I couldn't talk to my men about the things that were chewing at me. They had their own problems.

*Dear Mom,* I wrote. I began the letter by telling her where I was that day, describing every bush and animal in detail. Not that I felt she would be interested, but simply because I wanted to avoid the actual subject of my letter as long as possible. Finally, I could wait no longer.

*There is a question I need to ask someone, Mom, and you're the lucky one. What I would like to know is why I am here. Most of these people don't even know they are being oppressed by the Communist regime. All they know is that the Viet Cong and the U.S. are fighting each other and messing up their land.*

I stopped writing momentarily and checked the men and the area. Everyone was okay. I continued:

*Last night just as in every night in this hell hole, we killed more of the Viet Cong. As usual, we couldn't find their bodies. But we're convinced that we indeed did kill them. One thing that bothers me though, Mom. Why do we have to kill each other? Last night I killed a man just as I have done continually for the past seven months. The battles never change. When the smoke clears, someone's always dead or maimed for life. Our guys or theirs. Last night I killed a man because my country said he was the enemy. He tried to kill me for the same reason. What's ironic, Mom, is that in another day, another time I probably would have been shaking hands with the man and buying him a drink somewhere, sharing family photos. Instead, our countries told us we were enemies, so we fought each other. I didn't know the man, so*

*I couldn't hate him. He was no different than I. A man trying to serve his country and trying to understand why. My point is, Mom . . .*

I stopped to organize my thoughts and to fight back the bitterness that was rising up in the pit of my stomach. My pencil started off again.

*Just because my country, actually my country's politicians, decided that we had a responsibility to stop this "Communist aggression" in Vietnam, I have to kill every man they deem as Communist. We are supposed to rid this country of the oppressors. Okay, what then? Suppose we do annihilate every single VC and NVA over here. What then? Do we come in and put two cars in every garage? A swimming pool in every back yard? Give them all memberships to the country club? What do we do?*

*These people have no concept of our "American way of life" nor are they interested. They are simple farmers and mountain folks. They don't punch time clocks or drive fancy cars. They work from sunup to sundown trying to supply food for their own families, nothing more—nothing less. They are not interested in nor could they understand all of the modern conveniences we would like to Americanize them with.*

*These people remind me of the stories I read as a kid about the pioneers and settlers of our own country. Simple farm folks and country folks trying to live and let live. Simply to take life as God gave it. These people are no different than that. Their homes are crudely constructed huts made from nature-supplied materials, bamboo poles, palm leaves and vines, much like the homes of our ancestors. Different materials, of course, but much the same. They farm their land, raise their cattle and other livestock and simply take care of their families just as our own pioneers did. Most of the VC were just farmers, mad and exasperated because we, as Americans, either destroyed their crops, their cattle or their families. Any man would kill for that. To these farmers, "Communist aggression" means nothing. All they know is that their land has been invaded by a massive force of flag-waving Americans from one side, and from the other side by a bunch of soldiers that look just like them but who care nothing about them or their families, and each farmer and his family are caught up in the middle. Sure, there are Viet Cong who do nothing but try to kill us. The question is why? The answer is simply not here. Or is it? Someday we'll be gone and these folks can get back to their business, taking care of their families.*

*I love you, Mom. I miss everyone more than I could have ever believed. I know and you know that I will probably never make it out of these jungles alive. All I ask is that you not allow anyone to pin any labels on me. Don't let them call me anything but a soldier who fought and died for a cause, for a people. I'm not fighting for a democracy over here. I'm simply fighting to help these people survive in the way they choose. Good-bye, Mom. Tell everyone Howdy.*

I finished my letter, folded it, placed it into the special envelope they supplied us and stuck it back in my pocket to wait for a chance to send it to the rear. A couple of other letters, previously written, kept it company. It was not often that we were able to get letters in and out of the bush.

When I looked up, I saw Taan approaching me. "Chào, Corporal," he beamed.

"What's up?"

"Up?" he asked, feigning a look to the skies in mock memory of our first conversation.

"What do you want?" I rephrased my question as I stifled a grin.

"Oh, okay. Mamasan have gift for you," he said, trying to hide his laughter.

I was bewildered.

Mamasan started jabbering away at a speed that left my head spinning. I missed every word except "Lín," her daughter's name. "Is something wrong with Lín?" I asked, jumping to my feet.

"No!" Taan placed his hand on my shoulder to calm me down. "Come here," he said as he led me over next to Mamasan Tôu's cistern. "She want to give you her daughter because you top man of marines," he smiled.

"I, wha . . ." I trailed off in disbelief.

"True," Taan pleaded.

"But I'm no commander. I'm just an assistant squad leader."

"She not think so. She say you number one. She want you have her daughter."

"You mean to marry?" I asked hesitantly.

"If you want," he answered.

"Oh, no!" I slapped my forehead.

Taan got real serious. "She be hurt bad if you no want her daughter."

I settled down and considered the situation. Lín was a beautiful girl, but no older than fifteen or sixteen—a ripe age for the Vietnamese, but a child to an American. "Tell her I thank her for her daughter and that I accept her with open arms and that I accept responsibility for her as her man."

"Good," Taan started off to tell Mamasan Tôu.

"Wait." I said. "Dừng lại."

He stopped and turned.

"I'm not through. Lại đây."

"Okay," he smiled.

"Tell her also that I think her daughter is beautiful, uh, cô dẹp quốc tế," I suggested, using the words for "international beauty."

Taan smiled.

"One last thing, Taan." I looked him in the eye. "Tell her that I cannot marry her daughter. My country forbids me to marry her this young. She must be eighteen or nineteen before marriage can be considered. Tell her to pass the word around that she is my girl and that she must be treated with honor and respect."

Taan smiled. "It is good," he said as he turned to deliver my message.

"What have I gotten myself into?" My mind returned to the men and our new squad leader, the real "number one" man. He and Rodriguez were settled under a tree, talking. "A plan," I thought. "I promised the men a plan." I had an idea, but it was going to require in-depth thought and consideration. Men's lives hung on it, whatever it turned out to be.

We had started the concept of killer teams ourselves, but I had to wonder if it was a smart move to continue it on a regular basis. I remembered the previous times the VC had tried to divide us, then move in for the kill before we could regroup. The old saying came to mind, "united we stand, divided we fall." We had no choice, though. Sergeant Rivera was adamant about his decision. I just had to figure out how to make it work safely.

Mamasan Tôu approached, interrupting my thoughts. With her was an old man no bigger than she was. He was well weathered, and his feet and legs bore the calluses and sores indicative of many hours in rice paddies. I stood up to greet them: "Chào bà."

"Chào anh," she returned, then the old man began to speak. He claimed to be a farmer from School House Valley. He had heard of how we helped other farmers work their fields, build their homes, and tend their sick, and had come to seek our help for himself. My first feeling was suspicion. I never expected friendly action from School House Valley. I was also bothered by the relative ease he had in locating us. I questioned him about this and he said that news of our squad's activity and aid to the Vietnamese had spread throughout the Quảng Tin Province area. He was not sure he could trust us, but he had nowhere else to turn.

"Tại sao không VC?" I asked. "Why not VC?"

The man looked at me with disgust in his eyes. He spat on the ground and started jabbering away with Mamasan Tôu. He was obviously very upset. I caught bits and pieces of their rapid conversation. The VC, or actually, the NVA, had taken control of his farm, forcing him to secretly store supplies and arms and confiscating over half his food supply for their army. They had the entire valley terrorized. During the day, they remained underground in secret tunnels, hidden from our patrols and aircraft searching overhead. He had come to us today because the NVA had burned his hut and shot his wife as punishment for his disobedience to their "requests." Although he feared retaliation, he had to get help for his wife.

"Tôi biết (I know)," I said, reassuring the farmer that I understood. I called Taan over to talk to the old man to make sure I had the details right. I also wanted to see if Taan could smell a trap where I couldn't.

While the two talked, I informed Sergeant Rivera of the situation. "It could be a trap," I said, "or it could be an opportunity to start locating that mortar we've been searching for." Taan walked up and told me that the only thing I had missed was that the NVA had "recruited" the farmer's sons into their unit. The old man was concerned that we might kill them, but he needed our help so decided to take a chance.

"What do you think, Sarge?" I asked.

"Sounds like a surefire way to get shot up," he answered.

"Yeah," I returned, "but it could also establish a friendly eye in School House Valley. That is, if we can help his wife!"

Rivera nodded and checked his watch. It was 1415 hours. That gave us just shy of six hours of daylight to get in, help the woman and get out—or get set up in an ambush if the sergeant so desired. Rivera was undecided.

"We have to help him," I said. "If we refuse, he'll go direct to the NVA and give away our position, our numbers and our strength."

Rivera hesitated, then nodded. "Let's move out!" he yelled.

The farmer took the lead, followed by Taan, with the rest of us taking up positions in line behind them. I waved back at Lín as we disappeared into the jungle. We reached the school house about an hour later, with no sign of the enemy. We could hear the children inside singing their songs, oblivious to the death struggle that surrounded them. We kept moving across the rice paddies, lessening the chance that the kids would get caught in the middle of a firefight.

In a valley like the one we were crossing, not only were you visible from all directions, but your moves were predictable because of the patterns of the dike. If the Viet Cong opened fire, you could not hold your

A view across the rice paddies of School House Valley.

position. They'd zero in with mortars almost instantaneously. To get out of the rice paddies with any speed you had to stay with the dikes, which made you an easy target. In addition, paddy dikes were typical locations for booby traps. Although we felt like sitting ducks, we had no choice. The farmer's place was at the base of the mountains on the opposite side of the valley, north and around the back side of a hill from the "vil" where we had captured the girl.

It took about fifteen minutes to cross the valley and about fifteen years off our lives. Ever since Tết, we had known that School House Valley was the main area in which we needed to concentrate our efforts. We had not been eager, but the time had come to face the VC on their own turf. We crossed without even a sign of the enemy, so we assumed they were still underground.

The farmer's hut, or what was left of it, was located on a fertile, gentle slope encircled from the west by a mountain. The fence he had built to pen his hogs in was all but destroyed. Pieces of it lay everywhere. One hog lay inside the ruins, wounded in the back. As we approached, he fought frantically to pull himself to his feet, but his useless back legs failed him and he dropped back to the ground amidst the family pictures the VC had tossed out of the hut and into the mire.

The farmer's wife lay just inside the door of the hut, obviously in shock, staring into space. She did not even seem to realize that we were there. Doc checked on her condition, administering some morphine. She had been shot three times, all in the left leg. The VC had obviously wanted her to die a slow, painful death to keep the farmer under control.

"How is she, Doc?" I asked. Jones, Mendez and Lackey were setting up a perimeter watch.

"She's in pretty bad shape. We really need to medevac her to Chu Lai rear for proper treatment."

"If we don't?" I asked.

"She'll die," he said bluntly.

"Taan," I yelled him over. He came at a run. "Tell the farmer that we must medevac his wife to the hospital in Chu Lai. Tell him we can send him with her but if we do, the NVA might kill his sons. The best we can do is pass the word around that she died and we just flew her out for funeral preparations."

Taan nodded and relayed my message. The farmer was hesitant, not sure whether he should trust us or not, but he had no choice. He knew his wife would die without medical help. He grabbed her hand and stared at her, with pain showing in his tear-filled eyes. He turned back to us, engulfed in emotion. My heart went out to them both. In broken English, he muttered, "She go. I stay."

Taan patted him on the back to reassure him. I had Lackey call in a medevac and warn them that we were in an unfriendly zone. That would bring multiple choppers but it would also make them use their mufflers, so if the Cong were all underground, they would have a hard time hearing the approaching helicopters.

As we waited, Rodriguez and Rivera relieved Lackey and Mendez from perimeter duty so we could set about cleaning up the mess the VC had left. We salvaged what we could and helped the farmer set up a lean-to hut to temporarily shelter him from the weather. We put the wounded hog out of its misery with a quick slice of its throat, not wanting to risk the sound of gunfire. Housekeeping taken care of, we had settled in to wait for the choppers when I had an idea. "Hey, Sarge!" I yelled. "We could really impress the people of this valley if we helped the old man rebuild his hut." We talked over the pros and cons, and finally decided it was worth the risk.

"Let's do it," he said.

I pushed the transmit button. "Chu Lai Command, this is CAP One. Over."

"Go ahead, CAP One."

"Request one load of twenty sheets of metal roofing for construction of hut in School House Valley. Over."

"Roger. Stand by." A momentary silence. The radio crackled as the operator at Chu Lai rear depressed his button. "CAP One, this is Chu Lai Command. Be advised that shipment will arrive tomorrow at 1200 hours."

When Taan told the farmer what we were planning, he was elated, though he could not understand why we would risk our lives to help him rebuild his farm. I was reassuring him that we would return the next day to help him, when we saw three choppers enter the valley—two Huey gunships and one medevac unit. We could barely hear the faint "chop chop" of their muffled blades. I tossed a smoke grenade. "We see red," the medevac unit announced. "There's no other smoke in sight. We'll use that clearing just east of your smoke."

"Sounds good, but keep those other birds aloft and somewhat back," I requested. "We want to minimize any announcement of our presence."

"Roger. Will do."

The two gunships started a wide circle at about 1500 feet while the medevac settled into the clearing they had chosen for an "LZ," a landing zone. We hurriedly carried the farmer's wife to the waiting chopper, then settled back in the bush to wait for the medevac to rejoin its friends above. With a quiet "thump thump," the chopper reunited with the gunships and struck a path towards Chu Lai.

It was late afternoon. We gathered our gear, said our good-byes to the farmer and School House Valley, and headed out for the old French compound. Although there were no clouds in sight, there was a heaviness in the air, making it difficult to breathe. The humidity was definitely on the rise. "Must be a storm brewing," I said, more to myself than anyone else. Rain made things very difficult. A rain-soaked ground revealed very little noise, making it hard for us to hear approaching VC. That, coupled with the constant patter of raindrops on your helmet, cap cover, or body, made detection of movement impossible, except for actually seeing the approaching enemy. Even then, the rain cut visibility down to only a few feet. Then to make matters worse the constant patter of rain created a monotonous sound that lured you into a dream world, even sleep. You became an easy target for the searching Cong.

We reached the compound at dusk, just as the local folks were preparing their evening meals. On the blacktop, there remained only a spattering of people all scurrying around like mice searching for a hole to slip into. The sky was still clear.

Rivera wanted to send out his first killer team at 2000 hours. I was to take Jones, Rodriguez and Lackey, along with two PFs, and strike out for the area just the other side of abandoned railroad tracks which formed somewhat of a border marking the beginning of School House Valley. Rivera wanted us to cross over the tracks and check out each hut nestled on the slopes at the base of the bordering hill.

All too soon, 2000 hours rolled around. We had covered ourselves with mud and muck from a nearby stream and finished it off with a touch of our infamous buffalo dung. Sergeant Rivera was glad to see us go. As we slipped out the front gate of the compound, I had to chuckle at the idea of even having a gate, since there were plenty of openings around back.

 The blacktop was empty and silent. We quickly slipped across the road and momentarily settled in a palm grove. I turned to check the compound. It was dark except for the faint glow from the building where Sergeants Shôu and Rivera were having some sort of pow-wow. I hesitated. I hated to leave Doc and Mendez there, unprotected, but I had no choice. "Come on, gang," I motioned toward the waiting darkness. Taan had joined us along with another PF known as Naum Tôu, a boy no more than fifteen years old. He was eager to learn and adamantly hated the VC. Taan considered him his protégé.

Taan took point as we moved toward the mountains to the west. Thirty minutes slid by rapidly as we reached our first destination, the tracks. Years of neglect and lack of use had left them undetectable at night, except for the telltale mound of earth built as a base to keep them elevated above the waterline. That, too, had crumbled and washed away in various spots. The tracks had rusted over and were entangled in jungle growth and creeping vines.

We stopped briefly to get our bearings. To simply barge into the nearest hut could prove a fatal mistake, so Taan and I decided to quietly slip by each one in an effort to detect telltale signs of movement or activity. All five of us started over the tracks simultaneously.

That was our mistake. A sudden burst from a machine gun sent lead ricocheting in all directions. AKs backed up the gun with rapid fire bursts. The jungle ahead of us was teeming with Cong.

Everyone turned and dove for the cover of the embankment. I knew the VC would home in on our position in a matter of minutes, so in a quick crawl I led the men about fifty yards farther down the tracks. The Viet Cong were still searching our original position with their fire. Green ricochets and sparks filled the blackness of the night. The machine gun was a big one, probably equivalent to our 30-caliber. I silently sent up a quick prayer of thanks that the moon had not yet risen enough to illuminate our position.

The men lay with their weapons propped on the tracks, waiting for a command. My mind was reeling. Soon, real soon, the Cong would realize that they were not receiving answering fire. We had to act fast.

As if to motivate my actions, the moon was beginning to cast slivers of silver rays into the shadows around us. It was still below the treetops but high enough to make us want to seek better cover. Suddenly, a machine gun burst opened up from somewhere behind us, back toward the compound where Rivera and the others were waiting. It was an M-60. Our own men were firing at us! We scattered and rolled as we searched for better cover. There was none. We could only hug the ground and pray. I grabbed the radio transmitter. "Killer One to CAP One. Over."

"Go ahead, Killer."

"Stop the 60 fire! It's hitting us!"

The radio crackled. "It's not us," came the answer.

I was dumbfounded. We were pinned down by VC on one side and an unidentified M-60 on the other. As my mind searched for an explanation, the M-60 and the VC opened up simultaneously with a crossfire barrage that sent a deadly spray of lead plowing and ricocheting into our area. The noise from the gunfire and the ricocheting bullets was deafening. Minutes slid by. I knew I had to act fast or we were all going to die. The moon was clearing the tree tops. Soon, very soon, they would be able to pick us off with relative ease.

I pulled out my map and risked my flashlight. Taan crawled over to my position. "We are here," Taan assured me, pointing at a place on the map. I had to trust his judgment; Vietnam was his backyard, not mine. I grabbed the transmitter again. "CAP Base, this is Killer One. We have contact. Request fire mission. Over."

"Roger, Killer One. All units clear the channel for contact status. Go ahead, Killer," came the reply.

"Request 105 battery at 473075, mark with Willy Peter and standby with full battery of HE." I did not want to risk high explosive rounds with the initial barrage because we were less than a hundred yards away from the strike zone. With Willy Peter we at least had some chance of survival.

"Roger," was all he said.

I looked around. The moon was now full and bright so I could see, just a few yards down the tracks, a washout that looked fairly deep. I passed the word. No one hesitated. We half crawled and half ran to the hole, rolling into it and spreading out to prepare for the enemy. It was not as deep as I had hoped, but it was better than what we'd had.

"We'll just have to hunker down as low as possible and be ready," I said.

The 60 started strafing the area again. We could hold our fire no longer. The two enemy forces were zeroing in on our new position. We had to make a stand to keep the Cong busy until "Arty"[4] did its work.

"Hurry up with that Arty!" I yelled out. "Taan, Naum Tôu! Come on. Let's give 'em hell!" I led my two Vietnamese friends up the embankment to concentrate fire on the VC nest while Jones and Lackey opened up in the direction of the M-60.

I squeezed the transmitter one more time. "CAP One, this is Killer One. Over."

"Go ahead, Killer." It was Mendez's voice.

"Do you see any muzzle flashes from the 60?"

"Not sure," came the answer. "What's your position?"

"We're less than a hundred yards east and north of Arty's target," I returned, "against the tracks."

"The 60 is back toward us," Mendez offered.

"Open fire on it, " I said hesitantly, hoping the enemy with the 60 was not able to see us a half-mile away.

"Roger," Mendez said. The radio went silent, then I heard Mendez's M-60 join the battle. This attack confused whoever was firing the 60, which began to deliver a quick volley and then turn its fire back toward the compound.

We continued our own attack in the direction of the machine gun nest, and it wasn't long before I heard the faint "foomp" from Fat City a few miles away. Within seconds the burning fingers of Willy Peter had engulfed the hillside sheltering the Cong.

I grabbed the mike: "Repeat. Repeat!" The Arty commander must have been listening on my frequency. The second barrage was on its way.

"Keep firing," I yelled at the men. "We've got to keep them busy 'til that HE does its work." You could hear the shells whistle overhead as they searched out their target. The first one hit, followed immediately by the others. Screams echoed into the depths of the jungle as explosions and flames illuminated the night. The hillside was spotted with fires started by the Arty attack. Suddenly a secondary explosion sent a ball of flame streaking into the sky.

"Must have hit their ammo dump," I smiled at Jones.

The night had gone suddenly very quiet. The "unknown" with the M-60 had evidently turned tail and run. Lackey handed me the mike.

Sergeant Rivera was on the line. "This is Killer One. Go," I said.

"Roger," Rivera answered. "What's happening?"

"A direct hit," I answered. "We're moving in for the kill."

"Negative," came his reply.

"What?"

"Make your way back to the area near our position. The CO thinks that M-60 was the two American Chieu Hois.[5] Move in and try to bring on fire," he ordered. "The CO wants those men. Dead or alive."

"What about the machine gun nest?" Jones asked me.

"We'll come back after we find the 60 or when daylight hits," I said. "Right now let's hit the jungle."

With a quick glance toward the burning hillside, we turned and struck out into the darkness in search of our own men—our new enemy. The moon was at its peak, but some early morning clouds were gathering to darken the sky. The search was fruitless. I figured that the "Chieu Hois," if it had been them, were listening to our frequency and "dể đi 'd" when we were ordered to search them out.

The rain hit about an hour before daybreak. Weary from battle and the seesaw trek through the jungle, we made our way back to the compound. There we grabbed a bite to eat, joined with Sergeant Rivera and the rest of the men, and struck out toward the tracks and the machine gun nest to investigate the results of our counterattack.

With the rising of the sun the rain stopped. The clouds broke up and gradually faded away. A gigantic steam bath formed as the evaporating moisture created a fog-like cloud hovering along the ground. We reached the tracks around 0700 and momentarily stretched out along the embankment to study the scorched hillside. The steam, combined with the smoke rising from the smoldering remains of a handful of bamboo huts, left the jungle with an eerie foreboding look. The only way to know for sure if there were any Cong left was to search the huts one by one.

One by one we left the tracks and made our way up the hillside. Rivera took Mendez, Rodriguez and Lackey and set off to the right side of the hill to make a sweep back to the kill zone. Johnston, Taan, Jones and the rest of us made our way directly toward the smoldering huts. Just as we reached them a small group of Vietnamese villagers—men, women and children—came running to us from out of the jungle, waving and bowing to let us know they were friendly.

"Keep alert," I said. I told Taan and Naum Tôu to talk with the villagers as the rest of us searched through the rubble for signs of bodies, though we did not have much hope of finding any. As I listened to the rapid conversation between our PFs and the villagers, all I could pick up was that the VC had left the area. After a few minutes, when the villagers had quieted down and settled on their haunches to await our next move, Taan waved me and Rivera over.

"What have you got?" Rivera asked.

"VC move into village two days ago and force villagers to stay quiet. Villagers say a woman come to see VC everyday but only stay for short time. They think she tell them about us."

A shiver went up my spine. Whoever she was, she had to know at least one of us well enough to obtain an idea of our plans for each night.

Taan continued, "VC wait for us last night but not know exactly when. Our patrol surprise their outpost and force them to open fire too soon. They not see us. Just hear us move. Villagers say artillery kill fifteen VC, destroy machine gun nest, kill one water buffalo, some chickens and burn three huts."

"Oh, no!" I said. "We'll have to pay for that buffalo."

"No problem," Taan smiled. "Villagers happy to see VC killed and say no pay for buffalo. They want to cook buffalo now and be happy."

"A celebration sounds good to me. But what about the VC?" I asked.

"And the American Chieu Hois?" Rivera added.

Taan turned back to the villagers. They jabbered a few words and Taan said: "They say VC take wounded and dead and disappear into jungle that way." He pointed a finger toward School House Valley.

"And the Americans?" I asked.

Taan lowered his head to share our shame. "Two of them. One light hair American and one black American with machine gun. They say black man have radio. They not see them since just before dark yesterday."

I was confused, bitter and mournful over the idea that two of our men were fighting against us, but I could no longer ignore the facts.

Dawn ushered in the smell of roasting water buffalo as the villagers prepared a feast in celebration of our night's victory. Rivera told me to take charge of the squad and just keep him abreast of what was going on, so I sent Rodriguez and Jones to set up a watch post overlooking School House Valley. Taan sent two of his men along to assist. The rest of us set about reconstructing the burned huts. With all the natural materials growing in the jungle around us, the task took only a few hours.

Huts finished and debris cleaned up, we settled down for our first meal of roasted water buffalo. Taan and a couple of his men gathered choice chunks of the meat along with various other tasty items and trotted off to deliver a share to the men at the watch post. Right around 1200 hours, Lackey's radio crackled as a message broke the still of the noon day. "CAP One, this is Command. Over."

"Yo, Command," Lackey returned. "Go ahead."

"CAP One, be advised that your roofing materials are ready for shipment. What's your status?"

Lackey looked over at me, quizzically.

"Oh, my God! I completely forgot about the farmer!"

"Yeah, me too," Lackey agreed. "Standby, Command," Lackey said into the mike.

I spotted Rivera lying under a nearby banana tree, catching a few Zs. "Yo, Rivera!" I yelled.

He startled to his feet and looked in my direction. "Whatcha got?" he asked.

"The roofing is ready for shipment. If we leave now we could make it to the farmer's hut by 1400 hours. That would give us about four hours of daylight to get back."

"Yeah," Rivera agreed as he rubbed his chin and gazed off in the direction of School House Valley. "Let's do it. Round up the guys."

"Roger. Hey, Mendez," I yelled. "Prepare everyone to move out, and find Taan for me."

"Gotcha covered, man," he started off at a trot.

Lackey didn't wait for an order. "Command rear, this is CAP One."

"Go ahead, CAP One."

"Have the chopper meet us at the same grid as yesterday at 1430 hours."

We bowed to our Vietnamese hosts and offered our thanks for the hospitality and the meal as we struck out once again for School House Valley. We picked up Jones, Rodriguez and the two PFs on our way.

"How's the valley?" I asked, looking across the expanse of rice paddies.

Jones glanced over at Rodriguez. "Quiet, man, too quiet," he said. "The paddies have been empty all day with not a soul in sight, even in the huts."

I called Taan over. "Let's take a different trail this time," I suggested. "I think we should steer clear of that school house."

"How about that tree line crossing we used when we captured the VC woman?" Jones asked.

"How about it, Taan?" I asked. "That would put us within a half mile of the farm and would provide plenty of cover."

"No problem," he said, "but beaucoup booby traps. We must be careful."

He didn't have to say it twice. Sometimes we relaxed a bit but never on an entry into School House Valley, and it was a good thing. Just as we entered the tree-covered trail, his hand flew up with a firm command to stop. I made my way up to him. He was pointing at two bamboo sticks lying in the trail, each carved to a point on one end indicating direction. My eyes studied the trail ahead of us in search of the hidden death. There it was—not ten feet in front of us. The trail split around a clump of growth about two feet high. The left side was clean, but on the right side of the trail was the telltale glimmer of the deadly tripwire awaiting the careless foot.

We didn't bother trying to deactivate it. Instead, we moved the markers to the other side of the trail in hopes the VC would fall into their own trap.

"Pass word back to keep to the left," I ordered Lackey.

"Roger," he said as he turned to the PF behind him.

Taan moved out. I followed about ten feet behind. In no time at all Taan stopped again. Saying nothing, he bent down and relocated identical markers that were meant to warn those coming from the opposite direction. "Now," he whispered, "we go."

"Thank God for these PFs," I thought. "If it weren't for them one of us might have bought it back there."

I motioned the others forward as I followed Taan down the trail. Our searching became even more intent as we closed in on the valley's opposite side. We were almost there when Taan's hand reached for the sky once again, violently waving us back. We all hunkered back like cowering dogs.

Taan was frozen in his tracks. He was so still I thought he might have already tripped the mine or be standing right on top of it. He turned his eyes upward, searching the trees on our right. I followed his gaze. Once again, Taan had saved us; this time the whole squad would have been blown up. Dangling loosely from the branches for a stretch of about sixty feet were Chi Com grenades with pins connected to a common tripwire. The pins were still intact, so Taan evidently had stopped just in time.

I slowly approached his position. He pointed, not to a tripwire but to a vine lying across the trail. It was only then that I noticed it stretched straight across the trail rather than lying in a random formation. This trap had no warning marker other than the vine. I risked a deep breath as Taan and I stepped over the vine into a clearing. We surveyed the surrounding area and then returned to the waiting men. I motioned the men forward, directing each man's step around the deadly vine.

Finally every man was clear. I moved back up to where Taan sat peering into the depths of the jungle. He looked up as I approached. "Not look good," he smiled weakly. I checked my watch. It was 1400 hours already and we still had half a mile to go.

"Good or not, Taan, we have to go!" I motioned him forward. "We've lost too much time already."

He nodded, turned, and went ahead without a word. I waved the men on, then turned and followed Taan into the jungle. The rest of the trip was uneventful. The Viet Cong evidently were confident that their traps along the trail were enough to warn them of our approach, as they would have heard the explosions.

We reached the farm just as the faraway sound of the approaching chopper echoed through the jungle. The farmer was nowhere around, but the animals that had been left alive were still in their pens, munching away at food they'd been given earlier that morning. We searched the nearby jungle, but found no sign of the farmer.

We set up a perimeter guard with Jones, Rodriguez, and the PFs. Taan, Rivera and the rest of us unloaded the chopper and set about the construction of the roof. The farmer's absence made us all jittery, so we decided not to spend a lot of time trying to "do it right." We simply laid the corrugated tin across the existing framework and tied it down with vines we cut from the nearby trees. Our mission was accomplished in less than an hour.

"It'll do the job," Rivera stated.

"That's all that matters," I answered.

Taan was the first to notice that the jungle had grown overwhelmingly quiet. Jones and Rodriguez came running towards us. "Gooks!" was Jones's frantic whisper. "A bunch of 'em!"

Quickly, I looked around. The fastest escape route was across the paddies to the school house, but we'd be sitting ducks in the paddies. I turned to Taan and pointed back the way we had come. He rounded up his PFs and we silently melted into the jungle in a half run. Our only hope was that our "work" would detain the VC long enough for us to make our way back through the booby-trapped tree line.

We wasted no time. Taan stopped at the vine to remind us of the trap hidden there. We shot past him in a full gallop, stretching across the paddy area in a long line. We could hear the noise of the VC in hot pursuit. It sounded like Jones was right—there was a bunch of them.

Suddenly, AKs broke the silence as the VC in the lead decided to give us more to worry about. Fortunately, the dense tree line stopped the barrage short of our position. It did, however, add wings to our feet. I thought we would never reach the opposite side. Pain was shooting through my lungs as they struggled for more air. With a sudden burst we exploded from the tree line and spread out behind the nearby palm trees to await our enemy.

Just as I was contemplating a call for help to our local artillery base, an explosion erupted from the depths of the tree line. The relocated markers had confused the Cong in their hot pursuit, and one of them had tripped the very trap they had set for us. We grabbed the moment and vanished into the jungle behind us, again in high gear. We stopped about a hundred yards farther on to study our next move. We could hear the wails of the VC, but we didn't know how many of them were wounded or killed.

"Let's split up the group," Rivera ordered. "It may throw them off." He struck off on a trail leading northeast. Taan's PFs, Rodriguez and Mendez followed after him in a hard run. Taan and the rest of us struck off on a well-traveled trail heading south.

"We'll meet at the compound," Rivera yelled back. I didn't bother answering. I had distance on my mind, a lot of it.

---

[1] Two of the best studies on the anti-war movement and its impact are Charles DeBenedetti and Charles Chatfield (assisting author), *An American Ordeal: The Antiwar Movement of the Vietnam Era* (Syracuse, New York: Syracuse University Press, 1990) and Melvin Small, *Johnson, Nixon, and the Doves* (New Brunswick, New Jersey: Rutgers University Press, 1988).

[2] A B-122 is a Russian- or Chinese-made 122-millimeter rocket used by the North Vietnamese Army.

[3] The beetle nut tree produced a leaf that the Vietnamese elders found quite tasty even though it blackened their teeth. It also produced some sort of painkilling agent which they all needed due to their rotted teeth from lack of adequate dental hygiene. They also chewed and smoked opium in many forms.

We had toyed with the idea of getting dental care established in the bush along with instituting an educational program to help alleviate their addiction to the two drugs. We also considered offering our own painkiller drugs to replace theirs. Somehow that didn't seem to be the answer.

The beetle-nut/opium habit was a traditional cure passed down from generation to generation. To even attempt to alter its course was futile. Besides, even if we could get Mamasan Tôu and her friends to switch our drugs for hers, we knew we would sooner or later return to our comfortable homes in the states. At that point, unable to obtain anymore painkillers, the old people would return to their old ways. We left it alone.

[4] A slang term for artillery.

[5] "Chieu Hoi" refers to the U.S. Chieu Hoi Program, which offered amnesty and "rehabilitation" to defectors from the Viet Cong. It was also called the "Open Arms" program. U.S. forces distributed leaflets and other forms of propaganda to entice Viet Cong to rally to the South Vietnamese side. Douglas S. Blaufarb, *The Counterinsurgency Era* (New York: Free Press, 1977), 226–74.

# Chapter 8
# Quảng Tin Province Chieftain

**B**oth groups reached the compound without incident and, we hoped, undetected by the VC and their informant. Since nightfall was close, I doubted anyone would follow. The sun had settled into a faint glow covering the western horizon with a brilliant orange that illuminated the distant mountains. Darkness was closing in fast.

"Tonight I want you to take a team out in the direction of the VC village," Rivera ordered as he and his men merged with ours. "I've already reported it to Command."

"You're the boss." I smiled, but my sarcasm must have shown through.

"That's right," he snapped. "See that you remember that."

As my mind was conjuring up a witty remark that would knock him down a notch or two, a frail looking Vietnamese man came running toward us waving his hands wildly as if he were fighting off bees. My snide remark faded away as I watched Taan intercept him. Something was obviously wrong. The intensity of his jabbering far exceeded my ability to understand his language. Finally, when Taan calmed the farmer down and told him to wait, he stood like a scolded child, hands at his sides, staring a hole through me with piercing black eyes. I nodded to him in the typical fashion. He responded with a quick downward jerk of his head. He obviously had no time for social greetings. Darkness was upon us. Rivera's VC village would have to wait.

"What's up?" I asked Taan.

"Papasan say bomb fall from sky and hit his house but no blow up."

"Didn't blow up? That's incredible. . . ." My memory stopped me. About every fifth round of explosive, in my own experience, was a dud. I had seen many good men killed or maimed because some idiot in Quality Control was sloughing off his responsibility. The fact that someone in the good old USA was helping the VC murder us made my blood boil. You never knew when that fifth round had your name on it. It could be a simple M-16 round or an M-79 buckshot round in a point man's gun. In fact, the unit just north of us had been wiped out due to a dud M-79 buckshot round. According to the reports, a gook rounded an outcropping of a hill and came face to face with the point man of CAP Two. Both men fired, the point man a fraction of a second sooner than the VC, but his lifeless body fell to the ground as harmless buckshot rolled out the end of the barrel of his M-79. The Viet Cong then closed in on the unit and killed each man. They were dead not because of the Cong, but because someone back home did not realize, or did not care about, the harm their defective product was creating.[1]

I motioned Rivera over. "The farmer says we have a dud bomb beside his hut."

"A bomb?" Rivera asked.

"That's what he says," I stated, "but I doubt that it's actually a bomb. I haven't seen or heard any jets today. It's probably a Howitzer round. Fat City was firing harassment rounds earlier today."[2]

"Well, let's see what the CO wants to do."

I nodded and waved Lackey over to our little group. I checked my watch. It was 1945 hours as I took hold of the transmitter.

"Base, this is CAP One. Over." The approaching darkness was increasing my mental alertness. I knew that sound always traveled faster and farther at night. I could clearly hear villagers talking in their huts a hundred yards away. I wondered if the VC could hear us too.

Candlelight began to flicker in a nearby hut, creating an eerie glow that danced with the ever-darkening shadows. I felt like a sitting duck, silhouetted against the sky. Assuming that Command was going to send a "demo team" to fetch the round before the VC got their hands on it, I figured we'd have to set up night watch in our good old compound. The very thought of containment sent shivers up my spine. The Cong no doubt rolled in laughter after one glance at our "protective" perimeter, but I felt like a coward and a traitor when I sought shelter behind barbed wire and trenches. Vietnamese men, women and children faced every night not only without a protective perimeter, but also without a single weapon, short of a knife or machete, to ward off the enemy. I tried to shut off my memories of the mutilated bodies of children and the burned villages that had trusted the night. Worst of all, I realized that the Vietnamese people had more to fear than we did. We only had to worry about attacks from the Viet Cong and the NVA. The villagers had that worry coupled with the fear that a U.S. force could destroy them as well.

The radio crackled. "CAP One, this is Command. Go ahead. Over."

"Command, be advised that we have reason to believe a 105 dud has dropped next to a farmer's hut just south of our present location. Request demo team be sent out to remove the little devil. Over."

"Negative, CAP One." It was our good old CO's voice again. "Be advised that we do not send out demo teams after dark. Let it ride until 0800 hours tomorrow. Over."

I couldn't believe my ears. War was a twenty-four-hours-a-day, seven-days-a-week job. The very idea of "time off" was laughable, except for what it meant to us. I turned to Rivera. From the look on his face, he was taken aback, too. "You know what this means, don't you?" I asked.

For a moment, he just stared at me. "Well, rules are rules." He turned his back and walked away.

"Hang the rules," I said. "This war can only be fought with one rule—survival." I squeezed the transmitter again, trying to gain control of my anger. "Command, be advised that if we let the round lie unattended for that long the VC will have it booby-trapped by 0800 hours."

"Negative," came the CO's reply. "We cannot risk the lives of a demo team for one lousy 105 dud. I order you to drop the subject until morning."

All of my little visitors converged on me instantly: fear, hatred, bitterness all crowding in together, taunting me. I attempted to crush the transmitter in my grip, but I calmly stated, "Roger, Command. Over and out." I tossed the transmitter back to Lackey. "I don't know why I make you carry that radio. . . . We never get any help from it."

He smiled. "What're we going to do? You're not going to let it lay there are you?"

I was torn. I did not want to defy authority, but there was no question in my mind that by morning the round would be either booby trapped or carried off by our enemy to some more deadly location. My dad had taught me respect for authority, but basic logic and a strong sense of responsibility to my men and the Vietnamese people finally shoved that habit aside. I glanced over at the waiting farmer. He was visibly shaken with fear and bewilderment.

Memories of my grandparent's farm brought back visions of my grandfather and his approach to life. "Work your ground, respect life, honor your neighbor and worship God," he would say. "Just let me work my farm by day and sleep in peace at night." I saw a common bond between two farmers thousands of miles apart.

I checked the farmer's fearful face. If we told him to wait until tomorrow, he would no doubt hunt up someone else to help him out. Also, we would lose face with him, and his trust and loyalty would easily be won over by the enemy. I knew we had no choice. Too much was at risk to blatantly toss the problem aside until morning.

I looked back at Lackey. Returning his smile, I patted him on the shoulder. "Not a chance, Lackey, not a chance."

My eyes penetrated the darkness in search of Rivera. I felt I knew what his answer would be, but it was still his call. I had to check with him before I set out to fetch the "bomb." He was in the center of the compound, resting against the flagpole. His eyes met mine as I stopped in front of him.

"Rivera," I began, searching for the most convincing argument. "You've been in the bush long enough to know what will happen if we leave that round until morning. We're out here to help these people. All that farmer knows is that he and his family are being threatened! If we wait until morning, he'll find someone else to take the threat away and will, at the very least, become a VC sympathizer and informer." I stopped to let it all sink in.

He studied the ground for a moment. "Yeah, I'm sure if we wait for the demo team, we'll only be asking for trouble." He looked up. "But the CO can spell trouble, too!"

"There's no doubt about that," I agreed, "but I'd much rather face *him* than a booby trap or another informer."

"Let's go get it," he stated. "We'll deal with the CO later."

I could not believe what I had heard. Elation overwhelmed me.

"I'm already on my way," I said. "I'll take Johnston in case it blows. You keep the rest of the men and set up a defense perimeter until we return."

"Good idea. Any inkling how long you'll be gone?"

"None at all. In fact, it could be a trap. You may be requesting a new assistant and new corpsman tomorrow."

Rivera smiled. "Get back as soon as you can. And good luck."

I left him standing by the flagpole. I was happy. Rivera had revealed a side of himself that I hadn't seen before. He valued his men and was willing to risk a court martial to protect us. I smiled as I joined Johnston, Lackey, and Taan.

"I'll go with the farmer and take care of the bomb," I told them.

Taan beamed from ear to ear, obviously elated with my decision. "Me go with you?" he asked.

"Not this time. Stay here and watch over our beloved sergeant and the rest of the pack."

Taan laughed as he turned to the farmer with the good news.

My gaze turned to the compound as my hands automatically checked my M-16 and ammo for any misalignment or shortage. I could just make out the outlines of each of the other men as they sat on top of the collapsed bunkers.

Taan touched my arm. "Farmer is ready." He stopped, squeezed my forearm firmly, and continued, "and farmer say 'thank you.'"

I smiled and nodded to the farmer. "Let's dễ đi!" I yelled, motioning for the farmer to lead the way and urging him to hurry.

"Wait," came a yell from behind me. "I'm going with you." It was Johnston.

"Oh yeah! I forgot to tell you that you're invited to join us." I laughed at my own eagerness to move out.

"It wouldn't do to tell me otherwise," Johnston stated in his Australian drawl. "Someone's got to be there when the blimey thing blows you to pieces."

"Yeah, and what about me?" Lackey said. "You'll need a radio out there."

"No way," I said. "This is a hush-hush operation. Besides if we run into any contact, we'll just have to outrun the little critters. You stay here and help Taan take care of Rivera."

"Thanks a lot." Lackey surrendered, shook his head, and melted into the darkness in search of Taan.

The farmer jerked at my sleeve impatiently. "We dễ đi," he chided as he pointed a shaky finger in the direction of the farm.

I swallowed a lump that had suddenly grown in my throat. "No time like the present," I said. The three of us headed south, straight down the blacktop, into what I knew could be a trap.

Our mental alertness at the max, we finally stepped off the blacktop and into the jungle about a mile and a half southwest of the compound. I took a quick glance back in the direction of Rivera and the base camp, but all I could see was darkness. Thirty minutes later, the jungle trail abruptly opened into a clearing that revealed the outline of a tiny bamboo hut surrounded by crudely constructed bamboo pens built to shelter the farmer's livestock. "The only thing missing is the baling wire," I thought, as memories of my grandfather came back again.

"Ở đâu bomb?" I asked just as we reached the hut. The farmer grabbed my hand and led me inside. The flickering candlelight revealed the telltale glimmer of a 105 round lying in silent, deadly wait for our arrival. The farmer had not lied. In a way, I was relieved: "Thank God. No trap."

The north side of the hut was constructed of concrete blocks, a luxury usually only available to the more well-to-do farmers. "He's probably proud of that wall," I thought. My eyes searched it for signs of damage as I listened to the farmer's story of how the "bomb" had struck the side of his hut and then fallen harmlessly to the ground. There it was, a scrape about three feet long, along with a slight shift of the blocks in the impact area. The farmer and his family were lucky to be alive. By all rights, the 105 should have left only smoldering remains of his hut and his family in lieu of a simple scar on a concrete wall.

I bent down to inspect the round. The impact had knocked the fuse section completely out of the nose of the projectile. I pulled out my flashlight to study it closely. The faint red light revealed that the primer was not even scratched. "Thank God for my third MOS," I thought, thinking about the short time I had spent in Okinawa studying and working with all types of explosives to pick up my MOS in demolition.

I continued checking out the round. Other than the missing nose fuse it seemed harmless, yet training warned me of the true potential of the deadly explosive. Once a 105 round leaves the barrel of a Howitzer it has spun three complete revolutions and is armed and sensitive to the slightest movement or contact. Sweat rolled down my forehead. Normally, in lieu of attempting to move a dud to a more suitable location, the explosive would be detonated in place. In this case, I did not have that option. If detonated in place, the round would finish its assignment of destruction, and the farmer would lose everything. Feeling the eyes of both Johnston and the farmer on my back, I searched for the courage to break the rules and pick up the deadly round.

The courage came from Johnston. "Want me to tackle the thing, mate?" he asked, looking over my shoulder.

"No way," I snapped. "It's my job. Besides if it blew in your hands who'd piece you back together? Not me. I'm no corpsman." I laughed weakly as I reached out and touched the cold steel. My fingers slid forward until my sweaty palms rested against the main body of the round. "Here goes," I said, more to myself than to anyone else. The farmer sensed the danger and fled to a protective corner of his hut. Johnston backed up a step or two.

The moment of truth came. I tightened my muscles and dug my fingers under the round, lifting with a slight tug and allowing it to roll into my palms. Then, with a slow easy movement, I stood up and swung the cold steel projectile onto my shoulder. I stood there with clenched teeth waiting to see if it would blow. Sweat trickled down my spine as a chill crept past it to some spot between my shoulder blades. I fought back a shiver. Nothing happened. Only the silence of the night echoed back as I automatically released a quick sigh of relief.

I glanced over at the farmer. Nothing moved but his eyes, jerking from the round to my eyes with an obvious question: "What are you waiting for?"

I gave the farmer a slight nod of my head. "Chào ông," I said as I turned toward my trusty corpsman with an order. "Let's để đi mau, and you stay several yards behind me just in case this thing changes its mind. There's no sense in both of us buying the farm."

Johnston did not argue. He stepped aside to allow me to pass. We left the happy, grateful farmer behind and started our trek through the jungle back to the blacktop. "See you at my court martial," I whispered back to the papasan. He only smiled and waved us on.

The heavy round made every step seem laboriously slow. An hour slid by while I fought my way through the jungle. My attempts to walk silently were futile; I felt like I was wearing lead boots. "Might as well send up fireworks telling them 'here I come,'" I said to myself.

It seemed like eternity, but finally the black shadow of the asphalt loomed before my eyes. I was actually glad to see the old blacktop road in spite of its obvious dangers. I trudged up the small embankment and stepped out onto the hard surface. "No sense trying to conceal myself," I thought. I might as well walk smack dab down the middle of it." My legs stretched their way toward their destination. Now that I had the 105 round, I had no idea what to do with it. If I blew it, every VC in the area would investigate.

The cool night was filled with a multitude of odors radiating from the roadside huts I passed. Some people were fixing an evening meal while others were burning incense and worshipping their dead family members. Every hut boasted a crudely constructed shrine, usually a wooden shelf hidden by a drape of some sort. At least once a day the head of the family would light some incense, slide back the drape and send up prayers of worship and praise to Buddha in behalf of the family's dead loved ones.[3] Tonight everyone seemed to be caught up in their worship. The smell of incense flooded my nostrils from every direction.

As I studied the huts and their respective odors, I was suddenly interrupted by the sound of boots running up behind me. I stopped, turned and squatted down to reduce my size as target. It was Johnston. "What is it?" I asked, looking behind him and trying to sense the danger.

"Not a thing, mate. Not a bloody thing. I just decided that if that blimey thing blows, we might as well go together."

I smiled at his courage. "Okay," I said as I stood and once again faced my destination. "Let's go, but no talking. We're already sitting ducks as it is." I looked him in the eye. "Now who's the craziest?" I asked. "The Texan or the Australian?"

Johnston laughed and fell in step beside me.

I thought the sun would come up before we reached the old compound, but in reality, only a little over an hour passed before we stepped off the road onto the path that led to the main gate. I was always apprehensive returning to any compound at night because of the danger of the men inside opening fire before you could signal your "friendly" presence. Another danger lay in the possibility of an enemy takeover prior to our arrival. Again, we could be walking into a trap.

"Better let them know it's us," I ordered. "Flash your red light twice, but cup your hand around it to lessen the reflective light." He obeyed without hesitation. At first there was no response. Thirty seconds passed. Just as I was about to order a repeat performance, a single red light flashed from the darkness ahead of us. We moved forward, but I was uneasy until I heard Jones whisper.

"Sorry about the delayed return signal, man. I couldn't find my dadburn flashlight."

"No problem," I offered. "Everything okay?"

"Yeah. Nothing but pure silence out there."

"Yeah, I noticed. That's what bothers me." I turned to Johnston. "Let's put this baby to bed."

Johnston and I headed for the remains of the closest bunker. I laid my burden down in a corner and then we began laying sand bags ever so gently on top of it. Satisfied with the coverage, I stood up, stretched my muscles and searched the darkness for our remaining men.

"Get some rest," I ordered Johnston as I extended my hand, ". . . and thanks." He shook my hand firmly, turned and disappeared into the night.

I slowly made my rounds until every man had been accounted for, then came back to Jones. "See anything yet?" I asked.

"Nothing, man, absolutely nothing."

"Maybe it will be a quiet one."

"Maybe," Jones answered half-heartedly.

Actually, even the quiet nights in Vietnam were nerve-racking due to the continued anticipation and fear you felt until relief came with the first rays of the sun. This was one of those nights. We sat in total silence, each caught up in his own thoughts, with eyes piercing the night for any movement outside of the ordinary. Anything—a sudden snort from a nearby water buffalo, a chicken flapping its wings, or simply a child crying in his sleep—would send us into instant readiness for battle. The night continued with its little false warnings until the cool gray of dawn began to melt away the edginess. Sounds became more familiar, and could be attached to their true owners. I patted Jones on the shoulder. "Let's round up the men and see what the sergeant wants to do today."

We all gathered at the front gate, stretching our tired muscles in an effort to release the tension of the restless night. The local vendors mingled with us and our fellow Vietnamese soldiers, offering various assortments of morning meals.

"I'll take ham and eggs with toast, a large juice and a tall glass of cold milk," I told the vendor nearest me.

He simply smiled and continued to offer the bug-infested sourdough roll he was guaranteeing to be fresh.

Jones sided with me. "Yeah, man, we need to teach these guys the fundamentals of a good basic breakfast."

"That's right," Lackey chimed in.

We all started to chant and wave our weapons in the air. "We want breakfast! We want breakfast!"

Our fellow PFs, already engrossed in their morning rice, momentarily stopped in an attempt to decipher our meaning. They decided we were "beaucoup điên kiện đầu," and returned to their meal. Even Taan looked at us like we were crazy.

We'd had our fun, and regardless of how little we liked the vendors' offerings, we were still hungry. I stopped my chanting, turned and looked at the same old vendor offering the same old roll.

"You like?" he asked, shoving his wares gently in my direction, hoping the aroma would entice me. I took the roll, cleaned out all the obvious bugs and handed it back to him with orders to fill it with the typical strips of pork and fish smothered in a Nước Mặn sauce. Breakfast in hand, I settled under the nearest palm tree with canteen at ready to wash down any critters I'd missed. The others followed suit. Jones chose a couple of what passed for "sweet rolls" in Vietnam. My theory was that they were the old sourdough rolls that hadn't sold, covered with sugar to hide their age. Jones agreed, but felt he could lie to his stomach with that little bit of sugar.

The demo team arrived at 0830, riding in a jeep with a 50-caliber machine gun mounted on a turret in the center. They screeched to a halt and two men jumped out and headed in our direction. We all wolfed down our remaining breakfast in fear that these newcomers would want us to share our feast with them.

"Corporal Goodson?" Only one spoke, but both men searched our ranks with questioning eyes.

I could imagine how we looked to them as we stood there covered in a week's worth of muck and mire, our uniforms so soiled we easily blended in with the surrounding rice paddies. It wasn't quite time for one of our occasional baths.

Our visitors looked as if they had just stepped out of a laundry chute. They were clean as a whistle and smelled like a local perfume parlor. The man closest to me was lanky, around six feet tall, and shouldered the stripes of a sergeant. His partner was a PFC (private first class) who looked like he had just stepped into Vietnam. He was short and untanned, with nervous eyes.

I stepped forward, extending my hand. "I'm Corporal Goodson. Y'all my demo squad?"

The tall one nodded. "Yeah, I'm Sergeant Rodowski and this is PFC Alverti. We came to relieve you of that nasty 105 round." He looked back over his shoulder. "The CO tells me that it's by a farmer's hut just south of here."

"It was," Johnston offered as he decided to join the conversation.

"Was?" Sergeant Rodowski asked.

"Yeah, mate," Johnston answered with a note of sarcasm in his voice. "We weren't about the leave the blimey thing. . . ."

I cut him off. "What our corpsman is trying to say is that we decided not to take a chance and leave the round out there overnight. So we sent two men down, retrieved it and tucked it safely away in our little compound here."

"Hey! You were ordered to leave it alone until we arrived," the PFC jumped in.

I glared at him for a moment, controlling my desire to choke his little white throat. I turned back to the sergeant. "It has been my experience, Sergeant, that any explosive left in the bush overnight is a guaranteed booby trap by morning. We simply opted not to take that risk. Besides, an explosive of that size could wipe out our entire unit. It might even have ended up being placed in the roadway somewhere as a trap for ambushing travelers heading out from Chu Lai." I looked back towards their jeep, then turned back to the PFC. "And that's why some orders are not received," I concluded.

"You're lucky it didn't blow," the sergeant said.

"Yeah," I agreed. "I never thought I'd be thankful for a demolition MOS."

"But what about . . . ?"

"Can it!" the sergeant ordered as he turned to his PFC with a cold stare.

"*Some* sergeants have good sense," I thought. "This way," I said, and led them to the dilapidated bunker. I bent down and started removing the sandbags. The sergeant helped. He shouldered the round and turned back toward the jeep. The PFC stood still, his gaze shifting from the bunker to the rest of the ruins of the compound. I stood there beside him, following his gaze.

"Something wrong?" I asked.

"You guys stay in this ruin?" he asked.

"Only on occasions such as this," I laughed. "Our home is out there." I turned and pointed to the surrounding jungle.

His eyes widened. "You mean this is it?"

"You learn quick."

He looked at me a moment, his eyes full of bewilderment. "You guys must be out of your ever-loving minds," he stated, waving his hands in disbelief.

"It helps!" I laughed as I slapped him on the back. "It helps."

He turned toward his waiting partner and headed his direction. The sergeant fired up the jeep as we all gathered together to prepare for the day. The PFC jumped into the passenger side. Tires spun in the loose dirt, the jeep pointed its nose south and suddenly we were alone. The potential booby trap was gone.

I checked my weapons. A slight shade of brown had developed on the metal parts of my M-16 and .45. I thought wistfully about the VC's AK-47s. We never captured an AK that showed any signs of rust. Our theory was that you could drop an AK in hog slop, return a week later and finish a firefight without even wiping away the muck. In addition, the VC carried all their rounds wrapped in small burlap bags with no protection from the elements. That alone should have created problems. I didn't want to think that their weapon was superior to ours, but then again, I had never seen one jam.

My eyes returned to my good old M-16. "No such luck here," I thought, recalling the times it had failed me because I missed a day of cleaning. At that point, the weapon was useless, except as a club. That was probably part of the reason we were trained to fire in short, five-round bursts.

"Hey, Sergeant," I yelled to Rivera. "I suggest we take this opportunity to clean our weapons before we hit the bush." I showed him the brown build-up.

"Yeah, good idea," he agreed. "We'll move out in one hour."

"Where are we headed?"

"The CO wants us to head up toward Fat City and search the area north of the base for signs of VC activity. They received a few AK bursts from there last night."

"What about that village?" I asked.

"Especially there," he said.

I was glad. That village was trouble. I thought that the more often we visited it, the more likely we would uncover the little pests hiding in it. We had dubbed it "Charlie's Village."

I settled in to clear my M-16 of rust. Weapon-cleaning time was dangerous. For one thing, parts could be lost. Also, it required about an hour's time, since only half of us cleaned while the other half maintained a constant watch for "Charlie."

The hour passed slowly, each of us caught up in his own thoughts. Mine traveled from home to Vietnam and back to home again, although I tried not to think of home too much. It was thousands of miles from me, tucked away in a land I no longer knew much about. Memories of home only opened the door of bitterness. "If I make it out of this hellhole," I thought, "I'll visit my family, then move up to the farm and set up a stronghold there that will keep the name-calling cowards away from my door." I forced those thoughts aside. In a very real sense, I had become a resident of Vietnam. The present day was the only time that mattered. Dealing with the "home front" could wait.

It was time to go visit Charlie. I stood up and began to make my rounds, checking the weapons of every man, not out of distrust, but just as a precaution. The slightest oversight could be costly. I had one of the men check my weapons. Halfway through the inspection, Taan appeared. His eyes focused on me. For some reason, he seemed different. Not scared or worried, just different. He stopped right in front of me. "You must come with me," he stated.

"Why?" I asked.

He smiled. "Quảng Tin Province chieftain want to see you."

"What!" I exclaimed. "Why would he want to see me?"

Taan shrugged. "He asked to talk with you."

"Incredible," I thought. "Simply incredible." I yelled at Jones and motioned him over.

"Yeah, man. What's happening?" he asked.

"I have to go with Taan, so finish the inspection for me, please."

"No problem," he said. "Everything's copacetic."

"Come on, Taan, let's find the sergeant." Taan frowned at the thought, but understood and respected the chain of command. We found Rivera with Sergeant Shôu, sitting around a fire in Shôu's hut. The entrance was covered with a heavy handwoven blanket. The interior, dark and damp, boasted the telltale odor of incense. The two sergeants grew silent as we approached.

"What do you want?" Rivera asked.

I studied him for a minute, wondering what really made him tick. "Taan has a request from the Quảng Tin Province chieftain. He wants one of us to pay him a visit."

"Why?" Rivera asked.

"Who knows? Maybe he wants to welcome us to Vietnam."

"Don't be ridiculous," he stated. "Well, forget it. We have orders to patrol the area near the firebase today and I don't intend on changing them."

"Fine with me," I said as I turned to go.

"Wait." It was Sergeant Shôu. He turned to Taan and started jabbering away at him. I caught bits and pieces of his questions. He was basically asking Taan what the chieftain wanted and if he thought it might be a trap. Sergeant Shôu turned back to Rivera with a very concerned look on his face. "Someone must go," he said. "Chieftain not want to see American soldier before."

"I take Barry!" Taan quickly suggested.

"Okay with me," Rivera said. "But the rest of us will hunt for Charlie."

We turned to go. Sergeant Shôu reached out and grabbed my arm. "Careful," he warned. "Maybe a trap. We do not know."

"Yeah," I said. "Let's để đi, Taan."

We stopped to fill the other guys in on our plans. Not everyone was excited about spending the day with Rivera.

"Maybe Charlie will stay in hiding," I said. "We'll meet up with you as soon as possible. Let's go, Taan."

We headed northeast into the jungle flatland bordering the ocean. The chieftain lived in the village of Kương Phú, located in the northeastern sector of our area, about a half mile from the bay inlet leading to the South China Sea. The going was slow, due mostly to the maze of rice paddies that created a checkerboard pattern across the flat region. In addition, we had to pay our respects to every local farmer or kinfolk of Taan's who ran across our path. Shortly before noon, we reached the edge of the jungle bordering the chieftain's village.[4]

We stood at the edge of the clearing, searching the rice paddies that lay before us and the cluster of huts nestled in a palm grove on the opposite side. "I wonder who's staring back at us," I thought.

"Looks okay?" Taan questioned.

"No time like the present." I attempted a grin, but the thought of just the two of us contacting an enemy force did not thrill me at all. Taan was not crazy about the idea either, but he took the lead as we stepped onto the first dike that zigzagged across the paddies. I noticed off to my left a somewhat larger path that led straight to the village, and for a moment considered switching to it. Then my mind took another set of memories off the shelf, polished them up a bit and set them out in plain view for me to see. "The most obvious path can be the most deadly," I reminded myself as images of every booby trap I ever saw came to mind. "Follow your point man—always." I returned to negotiating my way along the narrow dike we had chosen.

We reached the village in a matter of minutes. Everything seemed normal. The chickens were scattered around the huts chasing bugs. Immediately, thoughts of fried chicken, gravy and hot biscuits filtered into the conscious part of my mind. I picked out a chicken and mentally wrung its neck just as my grandma used to do. "Lucky chickens," I thought, remembering that the Vietnamese in our area never ate them. Chickens were considered strictly as suppliers of eggs and controllers of the bug population. The people loved them and treated them like pets. The children, who enjoyed sneaking up on them, capturing and then swinging them around, seemed to be their only threats. Even then, some mamasan generally put a "whoa" to the scene, since it was believed that such activity had a direct correlation to the chicken's interest in laying eggs.

The pigs were enjoying a brief period of freedom from the pens on the sides of each hut. They milled around with the chickens, their massive bulk towering over their feathered friends. The scene prompted a memory of the book *Animal Farm,*[5] where the pigs set themselves up as dictators over a farm after ousting the farmer and his wife. "Chào, General Pig," I greeted the nearest one. He lifted his head to see if I was worth greeting or not. He worked his nose back and forth, then with a toss of his head, let go a snort that scattered his feathered friends in all directions. I took the snort as a return greeting.

A water buffalo was wallowing in the mud of a rice paddy off to my right. He lowered his ears and let forth a sigh as if to warn me to keep my distance, then returned to his mud without further concern. The buffaloes were becoming less and less troublesome to us, I assumed because we had developed a more palatable scent by living on a Vietnamese diet and living in the jungle without the benefit of frequent bathing.

The villagers seemed to be concentrating on their daily chores. We greeted them with the salutations appropriate to their sex and age. A group of men gathered in the center of the village, mending fish nets after a long morning's venture in the nearby ocean. Due to the location of the village, its inhabitants were primarily fishermen, raising rice and potatoes more as supplements than anything else. Their main product was the Nước Mặn I sprinkled on all my sandwiches, created by pouring vinegar wine through a vat of fermented fish. Occasionally they would venture out on the blacktop and sell the sauce and any excess fish.

The men momentarily stopped their work and nodded a greeting to us. They all smiled as if they knew why I was there, making me wish I did.

We stopped at a large hut near the center of the village. Although it had the typical bamboo walls and palm leaf roof, the decorations were different from any I had seen. Wooden posts at the entrance boasted paintings and symbols along with Vietnamese writing. The entire hut was covered with colorful painting. Smoke filtered through the cracks between the bamboo poles. The smell of incense hung in the air, blanketing the hut in a hazy cloud. Taan stopped at the entrance, sat down and removed his boots, then laid his 30 carbine and his knife alongside. I stood and waited. I wasn't about to take off my boots or put down my weapons until I knew I wasn't going to have to run. Taan said, "You wait, okay?"

"No problem, but be careful."

Taan disappeared behind a black silk cloth covering the entrance to the hut. I waited, clenching my rifle in anticipation. The moments seemed like an eternity as I visually searched the surrounding area for signs of anything out of the norm.

Suddenly, Taan's head appeared from behind the cloth, beaming from ear to ear. "Take off boots and weapons, then come in on hands and knees."

Of all the things and people I did *not* trust, Taan was *not* a member of that set. If Taan had asked me to run buck naked through a leech-infested swamp and slap every water buffalo I saw, he would have had a good reason for it, and I would have done it. I laid all my weapons, including grenades, alongside Taan's. "Now I feel naked!" I said to myself.

Taan had disappeared back into the hut. I could hear his voice, along with one other.

"Well here goes nothing," I muttered. Settling down on my hands and knees, I started crawling into the hut. About halfway in, my mouth fell open so wide I was sure my chin was dragging on the dirt floor. The scene before me was spellbinding. Remembering that I'd left my butt exposed to the outside, I continued my crawl until I was all the way in. I sat in a squat position beside Taan.

The interior of the hut was illuminated by what seemed to be hundreds of candles. The iridescent glow created by the flickering flames produced dancing shadows on every inch of the walls, making the place seem alive with spirits. At the back of the hut was a shrine boasting photographs of deceased friends and relatives. The center of the shrine was a carved Buddha, which seemed to be made of white stone or ivory, standing about four or five feet tall. Sitting at the feet of the Buddha was a man who looked a hundred years old, although I doubted he was because typically, the Vietnamese people only lived to their late forties. There were, however, tales of men who had been allowed by the Buddha to live many years to enable them to complete a specific task. Physically, the man was small and frail looking, yet I sensed a strength in him. His snow-white hair flowed past his shoulders and down his back, and his white beard was about six inches long, but sparse around the chin line. His eyes were coal black and pierced through me. "Don't try to con this man," I warned myself. I let my eyes drop from his as I continued to inspect him from head to toe.

For clothing, the chieftain wore white silk "pajamas," as we called them, rather than the black I was used to seeing. The silk was decorated with red emblems, a type of which I had never seen before. He sat cross-legged with his hands lying crossed in his lap. What caught my eye was that his fingernails were three or four inches long. I could not believe it. I stared at his hands until it dawned on me that I was being rude by doing so. Blushing with embarrassment, I returned my eyes to his and nodded with a slight reverent bow of my head.

"Chào ông," I greeted him with as much reverence and respect as I could muster. He smiled a contagious smile that set my mind at ease, and returned my greeting with a slow, equally reverent bow not only of his head but also at the waist, placing his hands on the beautifully woven mat that lay before him. He did not utter a word, but his actions told me that I was more than welcome.

He turned to Taan and spoke in a dialect unfamiliar to me, and I wondered if it might be closer to the original language of the Vietnamese people than any of the others I had heard. After speaking, the chieftain turned his gaze back to me, those cold black eyes reaching for my soul once again. With the long fingernails of his outstretched right hand he motioned Taan to relay his message.

Taan bowed his head in obedience. When he turned to me I saw that he had adopted the old man's contagious smile. "Chieftain say he very happy with you and your men. He say he know you are here to help his people, not destroy them and the land as others before you. He has heard stories how you protect our people from Viet Cong *and* U.S. Armies."

My mind flashed to the time the army had sent a truck into Chu Lai for supplies. On its return trip, one of the soldiers started throwing rocks at the local Vietnamese just as we came out of the jungle. I ran out on the road screaming and leveled off, ready to empty my 60 into the truck. The rocks stopped immediately as the army guys fell to the floor of their truck. My men, although sharing my outrage, maintained sense enough to knock me to the ground before I could squeeze off a single round. Later, I thanked them, knowing that killing a fellow American would have haunted me to my last days.

I also thought about our first Operation Mead River battle. We thought we were engaged in heavy combat with the Viet Cong, but a message came over the radio to cease firing because the enemies we had engaged were Americans. Although the CO assured us later that we had definitely been fighting the Viet Cong, I was never sure what to believe. All I knew was that I had shot a man and watched him die. He hadn't looked like an American to me and my mind reassured me at the time that he had indeed had on the typical NVA jungle helmet. A question remained in my mind only because the man had been so far away that my mind would not now produce an accurate picture of him.

Taan's voice returned me to the present.

"Also he say he heard of many people you treat for sickness and wounds. He talk with farmers you teach to plant foods better. Chieftain like you and is honored that you take time to help our people."

I turned to the chieftain. "Cám ơn u la," I nodded to him, in thanks.

The chieftain turned back to Taan with another barrage of the "old" language. After a few moments, Taan turned again to me.

"Chieftain say he thank you for speaking in his language. Also, he say you and your men are respected warriors in his province. Even VC respect you. He know about bounty VC offer for you and has warned people not to turn you in. Also, he now send runners to tell you where and when VC enter this province. You no longer to be attacked by surprise!"

My heart leaped for joy. "Mission accomplished," I thought. I wanted to hug and kiss the old chief. He had no idea how I had longed for a pur-

One of the Quảng Tin
Province chieftain's infor-
mants, a girl about seven-
teen years old. The men of
the CAP Một unit knew her
only as "Linda."

pose, a reason to justify the killing. He could not know how I longed to set
aside my weapons and just help his people live in peace. I knew it was a
stupid goal. Our own country, as civilized as it was, still had its own form of
Viet Cong who harassed and murdered people.

That was the extent of the conversation and the purpose behind the
meeting. We exchanged thanks and gratitude, finished our bows and Taan
and I left the hut. I would never have guessed the impact that meeting
would have on our lives.

Taan and I put our boots back on, donned our gear and allowed our
elation to carry us from the village. Only the sight of a bomb crater in the
center of one of the rice paddies brought us back to reality. The old man
would help as much as he could, but we still had to fight the war. The only
thing that had really changed was that now we would have a spy in every
village except, I thought, the VC village near the firebase.

Our minds back in tune with present dangers, we set out in search of
Rivera and the rest of the men. I prayed that there had been no VC contact

without my being there with them. We reached the village just as they were finishing their search. I hoped Rivera had made some effort to befriend the villagers. I couldn't help feeling that their close proximity to Fat City played a major role in their remaining VC-controlled. They were in a strategic location for contacting and observing the soldiers coming to and from the firebase. I suspected that an entire unit was tunneled in under the village and no doubt Fat City itself. The Viet Cong had always been dubbed as expert jungle fighters, but in reality, I felt their true expertise lay in the construction and use of tunnel networks.[6]

Taan joined his fellow PFs to fill them in on what the chieftain had told us. He was as anxious as I was to get the news out.

"Any luck?" I asked as I joined up with the group.

"Naw," Jones drawled out. "Just as friendly as could be."

"Too bad," I grinned at him. "Hey, Rivera, let's find a safe area to stop. I have some kind of news for you guys."

"Okay," Rivera said. "How about the tracks?"

"Works for me," I said. We left the village behind and headed southwest. The tracks, or rather the ruins of them, were on the way back to our old compound. I could read Rivera's mind. He was ready to spend another night there. "God help us," I thought. He was setting up a predictable pattern. If I could read him, so could the enemy. We reached our destination, settled in and everyone broke out snacks while I saddled up to fill them in on my day.

"Well, y'all aren't going to believe this," I started, suppressing the grin and eagerness that no doubt showed anyway.

"Well, come on. Tell us," Lackey chided.

"Yeah. What ya bellowing about, mate?" chimed in Johnston.

"Okay! Okay!" I said. "Here goes." I told them everything, beginning the moment we entered the village and ending the moment we left. "Well!? What do y'all think?"

"Unbelievable!" Jones said.

"Yeah, too unbelievable," Rivera added. "I don't believe a word of it."

"What are you saying, Rivera?" I asked, anger lodged in my throat.

"I think you've been duped into trusting these idiots," he answered.

"Let me tell you this, mister. If I hadn't trusted Taan, I would not be here today. You wait, that chieftain will send info some day that will save your ugly hide. Then you won't be so cocky," I ended my rampage, turned and started heading south.

"Where do you think you're going?" Rivera yelled.

"To the stinking compound you're so fond of," I said.

He blushed with the realization that I knew where he planned to spend the night. He said nothing.

"Well, are y'all coming or not?" I asked.

Everyone started forward but then stopped to see what Rivera was going to do. He had fallen in step behind the rest of the group, his mind obviously thinking of ways to get even with me. I figured he wouldn't do a thing, because without me as a buffer the men would chew him up. Besides, he would have no one to make his decisions for him. By the time we reached the compound around 1600 hours I had my mind on other things. It was definitely not good practice to develop a pattern of returning to the old French quarters, especially not with three hours of daylight left. We knew there was a VC sympathizer out there somewhere, probably close by.

To calm my nerves, I began systematically inspecting my weapons for readiness. I figured Rivera was going to put me in charge of his "killer team" night patrol again. But I was not to go roaming that night.

A neighboring PF unit from just north of Chu Lai was visiting our sector to allow the men the opportunity to visit their wives and families under the new "polygamy" law, instituted by the South Vietnamese Government in an effort to aid in increasing the population. In fact, the men were more than eager to participate, most seeking out a different wife in each of the major villages. The visiting unit consisted of around forty young men. The average age looked to be around sixteen, with the youngest being fourteen and the oldest pushing the ripe old age of twenty. In terms of physical age, they were kids. But in terms of war, they were the seasoned veterans and the Americans were the babes in the woods. Most of us had less than a year of combat under our belts.

CAP Command decided to take the opportunity presented by the visiting PF unit to send out a chopper loaded with "propaganda" films designed to help the Vietnamese understand why we were there helping them. Of course, Command referred to the effort as "American hand-in-hand involvement with Vietnam," rather than propaganda.

No matter what Command called it, I was furious with the stupidity of the effort. They weren't the ones flying a chopper into the bush near dusk, unprotected by gunships. They weren't the ones who would be attacked when the Viet Cong read the thousands of leaflets meant to invite the villagers and farmers to our movie. I could not believe they would actually require us to ignore all the rules of the bush and let Charlie know exactly where we were going to be. To make things worse, we would have a generator reverberating a signal into the jungle in all directions, along with noisy loudspeakers broadcasting the movie sounds, to help Charlie locate our position. To make it even easier for our enemy to do away with us, we were to cram everyone—two PF units, one CAP unit and a fair number of Vietnamese women and children—into one little area to watch the movie.

I felt like an idiot carrying out the CO's orders, but I did it anyway. I stood back away from the crowd, hidden in the shadows of the surrounding bush. The sound from the speakers and the generator was deafening. The crowd of villagers sat before the brightly lit screen. I checked the jungle around me wondering when Charlie would strike at such a perfect target. I had set up watch posts around the entire perimeter, with strict orders to the men not to leave their posts for any reason. Rivera said he would stick with Rodriguez and help him with his watch.

As the hour-long movie reached its downhill side, I left the post I was sharing with Jones to make sure all was well with the other men. Lackey and Mendez were intact and just as alert as I hoped. They shared their concerns about our vulnerability, followed by rather explicit suggestions about what we should do with the CO and his movie. I laughed and advised them I would take their plan under consideration. Part of me was dead serious. Our CO had become a thorn in our side—an infectious one.

I left Lackey and Mendez and headed toward Taan's and Johnston's post. They were wide awake and just as nervous as the rest of us. Taan forced a weak smile. He was not the least bit happy with the situation. "American CO beaucoup điên kiện đầu!" he blurted out, shaking his head in disbelief.

Johnston assured me that he could not improve on Taan's statement. I took a moment to share my fears of an imminent attack from the VC. Taan agreed, but doubted an attack until all was quiet again. His prophecy echoed in my brain as I left them and set out in the direction I'd last seen Rivera and Rodriguez. I tried to picture where and when the Cong would attack. I knew that something was bound to happen. "Try not to worry about it," I told myself. "Just be ready!"

Rivera and Rodriguez were supposed to be at the extreme south end of our perimeter. "Rivera? Rodriguez?" I whispered into the darkness where they had chosen to set up watch. Nothing but silence. They weren't there! My adrenaline pushed the blood through my veins as I squatted down beside a small palm tree and allowed my gaze to sweep the area. There were half a dozen huts off to my right about fifty yards from my position. I studied each one intently, searching for the slightest warning signal. There were no signs of a struggle, either by the huts or in the bush where the two men had been.

Suddenly, a sound I did not expect came barreling out of the hut nearest me—laughter. Checking my M-16, I headed over and sidled up against the bamboo wall of the hut, trying to maintain as much silence as possible. Locating a crack in the wall where the mud seal had broken loose, I peered inside, ready to see a bunch of gooks hovering over Rivera and Rodriguez.

"What the . . . !" I could not believe what I saw. Inside sat Rodriguez and Rivera, laughing and carrying on with a couple of girls. I burst into the hut with the finesse of an elephant. Neither man dove for his weapon. They couldn't have. They had left them lying by the front door. Rivera didn't even have his pistol with him. I stood there with rifle at ready. Their laughter had stopped. All four of them simply sat and stared at me—entranced by my beauty, no doubt. Suddenly the girls bolted out a back entrance I had not seen. Rivera and Rodriguez looked like two children caught skipping school.

To risk their own lives was stupid. To leave our rear unguarded and risk the annihilation of our entire unit was unforgivable. I fought to contain my rage. "How dare you!" I screamed between clenched teeth.

"Aw, man, nothing's going to happen with all that ruckus out there," Rodriguez said.

"Yeah, man. What do you think you're doing, scaring away our girls like that?" Rivera attempted to turn the accusing finger back at me.

All I could do was stare at him, a cold, bitter rage swelling up inside my gut. "Squad leader or no squad leader, you never leave a post," I spat at him. I waved my rifle barrel toward the front door. "Come on, let's get out of here before your girlfriends return with some friends you're not ready to meet." They simply sat there staring at me. "Now!" I screamed.

They both jumped to their feet, dropping little charms and trinkets they had been offering the girls. Grabbing their weapons, they hurried outside.

Once outside, Rivera's arrogant attitude returned. "How dare you order me around," he said. "I'm your squad leader."

"I'd shoot a general if he unnecessarily risked the lives of my men," I stated coldly.

Rivera dropped his eyes, turned and headed back to the group watching the final stages of the movie. Rodriguez hung back, staring at me. "You're on my list, man," he said.

"Great," I sneered. "I'll worry about that someday."

His bravado held. "Don't turn your back on me in the next firefight," he growled, pointing a finger at me. "I'll make sure you don't survive." He turned on his heel to make a grand exit and ran smack into Lackey.

"Don't try it," Lackey said as he shoved Rodriguez aside. He continued, his voice rising as Rodriguez disappeared into the night, "You try to shoot Goodson or even point a gun in his direction and I'll destroy you."

I jumped in to prevent a contagion of rage from spreading through the squad. "Whoa, cowboy!" I laughed. "You might bust a gusset with all that kind of talk."

"But he . . . ."

"Don't worry," I interrupted. "You know as well as I do that he's just blowing smoke. Besides, he's going to be too busy worrying about the pain Charlie can inflict to even toy with the idea of trying to kill me. By the way, where were you headed?"

"Oh, yeah," he answered. "Just wanted to know what to do after the movie is over." Just as he finished, the last strip of film slipped out of the projector. "Flap, flap, flap," it sang into the night.

"Shut that thing off!" I yelled.

Lackey ran over and shut down the generator. Silence engulfed us as the jungle regained its foothold over man's creations. As if by signal, the audience stood up and started the journey to their homes. As they filed out in all directions, I saw looks ranging from bored to bewildered, and I knew the movie had not had the effect the CO intended.

With all the civilians gone and the visiting unit tucked away in our neat little compound, we tried to secure the generator, projector and screen in as safe an area as possible. The chopper, of course, would not pick them up until morning. The visiting PFs obviously felt they were in a secure area. They lit up cigarettes and built a campfire right in the middle of the compound.

We all scattered ourselves among the bunker ruins in an attempt to set up some form of protective perimeter. Rodriguez and Rivera took the extreme eastern end of the compound, still enraged with the night's events. I chose the bunker overlooking the area to the south, into which the girls had vanished. "God, make morning come early," I prayed.

As I gazed into the night, I could hear bits of the conversation going on in the group of PFs huddled around the campfire. Suddenly, I realized they were talking about us, laughing and exchanging comments about how stupid Americans were. I was astounded. Our unit was renowned for its attempts to help the Vietnamese. Of course the film had added fuel to their fire. My rage returned. I leaped off the bunker, walked right into the middle of their ring and stood, my back to the campfire. Silence fell over the group as all eyes were focused on me. "What you want, American?" asked the PF in charge.

Suddenly it dawned on me. They didn't know that I understood their language, so they thought my jump into their midst was just another stupid stunt. With a smile on my lips, I spoke to them in their own language, telling them exactly what I thought about their comments and where they could put them. I don't know how long it was before I talked myself out, but I got no response from anyone in the group. With nothing further to say, I walked back over to my bunker to resume my guard position. "That was a pretty stupid move," I told myself.

Their party was over. A couple of them kicked dirt on the fire while the others made their way to a sheltered spot for the night. I could smell the smoke as the smothered fire tried to rekindle itself. The PFs were no doubt planning my demise. They could not let an "American" get away with such a thing.

Silence, welcome silence, once again settled on our little haven. I checked my watch. It was 0200 hours. It had already been a long night. A cool breeze filtered in from the ocean, cleansing the air of the remaining fragments of smoke. I took a deep breath, filling my lungs with the cool morning air.

Just then, a flash! . . . followed by a tremendous boom. I expected more explosions, but heard nothing else except the wailing cry of a woman. The attack had been so abrupt that it was difficult to pinpoint its exact location. The best I could judge was that it was a hundred clicks[7] south of our position and close to Highway One.

The area south of the compound was filled with a spattering of huts, most of which were nestled along the roadside. Some of them were built with concrete block walls. I assumed, since there was no immediate ball of flame following the initial blast, that the round had exploded against such a wall. If the blast had been low enough, there was a chance that the palm leaf roof had not ignited. An unseasoned observer's initial response would be to jump up and run to investigate. We knew better. All too often our enemy had staged a mock attack to entice us to the scene, where certain death awaited those who fell victim to the scam.

The attack was over as abruptly as it had begun. No fire resulted from the explosion. We simply sat, watched and waited. The woman's wailing was chewing at our insides, but we had to wait for a confirmation from the villagers—usually delivered by runner—that we needed to be involved. Unthinking action could spell death.

Suddenly a voice from behind me whispered into the night. It was Taan. "Corporal Barry?" Taan asked.

I slid off my bunker, my thoughts turning to our visiting PFs. I could just make out their silhouettes where they lay in wait for an attack to follow the explosion. Taan filled me in on further details of the story. A young boy about six or seven years old had sneaked into our compound and sought Taan's help in bringing us to the scene of the crime. A chill crept up my spine as I thought of how easily he had penetrated our perimeter.

"VC shoot RPG at PF Nguyen Tinh's home. They hope to kill him." PF Tinh, a member of the visiting unit, apparently held quite a reputation as a "Cong Killer," and was wanted by the VC as badly as they wanted us.

I checked with Rivera and told him what had happened. "They want us to check it out and help with the wounded," I told him.

"Fine. Take Doc and report back to me," Rivera ordered.

My trusty Australian was already at my side. "Come on," I said. "Let's go check out the damage."

PF Tinh's house was roughly a hundred yards due south of the compound. We followed a path that led directly in front of the house. A crowd, sensing that the VC had left, was quietly gathering around the makeshift bamboo fence that enclosed the yard surrounding the hut. As we approached, the woman I assumed to be Tinh's mother let go with more wailing, interrupted only by sobs and moments of silence as she caught her breath. She was standing outside her hut, facing the doorway. Her hands extended toward the opening, but it was clear that fear held her in check.

A hole about the size of a baseball allowed light to filter from the hut into the darkness. "An RPG concussion round," I remarked.

Taan followed my gaze. "RPG hit there," he confirmed. He then disappeared into the hut. In another moment he appeared again in the doorway, illuminated by the yellow light of a candle behind him. "Come," he said as he motioned us forward. The look on his face warned me of the death inside. I swallowed the lump in my throat and stepped forward as Taan held back the silk drape covering the entrance. Johnston was right on my heels, eager to "patch up" any wounded inside.

The entrance hallway about six feet long turned abruptly to the right and opened into a large room that served as bedroom, kitchen, living room and den. Mamasan Tinh followed along behind. Her small hand clenching my sleeve, she looked up at me with red swollen eyes as I walked down the hall with her. She reached out and grabbed my hand as I reached the end of the hall. She started crying again. "Tại sao?" she wailed, "Why?"

As I rounded the corner opening into the room, I stopped and turned stone cold. My stomach tied itself into knots as my eyes searched the room for the wounded and the dead. Mamasan Tinh continued to jerk on my hand with her continual question. My eyes took in the horrible scene that lay before me. I had seen death and destruction before, but somehow this topped them all.

A boy, no more than thirteen or fourteen years old, lay on a wooden bed that backed up to the west wall, his hands crossed and a look of peace and innocence radiating from his face. Except for the fact that he was completely white from the loss of every ounce of blood from his body, he could have still been sleeping.

A piece of concrete, no larger than a baseball, had struck the boy right between his right shoulder and the base of his neck as he lay dreaming the dreams of a young boy. It had torn its way through his body and come out near his groin, taking with it every piece of the boy that it could. The concussion from the concrete and the explosion spread blood and pieces of bone and body parts over the entire interior of the room. Blood dripped from the palm leaf roof and slowly flowed down the walls to puddles of red on the floor. A family photograph hung on the wall. It, too, was drenched in the blood and the horror of it all. Mamasan Tinh dropped to her knees, engulfed in her grief, wrapping her arms around my legs. I looked down and stroked the graying black hair in a feeble effort to comfort her. I returned my gaze to the horror before me. A tear welled up in my eye. My bitterness and outrage at the war overwhelmed me as I stood there transfixed in a scene and a memory that would follow me to my grave.

Johnston turned suddenly and hurried outside. I heard him throwing up somewhere in the darkness. My own stomach wrenched violently, but I fought it back. Forcing my eyes away, I reached down and pulled Mamasan Tinh to her feet, wrapped her in my arms and guided her outside. Taan was waiting there with men ready to take away the body and destroy the hut. After such a horrible death, Mamasan Tinh would not be able to live in that hut again. Two men removed the body while the others removed her belongings. Hut cleaned out, they set fire to it as a semblance of their effort to erase the memory, but I knew it would not be that easy.

We all watched the hut burn, impervious to the silhouettes we cast from the illumination of the fire making us open targets for the Cong. We knew; we simply did not care. Somehow the boy's death had changed us all. Bitterness and hatred engulfed us even more than before. The senseless murder of a sleeping child was almost more than any of us could stand. Mamasan Tinh was led away by her Vietnamese friends and relatives to prepare for her son's funeral. I remained by the flaming hut, her question echoing in my brain: "Tại sao?"

Morning finally came, bringing fresh cool air and a promise from the rising sun, but we refused to be refreshed. The smell of death hung in our nostrils and controlled our minds. Even though they had killed a young boy instead of PF Tinh, the Cong had done their job well. They achieved their goal of disrupting the peace and tranquillity of our little village. People were doing their morning chores, but with an unusual somberness. There was none of the typical chatter between neighbors, and the children sat staring into the jungle, probably wondering if they, too, would be killed by the VC.

I sat down with my back against one of the bunker ruins and began to clean my rifle. My thoughts turned to my own childhood experiences with fear, and somehow everything I could think of fell far short of the horrors the Vietnamese children had to face. It was no wonder the words "fun" and "play" were absent from their language. For an adult to cope with such horror and cruelty was one thing, but for children to have to go through it was too much. It seemed like God had abandoned the entire country. These people had no chance to really enjoy life, existing not just from day to day, but from moment to moment, from death to death, from horror to horror. They weren't concerned about tomorrow or even this afternoon. Survival was their only goal.

Rifle clean, I gathered up my gear and my thoughts and headed toward the men. I wondered how they were handling the morning's death. From the looks on their faces, they had done the same as I had—put the tragedy on a shelf in the back of their minds to be dealt with at some more convenient time.

Breakfast seemed like an impossible idea. Somehow my typical Nước Mặn and pork/fish sandwich did not sound appetizing, but I knew my body needed nourishment. "Maybe some fresh fruit," I thought, "bananas or a coconut." I looked around for a nearby tree. There were none. Just as I was about to concede to the sandwich, a visiting PF approached with a smile and a "Chào anh!" I returned his greeting with a question in my mind, but then I recognized him as one of those who had been badmouthing Americans the night before.

In his best English, he said, "My sergeant want you join him for breakfast. He . . . uh . . . embarrass by you understand our language last night. He want you come and eat with him. He want show you he okay guy."

I was amazed. After my stunt, I figured the last people I would ever hear from would be the visiting PFs. I looked around for Sergeant Rivera to tell him I was leaving, but he was not to be found. I turned to the PF. "Lead the way," I said, then yelled back at Jones. "Hey, Jones! Cover for me. I'm going to chow down with these guys." He nodded and waved me on.

As it turned out the visiting sergeant was embarrassed not only because he and his men had been caught badmouthing us, but also because he had been told off in his own language. Because he had "lost face," he was giving me breakfast as a peace offering and as a sign to his men that he and I were friends. He was honored, he said, that I had spent so much time studying their language and their culture. After the sergeant had spoken, there was very little conversation during the meal. They gave me the bananas and coconut I had longed for and we ate in peace. The Sergeant was pleased with my willingness to share a meal with him, which allowed him to regain face in front of his men.

Meal over, I returned to the compound. Jones and Mendez were writing letters home, no doubt trying to relate the horrors of the night before. I sympathized with their efforts. I had long since ceased any attempt to describe the hell of Vietnam to friends and relatives back home.

"Hey, y'all ready to move out?" I asked.

"Yeah, let's get out of this hole," Jones said.

"Yeah, mate, let's hit the bush," Johnston added.

They hated the compound as much as I did and were eager to put the whole scene behind them. We readied for the bush. I began checking each man's weapons to ensure everything was clean and in perfect working order. Through the entrance of the compound I could see Sergeants Shôu and Rivera.

We stood ready as they approached. "Chào anh," I greeted Sergeant Shôu. He nodded. He was never a man to get involved. In fact, we rarely saw him. He never hit the bush with us. Rivera had taken to him, but I didn't totally trust him. But it didn't matter what I thought; he was obviously powerful because Taan respected and even feared him, jumping at his every command.

"Sergeant Shôu has located the VC informer," Rivera stated. "We are to stay in the compound today, and you," he said while pointing to me, "will take two men and a radio along with Taan and arrest her."

"Her?" I asked, but I was not surprised. Women as well as children commonly served as fighters in this war. Taan conferred with Sergeant Shôu briefly to obtain directions and instructions. I could see disgust in his eyes when he learned the identity of the VC woman, so I discerned that he knew her. I turned to pick my men. There was no need. Jones, Lackey and Johnston stepped forward simultaneously.

"We're ready," Jones smiled.

"Good," I returned. "Three's as good as two. Let's move out."

We walked over to join up with Taan, who had just finished his debriefing with Sergeant Shôu. We stood in silent respect as Shôu dismissed him. When Taan approached, I called the men to attention and stepped forward to greet him. It was not necessary that we do so, but it showed respect for Taan and gained him favor in the eyes of his sergeant as well as his other men. He smiled weakly and motioned for us to follow him.

"You know the woman?" I asked Taan as we left the compound.

He looked at me with pain written all over his face. "She part of my family," he said, and left it at that. He never said her name. I presumed that she was a cousin. The Vietnam War, like our own Civil War, often divided families. In respect for Taan, I let the subject drop. We followed him southward, making no effort to leave the blacktop for the cover of the jungle. Evidently his thoughts blinded him to the reality of how exposed we were, but today we didn't care either. As I watched Taan, I wondered how I would feel if one of my cousins were an informer to the very people who wanted to kill me.

There was one other thing I knew was eating at Taan. His cousin was already dead and didn't know it. Not only was she dead, but she would also suffer horribly at the hands of Sergeant Shôu and his fellow interrogators before she died. I knew Shôu had chosen Taan as the one to bring her in because she was his kin. If Taan failed it would prove to everyone that Taan, too, was VC. Taan was well aware of the burden that had been placed on his shoulders. I could imagine the turmoil eating at his gut. Nothing could be worse than knowing that you had to bring your own kin into a situation that would lead to torture and a slow painful death. It would have been better for them both if Taan just walked up and put a bullet in her brain. That way her death would be sudden and basically painless. Yet that, too, would label Taan as VC. Whoever she was, she had to be brought in alive.

Taan stopped at the northern perimeter of a roadside village known as Kương Hiêp, about three miles south of our compound. It was a "shopping village" so it did not have the usual huts and animal pens. It looked like a set for an old western movie, with its box board construction, false fronts and wooden walkways. The only difference was that each store or building boasted colorful Vietnamese writing.

We stood in silence, waiting for Taan's command. Finally, with a deep sigh, he moved out, heading for a small store in the west side of the village. Without hesitation, he walked right into the building. We followed. His cousin stood behind a glass counter and stared in wonder as she saw Taan enter through the front doors of her store. Like Taan, she was tall for a Vietnamese, and was dressed in the typical colorful silk slacks and blouse covered with a contrasting silk shroud. "Chào, Taan," she smiled as she walked toward him.

Taan let her approach. No smile or salutation left his lips. He couldn't fake it and wasn't about to try. Realization hit her with full force, and fear flooded her face as she turned to run. Taan's 30 carbine broke the silence with a quick burst of lead which shattered the glass of the counter. She stopped dead in her tracks and sank to the floor with a sob as she realized that she had been found out. I sent Jones and Lackey to cover the front and rear exits to stop anyone, friend or foe, from interfering with Taan and his appointed duty.

He turned to me. "Search store . . . okay?"

Johnston and I set out in different directions and began our systematic search for evidence that she was VC, although we knew that once Sergeant

Shôu had labeled her as an informer, she would be tortured even if she were innocent. It did not take us long to find both VC and American ammo stored in the back room. We also found a roll of bills three or four inches thick.

"There must be thousands here," Johnston stated as he removed the string from the wad of bills. I wasn't as upset with the amount as I was with the type of money—good old American currency. Thousands of U.S. dollars in a country and a war zone where only MPC (military currency) or Vietnamese money was allowed. Simple possession of U.S. money, even by military personnel, could sign your death warrant. "Where did the money come from?" I wondered. My mind raced as I tried to visualize the source on the black market. I doubted that even torture would make her reveal anything, and we'd never find out the money's source.

Johnston and I returned to Taan and showed him the evidence. He sighed as his eyes locked on the money and the pain returned to his face. I was embarrassed that our country had contributed to his cousin's downfall. She had evidently been catering to someone with contacts in Chu Lai and was being paid good money to remain as an informer as well as supplier to the Viet Cong.

"We go," Taan stated suddenly.

I called to the other men. "Let's move out!"

As we left the store, Taan led the way with his cousin at gun point. A group of children were playing on the opposite side of the road. One of them stopped and watched as we walked away. He was strange looking for a Vietnamese boy—his blonde hair gave clear evidence of American influence in the village. I looked again at the remaining children and noticed they all showed signs of their American heritage. No wonder they were all playing together. They were outcasts in their own country, shunned and hated by their own people.[8] I shook my head at the sadness of the situation.

Our return trip to the old French compound was silent and uneventful. We delivered Taan's cousin to Sergeant Shôu, who immediately took her into his hut for interrogation. She turned and looked at Taan briefly with a look of fear and hopelessness. He turned away with his head down. I put my arm around his shoulders.

Sergeant Shôu shoved the woman inside and disappeared behind her. Rivera came out just as they entered. "I'm going to stay here as a witness to the interrogation," he stated.

"Your problem," I said flippantly. "How about me taking the guys north a ways to check out the possibility of VC activity in the area?"

He agreed without hesitation. It gave him an opportunity to strengthen his relationship with Sergeant Shôu.

"Let's head north," I said to Taan. He looked up with a tear in his eye and agreed with a slight nod and a sigh.

I didn't really know of any activity in the area. I just wanted to get Taan away before the torture began. I gathered my men, along with a handful of Taan's men, and we struck off into the jungle heading northeast toward a village I knew to be friendly, especially to Taan. He needed friends now. As we headed out, I had Lackey radio our report to CAP Command, advising them that a VC informer had been captured and suggesting that they send a truck to the village to pick up the "goodies" we had left behind. I had hidden the money under the cabinet of the glass counter. Hopefully, a truck would get there before the VC did. I had my doubts but I figured the knowledge of U.S. currency hiding there would motivate CAP Command to send a unit out "một phút" as the Vietnamese say—"pronto."

We reached the village around 1300 hours and settled into a pleasant coconut grove overlooking a shallow inlet from the nearby ocean. The men shed their gear and lost themselves in their own thoughts or activities. Lackey and Johnston played with the children while Jones, Mendez and Rodriguez returned to letter writing.

Sergeant Shôu had sent a battery-powered, handheld loudspeaker (another U.S. donation), along with his men to attempt to call the "Chieu Hois" in from the bush. There was not much hope of anyone surrendering from the area we were in, but I suspected that Shôu wanted to get the news out about the Tinh boy's death and Taan's cousin's capture. These particular people adamantly hated the VC and resisted their worst tactics. Still, I did not interfere with the efforts of the PFs to bring in the "lost souls" or to deliver their message.

Suddenly, Taan grabbed the speaker and let go with a barrage of Vietnamese language that shattered the jungle. His men shrunk back as if his words were meant for them. The outburst was what Taan needed. He finished with a threat and a promise to annihilate the enemy regardless of who they were. He turned, smiled at me and held the loudspeaker out. "You talk," he said, obviously feeling much better.

"Oh, no . . . not me." I shied away, but the other men saw what was going on and joined Taan as they cheered and chided me on.

I gave in, grabbed the loudspeaker and screamed into the depths of the jungle. "VC, give up! We kill you anyway!" Like Taan I let go with a barrage not fit for human ears. He was right. It did make you feel better. I started to hand it back to him when one of his men jumped in and shoved it back at me with a smile.

"Sing!" he encouraged.

"No way. Here, Taan, take this before I get in trouble."

"No way, man . . . sing!" Taan ordered.

Once again I gave in. With my best lousy voice I filled the jungle with bits and pieces of songs I knew. Everyone cheered me on as the jungle echoed with laughter.

Johnston strolled over. "The VC will no doubt surrender by the dozens now, mate. Now that they've had a taste of our secret weapon."

We all laughed. Taan and some of his men acted like VC swarming in from the jungle surrendering with pleas to "sing no more." Other men joined in and contributed their own musical singing talents to the jungle. More laughter came forth than singing as more mock VC flooded the area with pleas to cease. Soon we were all engulfed in a contagion of laughter.

One by one we settled back to the reality of the world we were in as the laughter began to subside, but somehow we all seemed happier, even Taan. As we each returned to our own thoughts and activities, Lackey approached me. "Hey, Corporal," he yelled out.

"Yeah, Lackey, what ya got?" I asked.

"Just this," he stated, holding out one of his frag grenades.

I took it from him and let it roll in my palm. Small holes, about one-eighth inch in diameter, were scattered on one side. The metal skin covering the outside of the grenade was so thin that the simple rubbing against his side had worn through to expose the explosive inside.

"Got any more?" I asked.

"No, but you better check the other guys," he suggested.

"Yeah," I agreed. "Gather them up for me, will ya?"

"No problem, Corporal," he answered as he headed off in search of rotten eggs.[9] Soon he returned with two more. "Mendez and Rodriguez each had one."

"Too bad," I returned. "I hate to get rid of something we may need, but Command says they're volatile when the explosive is exposed."

"Wanna pull pins and drop them in the ocean?" he asked.

"No, the water is only a couple of feet deep. There's too big a risk of the shrapnel breaking the surface and hitting someone. Unscrew the fuse and throw the egg into the inlet. Then pull the pins on the fuses and toss them in by themselves. The small explosion from the blasting cap will never break the surface."

"Good idea," Lackey stated. "Consider it done." He gathered the eggs and headed toward the edge of the inlet. A small group of children gathered around to watch. I started to warn him to watch out for the children, but decided there was no need. I watched them for a moment as he dismembered the first grenade, tossed the egg into the water, pulled the pin on the fuse, held it momentarily by habit and then tossed it into the water. From my position you couldn't even hear the muffled explosion of the blasting cap.

"Good," I thought, remembering a time when I was still with the 1st Marine grunts on patrol in Elephant Valley. We had stopped alongside a river for a breather. A couple of us had a few bad eggs and decided to toss them into the river, knowing the explosion would kill the fish in the immediate area, providing fresh fish for the Vietnamese kids who were following us. There was little risk of the VC hearing us because the depth of the river engulfed the explosion to a subdued rumble.

My thoughts turned back to Taan's cousin. I checked his face and saw that he was lost in thought. "I just pray she's already dead and not still suffering."

I was interrupted by a sudden scream from Lackey: "No!"

I jerked my head in his direction. He was chasing one of the kids along the edge of the inlet. Before he could reach him, the boy had already pulled the pin on the fuse he held in his hands. He must have thought the fuse was harmless without the egg, just a toy that he had stolen from Lackey. The other kids stood in horror as the blasting cap exploded, ripping the kid's fingers to the bone, severing one finger from the hand. The kid screamed with pain and fell to the ground. I thought he was dead. Lackey and I both screamed "Medic!" at the same time.

Johnston was ahead of us as he ran toward the crumpled child. Quickly, professionally, he bandaged the mutilated hand and checked the boy's vital signs. Fortunately, the child had not been wounded anywhere else.

The boy's mother came running from one of the huts, screaming. We tried to comfort her as Taan explained what had happened. I grabbed the radio and requested a medevac unit. Within minutes, the chopper arrived.

We loaded up the boy and his mother while Taan assured the boy's father that they would be returned.

Lackey was engulfed in self-condemnation over the child's wounds. The rest of us tried to convince him to blame it on the war. I tried to get him to blame me since it was my idea in the first place. Our peaceful respite shattered, we decided to head back for the old French compound. I checked my watch. It was 1532 hours. We still had four or five hours of daylight left. It would only take an hour to reach the compound. I prayed the interrogation would be over by then and that Taan's cousin would already be dead. Hopefully, Rivera would want to set up ambush in lieu of spending another night in the compound.

As we reached the old fort, Mendez and Rodriguez suggested that we visit the local "music mamasan," a merchant in a grass roadside hut across from the compound who had a battery-powered record player. Mendez and Rodriguez kept her supplied with batteries from home. The only catch was that between all of us there was only one record, and it only had one good song: "I Heard It Through the Grapevine." I had heard it so many times I could recite the words backwards. I was sick of it, yet it still soothed a certain part of me.

"Turn it up," I said, as we all faded away into our own thoughts and prayers for home, a place no longer real to us except in our minds. The violent realities we encountered every day made us sure we would never see "home" again, but our dreams and hopes kept it vividly etched into our memories. A tear fought its way out. I turned and walked outside.

Rivera was there, waiting as I stepped from the hut. He was pale, obviously affected by the torture Taan's cousin had endured. I didn't bother with a greeting. He nodded with a weak smile. "She's dead, man," he said.

"Yeah," I nodded, "Did she talk?"

"She confessed to being the informer, but held back any other information." His eyes searched the ground momentarily. Shortly, he glanced back up. "It was gross, Goodson," he started. "They tied her up and . . . "

I stopped him. "I know," I said. "I know." I turned and walked away.

Taan arrived to take the woman's body back to her kin. He wanted to make sure that she at least received the proper burial. He didn't want her soul lost forever along with the other VC souls. I watched him carry her away. She had been wrong, but she was still kinfolk. He knew that we all knew it. Another casualty of our war.

"I Heard It Through the Grapevine" filtered its way through my thoughts as I turned my gaze back to the hut where the men were escaping into another time, another place, away from Vietnam. My thoughts turned back to the war. I made a cursory check of my M-16. I had cleaned it that morning, but had only used a small amount of lubricant. I wasn't sure, but it looked like brown spots of rust were trying to take over.

"Dad, send that cleaning gear soon," I pleaded, sending my plea in what I thought was the direction of Texas. "Real soon," I thought, "or we're goners for sure."

---

[1]  As Goodson suggests, the M-16 was a controversial weapon in Vietnam because of the jamming problem. A 1967 Congressional investigating committee was critical of the U.S. Army's management of the development of the M-16. Ronald H. Spector, *After Tet: The Bloodiest Year in Vietnam* (New York: Free Press, 1993), 52–54; Thomas L. McNaugher, *The M-16 Controversies: Military Organizations and Weapons Acquisition* (New York: Praeger, 1984).

[2]  Harassment rounds, or harassment fire, was a term used by firebases to describe the times they fired artillery into areas of suspected enemy activity. The volley of shells was utilized to harass and impede the opposing force's progress or operations—nothing more, nothing less. In most cases firebases were not sure of the location of the VC/NVA units, so they based their selection upon recon and intelligence reports. Rarely were such attacks confirmed as to exactly where the projectiles fell, what or whom they destroyed, or whether the harassment was even effective in its purpose. In reality a number of innocent men, women and children were usually killed or maimed.

[3]  The vast majority of Vietnamese peasants were Buddhists. On the importance of Buddhism in Vietnamese rural society see Frances Fitzgerald, *Fire in the Lake: The Vietnamese and the Americans in Vietnam* (New York: Vintage, 1972), 18, 174–80.

[4]  Few of these villages really had any particular name or title. If it had to have a name it usually received the title of its most influential citizen. In some cases the name came by association with the Viet Cong.

[5]  George Orwell, *Animal Farm* (New York: Harcourt, Brace, 1946).

[6]  The tunnel networks in Vietnam were extensive. Some of them were begun by the Vietminh (armed forces of the Democratic Republic of Vietnam) in their war against the French, 1946–1954. The system was vastly improved once the Communist war against the South Vietnam government began in the late 1950s, and especially after U.S. firepower made it increasingly difficult to survive above ground. For background and commentary on the complexity of the tunnels, see Tom Mangold and John Penycate, *The Tunnels of Cu Chi: An Untold Story of Vietnam* (New York: Random House, 1985). Although the authors focus on the tunnel network northwest of Saigon, the book gives a good overview of the tunnels throughout the country.

[7]  "Clicks" is slang for kilometers.

[8]  The Vietnamese people believed in a pure race, and adamantly detested "contamination" from Americans or any other outsiders. Many of the Amerasian children were placed into local orphanages for their own protection. Many others were killed, along with their mothers, by members of the extended family.

[9]  "Egg" is slang for a grenade.

## Chapter 9

# CO's Night Out

We were in luck that night. Rivera not only agreed to setting up ambush, but we received orders from Command that we had to change our Killer Team tactics and stop setting up a base camp. The reason? Pressure was on from Fat City firebase to locate and destroy the Viet Cong who were constantly bombarding them with mortar fire. The attacks had become bolder and had increased from unpredictable random occurrences to regular night-by-night attacks, and sometimes even daytime appearances. Consequently, the firebase personnel were required to maintain a twenty-four hour alert readiness. The gooks were wearing them down.

The Army command was scared, and rightfully so. Every patrol they tried to send out came back nearly destroyed, if they came back at all. Patrols had evolved from priority activity to volunteer basis only, and from what CAP Command was relaying, CAP One had just volunteered.

We didn't begrudge the Army anything. We well understood the gravity of the situation. They were constantly being shelled by an enemy they could not see. Their efforts to return harassment barrages were typically thwarted by the accuracy of the mortars fired into the gun emplacements. The casualties were continuous. The psychological effects were taking their toll. Mentally and physically, Fat City was a shambles.

The Army did not understand how we could operate such a small unit without incurring casualties. In fact, they could not believe we had not been wiped out. Neither could we. We owed a large debt to the old chieftain, who had kept his word by sending us a network of informers. That, coupled with our knowledge of the bush and our ever-increasing ability to locate booby traps—thanks to Taan's tutelage—had literally kept us alive. The only areas for which our informers had failed us were the immediate area of School House Valley and the mountains bordering it on the west. The depths of the jungle growth there prevented the firebase, as well as us, from being able to zero in on the mortar's exact location. A muffled "foomph" was the only warning the tortured base ever received. Our intelligence efforts had failed miserably and the reason was simple: every farmer in and around the valley was under Cong control. To even talk to us was comparable to signing their own death warrant. They knew it. We knew it. We understood and respected their silence. The NVA and the VC had no qualms in utilizing their power to provoke fear. We fought desperately to win the villagers and farmers over with our genuine concern and offers to help. Fear tactics we saved solely for our enemy.

We established strategic patrols of School House Valley based on times that we felt might coincide with the mortar attacks. Yet even though we skirted the trails at the very base of the mountains, the VC all went underground, refusing to make contact with us. Why they didn't just wipe us out was beyond my comprehension. We knew by reports that there were hundreds, maybe even thousands of VC/NVA scattered throughout the valley. The surrounding mountains were honeycombed with tunnels, underground arsenals, and even complete facilities for companies of soldiers. Evidently the enemy was after much bigger game. We were a definite thorn in their side, but destroying Fat City was obviously a more desirable task.

As a CAP unit of only seven men, we were somewhat dubious about even patrolling the valley, much less trying to uncover the tunnel complex. I had a feeling that one reason we rarely had any contact there was that the Cong didn't want us meddling around in the area. That was why they were constantly sending patrols into our eastern sector. As long as we were receiving a regular line of informers from the other areas of our APR, they could rest assured that we would not mess with their valley. Up until now, their strategy had worked. However, their increase in mortar attacks had changed all the rules. The Army and CAP Command had made the "Mortar Gang" Priority One. The rest of our APR would have to wait. One hundred percent of our activity was to be spent patrolling VC Valley. Our clash with "Charlie" in his own territory was inevitable.

Their resistance was strong, however. In spite of our daily thrusts into the valley, we had to pull out to answer the calls for help from friendly villages. The Viet Cong knew that we would not be able to concentrate on searching for them if they kept us busy with attacks against other areas. They played upon our concern for the villagers' welfare. Nevertheless, we were determined to find them. After a brush with the VC in one sector, we would immediately return to School House Valley, but never from the same trail or the same direction. Our goal was to locate the Mortar Gang.

This type of action continued throughout the month of March. The Cong had us running back and forth so much that we were constantly on the move. We did not set up and wait, anymore, for them to come to us. In addition, we had no time for our other main duty, helping the people with their day-to-day work.

One day our illustrious CO decided that he was going to come out and show us how it was done. He was embarrassed by our lack of results with the Mortar Gang. His call came in at 0800 hours that morning.

"Go ahead, CAP Command," Lackey returned into the transmitter. The radio crackled with frequency interference as CAP Command keyed up to transmit the message.

"Say again, please. Your transmission was garbled," Lackey stated.

This time it came through. "Be advised that I am coming out to set up ambush with you guys tonight. We will heli-lift[1] to the old French quarters at 1830 hours and move out under the cover of darkness. Tonight we kick Charlie's tail. Over."

"Roger," Lackey said as he looked over at me. "You heard?"

"Yep," I answered, frowning with thought.

"What's the matter?" Lackey asked.

"It's his 'cover of darkness' idea," I said.

"Oh, yeah? What about it?"

"Tonight will be a full moon and a cloudless sky," I told him as I cast a gaze upward. "You and I both know that means Charlie will be in hiding tonight. They know that they are too visible on such nights. If we do much traipsing around Charlie will welcome us with an ambush."

"Yeah," Lackey agreed.

"Well, I'll go hunt down Rivera. You advise the rest of the men that we'll be spending the day in the immediate area," I ordered.

Rivera was where I expected him to be, with Sergeant Shôu. As I entered Shôu's hut, I was tempted to render a mock salute, but quelled the thought at the last minute. Rivera didn't worry me, but I figured Shôu could make life miserable, in many ways. I never knew what he and Rivera were planning—or whether it would be in behalf of the people or CAP. No great strategies or ideas came out of their meetings. In fact, all of our patrols and ambushes either filtered down from CAP Command or came from me, based on a tip from our Vietnamese informers.

I relayed the CO's message to Rivera.

"Where does he want to go?" Rivera asked.

"I have no idea. He didn't say, but it doesn't really matter. Tonight we have a full moon. If anyone sets up an ambush, it will be Charlie. But chances are they'll stay underground in lieu of being seen cavorting around in a full moon. At the most, they may set up a few booby traps." I finished my speculation. I didn't really know Charlie any better than anyone else. I just knew that on our previous full-moon nights we'd had little or no contact with the VC unless we just happened to surprise them.

"Okay," Rivera stated. "Let's just take the day off and stick around the compound. I'll stay here in conference with Sergeant Shôu."

"No problem," I answered as I spun on my heel. "You two have a great time now, ya hear!?" I yelled back as I left, while reminding myself that someday this mouth of mine was going to get me in trouble.

I found the men bunched up in the compound, milling around like grazing cattle. They had obviously been having some sort of pow-wow.

"What's up?" I yelled.

Jones waved me over. "We have a problem."

"I know," I said. "We're locked in Vietnam without a key."

He was not amused. "Seriously, Goodson," he began, "the thefts are on the rise."

For the past few weeks the men had been reporting thefts of various personal items. I had attributed the thefts to the "locals" and ordered the men to keep things locked away. However, the thefts didn't cease. I just figured the men were still being sloppy or leaving things lying around.

Jones continued, "Lackey was hit last night, or at least he thinks it was last night. It's a lighter his girl sent him from home, man. This stuff has got to stop."

"I agree. But I warned you guys not to leave things lying around," I reminded him.

Lackey overhead. "But I didn't," he protested. "I had it stored in my sea bag."

"Look," I tried to explain it one more time. "I've told you guys and you know it as well as I do, these people will steal you blind if you don't keep things locked up."

Jones interrupted, "Yeah, we know, except for one thing. . . ." He hesitated.

"Well?" I asked.

Mendez jumped in. "Well, there's one person in this unit who has never lost anything, or at least he's never complained about it," he stated. "Sergeant Rivera."

"Which means what, Sherlock?"

"Come on, Goodson. You know what we're saying," Jones chimed in.

"Yeah," Lackey agreed.

"You're accusing your sergeant of theft," I answered.

They all looked down momentarily, half ashamed of the accusation. They all knew Rivera as well as I did. They knew he was a good fighter when the chips were down, but there was another side to him—a closed side—a withdrawn side. He certainly had plenty of opportunity to steal from us since he stayed with Sergeant Shôu about half the time we were in the daytime bush.

They all stood there simply staring at me, waiting for my decision. "Come on," I said as I started off in the direction of our storage area, praying their suspicions were wrong.

We searched through the bags until we found it—a footlocker labeled "Sergeant Rivera USMC."

"You guys know that if you're wrong, Rivera can have them throw away the key on our cells."

"Hey, man, we're in hell already," Jones remarked.

"Yeah," agreed Mendez. "Jail would be paradise to this place. Besides, we know we're right."

"Stand back," I warned as I raised my rifle and slammed the butt down on the combination lock barring our entry. The lock was a cheap one and broke away easily. The men grew silent. Lock broken, we were committed. I bent over, removed the lock and tossed it aside. With one swift move, I swung the lid open. "Well, I'll . . . ." I couldn't finish the sentence. Rivera's footlocker looked like the inside of a five-and-dime store. Lackey's lighter lay right in the top tray, as pretty as you please, along with all of the other items we had previously attributed to the thievery of our local Vietnamese patrons.

Lackey broke the silence. "We were right!" he exclaimed in disbelief as he stretched out his hand to retrieve the lighter.

"All you other guys gather up what's yours and let's go pay the sergeant a visit," I ordered.

I was mad. So were the men. Whatever his excuse was, it didn't matter. His days as squad leader were over. I knew there was no choice. It was always bad when a man went down that way, but if we let him go there was no telling what would happen. He might turn against us in a sudden rampage, forcing us to kill him, or worse, one of us might decide to eliminate him on our own. Either way was no good. It was simple; he could no longer be trusted, in any way.

As we started across the compound, the telltale sound of approaching choppers echoed in the distant jungle. I stopped, searching the horizon. Suddenly they were there, two Chinooks closing in on our position.

Lackey came trotting, transmitter in hand. "It's the CO," he yelled.

I checked my watch. "They're two hours early!" I yelled, then keyed up the mike. "This is CAP One. Go ahead."

"CAP One, this is Bird Dog approaching your position. Give us a drop zone."

"You'll have to drop one at a time in the compound," I stated.

"Roger. Chopper Two will circle cover 'til we drop our load. Over."

I turned to the men. "Rivera's party will have to wait," I warned. "Right now everyone spread out and set up perimeter guard for the choppers."

They asked no questions. They knew the confrontation with Rivera would have to wait until the CO returned to Chu Lai rear. Each man spread out to the perimeter of the compound so that every direction was guarded. Chopper Two began a long sweeping circle with an inward lean toward the jungle below, keeping its bay door 60 trained and ready for possible sniper fire. The CO's chopper came down in a rapid swoop, with its massive blades chopping the air to maintain a hover position about two feet above the ground. The thrust of the blades raised a thick dust cloud that sandblasted our faces and momentarily blinded our eyes.

Without hesitation, the CO and his men jumped to the ground. The helicopter reached for the sky like an eagle in search of its prey, trading places with Chopper Two.

The last of the men leapt from the second chopper and joined our ranks as we turned our backs against the blast of sand left by the second chopper.

Reunited, the choppers struck off in search of Chu Lai rear and, no doubt, a cold beer and a warm nurse. I watched them disappear behind the treetops wondering what their part in the war was like. Did they have the same problems as our little unit? No doubt they enjoyed a few more luxuries than we did, but that did not overshadow the fact that they too had their "Hell on Earth."

"I still like my feet on the ground when I'm getting' shot at," I told Mendez. He let his eyes follow my gaze.

"Yeah man, but just think. One of these days one of those birds will be taking you out of this place . . . forever!"

As the dust settled and the typical jungle noises regained their foothold, we turned from our thoughts of home and mingled with the troops from CAP rear. My eyes searched out the CO. Deep down inside, I still wanted to blow him away for that night of Tết. Logically, now that emotions could be set aside, I knew that even harsh words with him would create more trouble than I cared to entertain. His eyes met mine. I swallowed hard and tried to convince my eyes to smile.

"Welcome. You're early." I extended my hand in lieu of a salute. "A salute would kill him for you," tempted a thought from somewhere in the depths of my mind. Although in the rear, a salute to an officer was mandatory, in the bush it was not a good idea to give away a leader's identity to any snipers who might be watching for a sign of leadership.

He shook my hand. "We decided it would be better to allow the men a brief time to get to know each other before we struck off into the bush," he said.

"Yeah, I guess so," I answered, turning to check out his men. I had to suppress a chuckle. The men were dressed in complete accordance with the book. Each one had the exact same issue: one canteen, one first-aid kit, two grenades, one bivouac pack with entrenching tool, brand new utilities and shiny boots. Even their ammo and rifles glistened from lack of use.

I turned my gaze to my men. Each one had four grenades, six belts of 60 ammo and an equal amount of their own ammo. First-aid bandages were the only other items we ever took with us, and we carried those in our pockets. We never carried canteens, packs, or entrenching tools. If someone had been comparing the two groups in a war movie, they would have thought that *we* were the crazy ones, the untrained misfits. In reality, our burden included only those items necessary to our survival. We had long since adjusted to the local wells and rivers, so we drank water where we found it instead of carrying canteens. If we got thirsty in an ambush, we simply chewed on a twig or a rock. We had discovered packs and entrenching tools to be absolutely worthless, since both were designed for taking care of a soldier who planned to stay in one place for a while. We didn't. We never dug a foxhole or a trench. As for food, the villagers and the jungle supplied all we needed.

"Hope your guys don't have to run tonight," I remarked to the CO.

"What?" he asked, not grasping my meaning.

"Never mind," I said, and wisely shut up before my mouth started the trouble I knew I had to avoid. Rivera was heading our way. "Here comes your man," I nodded toward him as I headed toward Jones and the others. "I'm going to make sure my men are ready. Call when y'all decide where we're headed."

Rivera and the CO shook hands and headed off to the shade of a nearby hut.

"What are they planning?" Jones asked as I walked up.

I glanced back in their direction. "Who knows?" I laughed, "But it's probably some place so safe you'll be able to take the time to write your folks a letter." I laughed again as the others joined in. The theft and Rivera were set aside for a more appropriate time.

"You guys all cleaned up and ammo checked?" I asked.

"We're ready," Mendez smiled, "except we can't find our canteens!" He acted shocked and dismayed as he started a mock search through his gear for the elusive container.

"Yeah, man," Jones smiled, "and what are those things on their backs? Are we going on a campout or what?"

"Good idea," Lackey piped in, "let's have a weenie roast."

Rodriguez was next: "Yeah, man, we ain't got no wieners or marshmallows or nothing."

That did it. We broke into a contagious laughter that proved to be the medicine we all needed to put the thefts out of our minds.

Suddenly very serious, Lackey grabbed my shoulder. I squelched a remaining laugh. "Yeah?" I asked, checking his face.

He was looking at our visitors. "Someone should warn them, don't you think? I mean, we may just hit some VC tonight."

"Yeah, you're right, Lackey," I said. "I'll go let them know they're overdressed, but I bet the CO's not about to let 'em junk it all." I headed off in their direction followed by Jones, Mendez and the others still muffling laughs.

"Who's in charge?" I asked. A tall lanky dude, a sergeant about nineteen or twenty years old, jumped up right at my heels. I stepped back a bit.

"I am," he said. "What can I do for you?"

"It's what we can do for you," I began. Jones and the others each picked out their own group to warn about their "overdress."

"It's the way y'all are dressed out," I said.

"What of it?" the sergeant said.

"Well, no offense, but if we find Charlie tonight, you're going to find yourself very overburdened."

"We're in standard Marine Corps issue."

"I know," I said, "but I guarantee that out here we never have the time or desire to dig in. We simply hit and run and then hit again. We are too small a force, even with y'all, to attempt to stand against the size of forces in this bush."

"I think I see what you mean," he agreed, "but the CO will never let us ditch this gear."

"No problem," I answered. "When we set up tonight, just take it all off and set it aside. If we have contact just keep your eyes on us. When we move, you move."

"Got it," he said. "By the way, I'm Sergeant Andrews."

"Corporal Goodson," I said extending my hand.

"Thanks for the warning," he said. "I'll make sure my men understand."

"By the way," he asked as he turned to leave, "do you think we'll see Charlie tonight?"

"Depends on what *they* decide," I nodded in Rivera's direction. "And of course it ultimately depends on the VC."

As I guessed, Rivera and the CO chose a spot that would allow them to say they attempted to locate the VC, but still stay far enough away to reduce the risk of contact. They chose a bunch of sand dunes about two miles east and north of the VC village just outside of Fat City. The area was definitely "VC," but far away from School House Valley and the Mortar Gang.

As the sun melted into the mountains to the west, we struck off to the north in search of the dunes. To make good time on the long march, the CO decided we should stick to the blacktop. The visiting platoon totaled about twenty men, including the CO. Counting us, that made twenty-seven marines and a handful of Vietnamese in search of Charlie. On one hand, it felt good to have so much firepower around. On the other, we had no idea how our new friends would react if a battle erupted. The long stretch proved to set me even more on edge than usual. Our visiting troops had obviously seen very little action. They marched along, poised in perfect military fashion, their equipment making enough noise to send alarms echoing for miles in all directions.

Jones made his way over to me. "What do you think?" he asked.

I looked at him and then at the rank of soldiers following us. "I think Charlie is too caught up in laughing at us to worry."

"Yeah," Jones agreed. "Let's hope he keeps laughing 'til dawn."

Just as the moon began its first glance through the dense growth of the jungle, we reached the dunes, which were laid out with a natural cover to protect us from the VC village. I spread my men out in a "lazy C" type ambush so we could detect movement from any direction. The CO intermingled his men with ours. As usual, I put Jones and his machine gun in the center of the ambush.

"Pass the word," I told Jones and Lackey, "every other man catch some quick Zs."

"Roger," they said.

I figured that we were in for a long night and that the men from the rear would probably fall asleep anyway. Allowing part of them the okay to sleep at least guaranteed half the unit would potentially stay awake during the waning critical hours of the night.

We all nestled down behind the windswept tops of the dunes, making sure that our silhouettes blended in with the contours of the surrounding terrain. Fortunately, the spot we had chosen had enough palm trees scattered around that even with the full moon overhead we were able to mingle with the shadows. My only concern was that a VC patrol might possibly approach us from the east, the ocean side. The probability was slim, since all the reported Viet Cong activity of late had been west and south of our position. Yet we were in VC country no matter where we were. To assume any area safe was suicide.

My thoughts drifted back to Everett's last night with us, when we had set up ambush in the same general area. Of course, there had been only six of us then, including the PFs and Taan, but it, too, had been a full-moon night, and the VC had not been afraid of it then. "Who knows," I thought, as my eyes searched the surrounding jungle east of us and slowly moved along to search the nearby dunes. The only rule I knew for sure was that Charlie was unpredictable.

The night seemed too still to me. The slightest movement—occasional sniffles and muffled coughs throughout our ranks—could be heard for a hundred yards. A chill ran up my spine as a wandering breeze reached me from the ocean. It moved among us like a ghost from wars previously fought. Suddenly it was gone—off to visit some other unit somewhere deeper in the depths of the jungle.

"If only I was a breeze," I thought, "I could visit enemy camps everywhere, label their numbers and weak points and slip away without the slightest trace." My eyes shifted toward the area surrounding VC Village. All I could see were the sand dunes vanishing into the dark shadows of the jungle. The village lay silent and deadly just within the dark covering of the tall coconut and palm trees.

"Where are you, Charlie?" I sent a telepathic message into the darkness, but got no answer.

With the grace of a hippo, the CO suddenly came half crawling, half running toward my position. I checked my watch: 2315 hours. The hippo plopped down beside me. "What's the deal, corporal?" he hissed. "I've found at least a half dozen men asleep and they claim you told them it was okay."

"Look . . . " I began.

"No! You look!" he half yelled. "No one sleeps in the bush. You should know that."

"With this many men, it's sometimes wise to allow half of them to sleep for awhile," I attempted to explain my strategy. "Half of them asleep provides a couple of things."

"Like what?" he sneered.

"Like for one, at least half the unit will be refreshed regardless of the timing of Charlie's visit. Secondly, with half the men asleep there is half as much movement and noise, barring any sudden outburst of snoring."

"Snoring!" he exclaimed. "That's all we need."

"Actually, I feel it's good strategy."

"You're kidding, I hope. You've got to be crazy!"

"Think about it," I whispered, trying to make him keep his own voice down. "Chances are very good that Charlie knows exactly where we are. In fact, I'd stake my life on it. So I figure that if Charlie hears a snore or two resounding into the night, he gets careless and just walks up boldly for the kill—when he does, we've got him!"

"Sounds stupid to me," he retorted. "Pass the word that all eyes are open," he ordered the guy next to me. He returned his attention to me. "One last thing," he whispered. "I want that M-60 in that growth over there." I followed his finger to a clump of small trees and bushes darkening the top of a sand dune about fifty yards in the direction of VC Village.

"Now you're the one that's gone Looney Tunes," I half laughed. "We never leave our 60 unprotected. Besides, if the VC approach from the ocean the 60 couldn't fire without risk of hitting one of us. No way, man. If you want it out there, you'll have to take it out there yourself or order one of your sidekicks to do it."

The moon illuminated the rage reddening the CO's face. "I've given you a direct order," he hissed through clenched teeth.

"Didn't hear it, CO," I stated.

"Neither did I," Lackey joined in suddenly.

The CO stood up like a brazen idiot. "You've talked yourself into a court martial, mister," he stated, pointing his finger at my face.

"Good," I smiled, "that'll get me out of this stinking place, and with skin intact."

Without further word the CO stormed off into the night, still fully upright, brazen and proud—a perfect target. A fleeting thought brought temptation my way as I watched him storm into the darkness. "Someone ought to put him out of his misery," I said, half to myself, half to Lackey.

"Yeah. Don't tempt me," he growled.

Suddenly, as if he had heard our little conversation, he dropped to the ground and jerked his head back in our direction. He obviously realized the stupidity of his storming tantrum.

"Now," I thought, as my gaze and attention returned to the VC village, "Charlie definitely knows we're here."

Evidently the Viet Cong were either sound asleep, on vacation or simply not in the killing mood. The rest of the night passed in complete silence with the exception of a half-dozen mortar rounds dropping on the firebase with its nightly barrage of destruction. The Mortar Gang had struck again.

"Those men must be nervous wrecks," I thought when I saw the flashes illuminate the night sky as exploding rounds causing havoc and mayhem throughout the base. To sit within a confined perimeter and wait for an attack from someone you could not see or retaliate against with any real hope of effect, had to be devastating.

The full moon faded to a faint glow on the western horizon as the approaching dawn turned the threatening shadows into the empty trails and bushes that they actually were. The tension of the night gradually subsided in retreat from the rising sun.

I passed the word. "Prepare to move out," I whispered. As the word went around, I searched out the CO.

Lackey followed like a man's best friend, radio in hand. "Choppers are on their way," he advised.

"Good," I smiled. "I guess he'll take me in with him."

"No way, man," Lackey scoffed. "We're not about to let him give you a vacation away from all this."

I laughed.

The CO was adjusting his gear and talking to the approaching helicopters. He finished his conversation, tossed the transmitter to his radio man and glared at me as I approached.

"Well, silent night after all," I once again tried the friendly approach.

"Knock off the humor," he ordered. "The only reason I'm not going to court martial you is that Command says we do not have a replacement available at this time."

"Good old Command," I sighed.

He raved on. "If it was up to me, I'd have you shot for disobeying a direct order during combat. So watch your step, mister. I'm gunning for you."

Rivera joined us.

"Rivera, you better get this man in line," the CO yelled as he watched the choppers start their descent.

"Roger," Rivera yelled back over the deafening prop wash. He shook the CO's hand, turned and frowned at me, then trotted off to the shelter of the nearby trees.

I smiled at the CO. "I enjoyed your visit. Come back any time!" I tossed him a salute, spun on my heel and headed off in the direction of my men. His answering remarks were drowned out as the choppers dropped out of the sky to give him and his warriors a ride home. I half turned a glance over my shoulder as I walked away, catching the look of fear on the CO's face as he stared momentarily at the hand that had swung up to return my salute. He quickly searched the surrounding area to make sure no one had seen his actions—especially the Viet Cong.

I continued walking toward the small group of men waiting for Lackey and me.

"You make friends easily," Lackey chided.

"Yeah," I returned as I turned to watch our visitors climb into the hovering choppers, "there goes a man we can trust—with our very lives."

Rivera gathered us all together and we struck out in the general direction of School House Valley. Nothing more was said about my pending doom. Along the way we paid a surprise visit to Mamasan Tôu. The men were due for a little refreshment and I wanted to see if she had any word on the Mortar Squad. Everyone settled down for a few hours of rest, letter writing and weapon cleaning. They each bought a beer or soft drink, carefully inspecting the cans for any signs of penetration or indentations. The VC were notorious for injecting poisons into cans and for putting bamboo shavings into bottled drinks. It was easier to detect tampering in the cans because of the absence of the telltale "hiss" of escaping air pressure when you opened it. Bottled drink tampering was harder to detect, because Charlie was an artist at prying off the lids so as not to scratch or damage the cap. The pulverized shavings he added, about the consistency of powdered sugar, couldn't be seen or tasted. Even the "hiss" returned with a properly-replaced cap. The reports of men drinking the stuff were gruesome. The bamboo passed through the stomach undigested, then lodged in the intestinal walls like thousands of little needles, allowing poisons to flow into the body cavity and causing massive internal bleeding. Death was painful and slow, lasting sometimes two or three days.

Mamasan Tôu had very little information that we didn't already know. She had, however, discovered that the VC were forcing the teacher in School House Valley to teach the children all the wondrous and honorable ways of Communism. "Hitler all over again," I thought. "Raise and train your own army of brainwashed kids." Charlie would also put pressure on the kids and their families to make sure the children showed up everyday. It was not unheard of for the VC to murder their own children as examples, to force obedience from the rest.

I thanked Mamasan and left to seek out Rivera. I found him off by himself, folding up a letter I assumed was to some loved one at home. Like the rest of us, he didn't write very often, simply because we rarely had an opportunity to "get it out of the bush." Besides that, the more we heard about the state of affairs in the states, the less incentive we had to put our hearts on paper.

I stood silently, waiting for Rivera to find a secure dry spot in his "jungle utes"[2] to stash the letter away for that magic day when a chopper could risk touching down. Letter secure, he looked up and asked, "What'd ya find out? Any sign of Charlie?"

"Yeah," I answered, "but no one's saying exactly where. I guess the chieftain's network breaks down in the School House Valley." I told him everything Mamasan Tôu had said.

"Do you think Charlie is in or around the school house all the time?" Rivera asked.

I thought a minute. "Well, Mamasan Tôu thinks so. And from what I could gather, the school teacher is loyal to our chieftain. So I would be willing to bet that she has VC visitors on a daily basis just to make sure she stays in line. In fact, I have no doubt that Charlie does his share of the teaching in person."

"Then we should pay the school house a visit and maybe try to get the teacher and the children out of there?" Rivera asked.

"No doubt we'll get some action there." I paused. "And if we're lucky enough to capture one, we'll get a little inside information." Again, I hesitated, hating the thought of what I was going to say: "Even if it means capturing one of the kids that may be a Viet Cong sympathizer."

Rivera caught my meaning and gave me an understanding sideways glance, then dropped his eyes to the ground. "Yeah," he said. "Get it set up with Command, then pick your PFs. We probably should head out right after dark."

"Roger," I answered and headed off to locate Lackey, who turned out to be by the roadside by Mamasan Tôu's hut, flirting with one of the local girls on her way to market.

"Giving away our secrets?" I asked.

He turned quickly to check my face for the telltale smile that would reassure him I was kidding. It was there. "Man, don't kid like that. There are enough suspicions around here already." Beads of sweat hung like morning dew on his forehead, which he swept away with the back of his hand. It was only April, but summer was on its way.

"Don't worry. You're above suspicion," I laughed, "but I know you weren't just passing the time of day."

He blushed all the way down to his boots. The girl fidgeted from side to side. "But . . ." he tried to protest.

I laughed again and waved at the girl. "Get her name and phone number. Maybe we'll be back through here in time for her high school prom." We both laughed, and the girl joined in even though she had no idea what we had said. When the laughter died down, I said, "Seriously, Lackey, send her on her way. We have eggs to fry."

He didn't hesitate. As he turned to make his final adieus, I sought shelter in the shade of a nearby palm tree and settled in to mull over the fast-approaching nightfall. Danger was in the air. I knew that tonight, full moon or not, a battle with the Viet Cong awaited us. It was getting to a point that I could predict a firefight with the same efficiency my grandfather had displayed in predicting the weather. His senses never failed him. I silently prayed mine didn't either.

We never wrote down any plans and we did not carry any orders on our bodies. The risk of them falling into the wrong hands was too great. However, as a form of personal protection, I always had Lackey act as my mouthpiece to the rear. That let them know that two people in our squad had heard the transmission from both sides, so the CO could never claim not to have approved our plans. Besides, it kept me from having to talk to our illustrious CO.

Lackey finally dropped the girl's hand and sent her on her way. As he stood watching her I watched her, too. "I hope she's not one of Charlie's girls," I thought to myself. "It would be so easy for her to disappear over the hill and then hurry to report our present location and numbers." I mulled it over as she did indeed disappear over the hill. An uneasiness ground away in my gut.

"What's wrong?" Lackey asked as he followed my gaze down the blacktop.

I looked up. "No offense about your girl, Lackey," I said, "but I have a very strong urge to get our unit back on the move."

He stood for a moment with pain showing in his eyes. "Yeah. She was awfully inquisitive," he said as he glanced back in her direction. "I'm with you."

"Well, let's call in our evening's plans and then head out. We have about ten miles to go and I'd just as soon not wait until the last minute to complete our venture into no man's land."

"Yeah," Lackey agreed again, staring at the place where the girl had vanished.

Mendez was heading our way. "What's up?" he asked. "Have you made any plans for the night?"

"Yeah," I answered. "Tell everyone we're heading out in ten minutes." I paused. "And if your weapons aren't clean, get it done quick, because tonight spells trouble."

His smile disappeared. "Roger," he said and hurried off to tell the others. Lackey and I completed our transmission to Command. I had urged them to advise Fat City about our plans and general location and also encouraged them to advise the army not to send out any patrols tonight, especially not in our area. I was not excited about an accidental firefight with our own men. Our objective was about a mile and a half from the firebase, where a fair-sized hill would separate us from them. I prayed that the army had gotten our message. We weren't allowed to talk directly to them and I feared that the message might get muddled up by the time it reached the right ears.

The ten minutes were up. "Everyone ready?" I yelled. Murmurs of agreement echoed back. Rivera and I inspected each man's weapon. "Today's the day," Rivera bellowed, "the day to kick Charlie's butt! Let's roll."

As usual, I spent a brief moment thanking Mamasan Tôu and Lín for their hospitality. I told Mamasan that we were going north to check on VC Village and that we would return in two days. It was all a lie and she knew it, but it gave her something to tell the VC when and if they paid her a visit. My thoughts returned to the girl Lackey had been flirting with earlier. I hoped beyond hope that she had no connections with our enemy, although the chances of her actually being a VC sympathizer far outweighed the odds that she was not. We could only hope that none of them paid Mamasan Tôu or Lín a visit. Their inevitable torture at the hands of some sadistic fiend was more than my mind could bear. I shook my head to dispel the mental picture, and I prayed that we would be around to prevent it. I knew, in reality, we would be far away if and when the torture began.

To add credence to my story, we struck off to the north straight up the blacktop in full view for all to see. We waved to every Vietnamese we ran into or saw by the roadside. I checked my watch—it showed 1600 hours. After about a mile, when we could no longer see Mamasan Tôu's hut, we left the blacktop and started up a trail which headed north by northwest toward VC Village. We continued for about another half mile until the jungle swallowed us up and not a soul was in sight. I called the squad to a halt and we spread out and settled down to wait a few minutes to make sure we were not being followed. Minutes passed as biting flies and mosquitoes tested our endurance. Finally satisfied that no one had followed us, we joined back up and struck out in the direction of School House Valley.

We stayed within the jungle, avoiding clearings and the farms surrounding the valley. Our only hope was to reach the school house undetected and surprise Charlie. We hoped that there would only be a small force and that reinforcements would be too far away to rescue them. I looked over our own men and "chosen" PFs, and realized that was exactly *our* position. Reinforcements were miles away at Command rear. Army artillery was supposed to be on standby, but all too often "Arty" was previously committed when our time of need arrived.

It was well after dark when we reached the clearing that opened out to the school house. We settled in and spread out so all eyes could search the clearing we had to cross. Fortunately, it was scattered with coconut and date palms, which offered very little shelter but did provide a spattering of shadows we could blend into. I checked my watch once again—it showed 2015 hours. Darkness had settled in and the moon was just beginning to glow in the eastern horizon. I made my way over to Rivera. "I suggest we beat that moon and move out under cover of what darkness we have."

"Agreed," he answered.

I put my hand on his shoulder. "What do you think about splitting the group up into equal units and sneaking in along the outskirts of the clearing? It will take a little longer, but would force their retreat into the rice paddies."

"Good idea," he answered. "Let's move out."

I passed the word. I took Lackey, Mendez, Taan and a couple of his men while Rivera led out with Rodriguez, Johnston, Jones and the remaining two PFs. We struck out into the rapidly decreasing darkness, keeping to every shadow like hummingbirds darting from flower to flower.

The school house was made of concrete blocks which had been painted white and were now covered with all sorts of Viet Cong graffiti and propaganda. It sat on a hunk of land that jutted out into the rice paddies sort of like a peninsula. As we made our way silently toward the school house, I studied it intensely. Rays of light from candles inside the building created dancing shadows in the cool night air.

"Someone is in there." I thought to myself. "Prepare to die, Charlie." I checked my safety. It was off. I turned to Lackey. "Prepare for action," I whispered as we settled down behind the last bit of protection left before we made it to the embankment leading to the door. Other than shuttered windows, the school house offered no exit except for the double front doors. It was one of the few buildings I had seen in Vietnam that actually had doors in lieu of a simple straw mat or a slab of wood slid into place.

A row of roughly finished concrete steps led up to the double doors. The roof was good old American corrugated tin, probably a gift from CAP Command sometime in the past. We stealthily approached the building from both directions. I could just make out Rivera and his men as they made their way over the embankment to within fifty feet of the school house.

All was quiet. Not even a breeze disturbed the muggy night air. We reached a spot directly opposite but on an angle away from Rivera's and settled in to study the area around the building. The sparse vegetation between us and the school house consisted of only a few scattered banana trees which provided virtually no protection. "This will have to be one of those all-out, one shot situations," I told myself. With no option available for a defensive stance, we had to make our initial assault one hundred per-cent effective. Anything short of success meant a sure death for all of us. The others sensed the same.

So far there was no sign of a guard or sentry of any kind. It looked as if they were not expecting us tonight. I glanced toward the sky and my jaw dropped about six inches. To my amazement the school house flagpole was boldly flying the North Vietnamese flag—Charlie's colors. It was unbeliev-able. It dangled limply, with an occasional flutter as the night wind un-furled the hidden bold red and blue stripes decorated with a single yellow star. The symbol of Communist oppression sent shivers dancing along my spine, not from my fear but from the memories of death and agony I had seen so many friends—Vietnamese and American alike—suffer because of the doctrine represented by that piece of silk cloth that hung from the pole above me. The flag unfurled again as a momentary shift of air made its way amongst our ranks. It seemed to look down on us in mockery of our efforts. "This school is mine!" it screamed. I had to wonder if the VC were brazen enough to fly it during the day. No doubt they were, as a trap to a searching Huey or a patrol sent out from Fat City firebase. Their patrol would have approached from the rice paddies, a clear, open target for the VC. "Clever," I thought, "clever."

Another chilling thought slid in unexpectedly. Another reason they may have flown the flag during the day was that Jets or Cobras[3] seeing the flag or even simply an army patrol, might see it and attack immediately without investigating what was inside. That would kill or maim the children and the teacher. The VC would, of course, retaliate—in mock defense of the children. They would become heroes overnight, fighting off the enemy they had adamantly warned the villagers about. No one would ever know the truth behind Charlie's schemes and plots. From their viewpoint, it would appear that Americans had murdered helpless children and a teacher for no reason. The flag was bait, I was sure, and if we failed tonight, the attack would come, sooner or later. The deaths would come, and the Viet Cong would have another stronghold.

Suddenly I heard voices inside. One of the double doors swung open with a loud creak. We flattened against the ground, still so warm from the heat of the sun that it sent a renewed energy through my body as I tried to blend in with the surrounding grass. The moon was well up over the trees and I felt sure that our bodies stood out like sore thumbs. Slowly, I stretched my hand to my belt to pull out a grenade. I could feel beads of sweat popping out on my brow. "That's all I need," I thought, as I envisioned the moonlight illuminating the beads of sweat like tiny spotlights shining into the darkness. I lowered my head and gently rolled it back and forth in the dirt. The beads turned to mud. I checked out Charlie.

He was gone! The door was still open but he was gone! Frantically, I searched the darkness around the school house. We could not risk him going out on a moonlight stroll to alert nearby reinforcements.

My eyes continued to search the darkness as I held my breath. Suddenly I saw movement. A single, solitary Cong stepped from the shadows to within ten feet of Rivera and his men. "Trouble," I thought. "He won't be able to miss them in this light." I froze as he took another step forward. We could not move from our position. It would mean sudden death to us all. Rivera would have to make a move.

A shadow moving across the doorway interrupted the dim light emitting from the interior. I peered into the opening. A second VC stood there, offering a perfect target as he was momentarily illuminated by the candlelight inside. The enemy snuffed out the candles as they prepared to head out, no doubt to harass Fat City. I hadn't seen a mortar anywhere, so I had my doubts that we had located out illustrious Mortar Gang. The teacher and the children seemed to be gone. Hopefully, they had been allowed to return to their homes in the nearby villages and farms. Nothing but the muffled voices of our bitter enemy broke the still of the night.

The rest of the VC stepped out of the building and squatted on the steps in their typical Oriental fashion, like a bull frog on a lily pad. Evidently, they were waiting for the man standing in front of Rivera. They darkened the entire steps of the school house. I tried to count but their bodies intermingled. "At least a dozen," I thought as I tried to formulate a plan of attack that would mate with Rivera's own thoughts.

I turned my attention back to the man who was now facing Rivera. He was taking a leak! I almost laughed as I thought of the situation. Rivera, no doubt, was far from laughing, but he wisely did nothing but watch the VC finish his duty.

Slowly, silently, I pulled the pin on a frag grenade, holding the handle tightly against the cold steel of the egg. Our lone Charlie finished his duty and turned back to his waiting comrades, completely unaware of Rivera and his men. I couldn't believe we were so lucky. He barked out an order to prepare to move out. "So," I thought, "here is our leader."

I let the handle fly as I moved my arm back by my side in a cocked position. A "flack" sound seemed to resound off the surrounding mountains as the handle bounced away into the night. One Cong turned his head in our direction but, unfortunately for him, must have dismissed the noise as being one of the creatures of the night. "He's right there," I told myself. "I am one of the creatures of the night." I mentally took aim at the leader as I counted off the seconds. "One . . . two . . . three . . . four . . . five." As I heaved the egg toward the unsuspecting Cong, I saw that Rivera's mind had been in sync with mine. He was unleashing his own messenger of death.

My grenade was a full eight-second one. I heard it plop and roll at the feet of the Cong. They heard it, too. They screamed and lunged away from the grenade in hopes of escaping the ripping metal following the inevitable explosion. It seemed like eternity passed as I waited for the three remaining seconds to tick away. Then it blew, breaking the still of the night with a loud, thunderous boom, illuminating the bodies of the surrounding VC. Three of them fell lifeless to the ground as shrapnel ripped their bodies apart. Another one screamed and momentarily clutched his left leg as he stared at what had once been his foot. Steam rose from the gaping wound as his warm blood flowed out onto the ground.

The remaining eight or so men dove for cover as Rivera's grenade exploded right in front of the man staring at his destroyed foot. His pain was over in a flash as his dismembered body was tossed into the shadows of the school house. Quickly we rolled and spread out on line to release a deadly barrage of gun fire on the remaining eight VC. They saw our movement and opened fire with their own barrage. The AKs filled the night with automatic fire as green tracers mingled with our own bright red tracers in a colorful dance of death.

Sand and debris stung my face as bullets ricocheted off the ground in front of me. We were sitting ducks! We returned their fire, knowing it would be only moments before they adjusted their night vision, zeroed in on our position, and picked us off. Our return fire was having little effect on the VC, who were all huddled behind the school house steps for protection.

"Fire!" I yelled at Rivera, wondering why he hadn't thought of it yet. Suddenly, the welcome sound of Jones's deep-throated M-60 bellowed out a hail of lead into the group hiding behind the steps. The barrage sheared the flagpole, sending it crashing to the ground. The Communist flag dangled over the school house steps, partially blocking our view of the enemy. Bullets were ricocheting into the night from all directions. Two more Cong fell under the hail of lead from the machine gun. The flag seemed to flinch in reaction as bullets and shrapnel ripped through its colors. As one of the Cong, already suffering from multiple wounds, attempted to flee, a hail of lead sent him careening backwards, ripping the flag from the splintered pole. The dead man rolled down to the bottom of the steps, his body stopping against a water basin at the base. Water trickled from bullet holes in the basin onto the dead Cong, while the "symbol of oppression" fluttered harmlessly to the ground beside him.

The remaining six VC suddenly jumped up and let go with rapid gunfire bursts, at first toward Rivera and his group and then toward mine, before they turned to run up the steps and into the school house. More sand sprayed my face as the rounds searched for their target. I rolled to my right as hard as I could. My fellow marines followed. Just as the VC reached the top of the steps we each fired simultaneous bursts. When Mendez fired his M-79, we all hugged the ground. The projectile exploded off the doors. Three more Cong released their spirits as their mangled bodies decorated the steps.

Jones downed another one as they all dove into the depths of the darkness of the school interior. We continued firing at the doors to keep them pinned down inside. Once the bullets passed through the dark opening of the doorway, they began a ricocheting dance off the walls inside. Another scream told us a ricochet had found its victim.

Mendez opened up with a barrage of M-79 grenades as fast as he could break open the breech and slide another shell into place. "Boom— Boom— Boom" echoed into the night.

I motioned my men forward to move in for the kill of what we hoped was just one remaining VC. As we ran toward the doorway, I pulled the pin on my last grenade. Mendez followed suit. We tossed our grenades as hard as we could through the doorway. Mine exploded first, ripping one of the doors from its hinges. As it bounced down the steps, Mendez's concussion grenade let loose its shocking explosion. A final scream filled the night air as the last Viet Cong staggered from the interior, clutching his head in agony. Blood was pouring from his ears and mouth. His eyes looked as if they were going to explode from within. I took aim with my M-16 and prepared to put him out of his misery, but death saved me from the duty as our sole remaining enemy stumbled over a friend's body and rolled down the steps, coming to rest with his lifeless body staring up at the moon.

Without hesitation, we burst inside the school house to make sure all the VC had been killed. The dark interior offered only the silent echo of our entry. The battle was won. The firefight was over. I heard single shots from Rivera and his men as they made sure that all of the VC were dead.

"Let's get out of here," I told Mendez and Taan as we satisfied ourselves that the building was indeed empty. On our way out, we quickly searched the building and the bodies for any information that might be of some use to us. The school house revealed nothing. The bodies had only ID cards and photos of loved ones.

The ID cards bothered me. They were supposedly only issued by the South Vietnamese Government to people they were sure were "anti-Communists." Anyone with an ID card could infiltrate just about any base, firebase or Command rear with virtually no resistance.

"Security is breaking down somewhere," I stated to Rivera.

"Yeah," he agreed, "that could prove dangerous for all of us."

"No doubt about it," I answered. "No one can be trusted anymore."

We gathered up the AKs and Chi Com grenades and tossed them into the muddy depths of a nearby river. We left the bodies as they had fallen, as a warning to the Viet Cong we knew would be coming to investigate the sounds of the battle.

"Hey, there's bound to be a VC patrol heading this way, don't you think?" Jones asked.

"No doubt about it," I answered.

"They why don't we set up an ambush?"

"Two reasons," I said. "First, we don't know how many there will be or how much fire power they carry. Second, I'm low on ammo and I bet the others are too."

"You're right. We're down to about 500 rounds of 60 ammo between all of us."

"As a final gesture we can booby trap a few of the bodies," I suggested.

"Good idea," Rivera said. "Who has grenades?"

"I do," Johnston offered.

"Yeah. Me too," Lackey joined in.

I took their grenades and pulled the pins on each one and lodged them under the bodies in a way that would keep the handle depressed until the body was moved again. Instantly, three bodies became deadly traps. I could only pray that no innocent villagers messed with the bodies before the VC got there.

Job finished, I turned to Rivera. "Let's move out fast. I can feel them coming already."

He didn't hesitate. He motioned the squad toward a trail that would take us back to the east and, hopefully, toward a short rest from the long night's events. I was exhausted. None of us had received any injuries, nor had any of Taan's men. The battle had been a complete success. We disappeared into the jungle, leaving the death and destruction behind, for a while. I checked my watch. It was 0300 and the night was but a memory. Yet I knew it was a vivid one that would be etched into my mind forever.

To confuse any VC that might be following, we changed directions constantly, although it was risky because they might have already set up ahead of us. It was a risk we had to take. The hours ticked by. Finally, just as we left the steaming jungle and stepped onto the blacktop, the sun greeted us. Rivera had us all settle down for a rest. We watched the blacktop begin to show signs of a busy day as a few people walked down the road in hopes of beating the heat. Each one nodded and smiled knowingly at the small group of marines covered in dirt, muck and blood. Taan and his men mingled with the crowd of their fellow Vietnamese, and soon headed off by ones and twos. The passersby never questioned our condition. The scene was all too familiar to them; they knew somewhere in the jungle someone had died last night. It wasn't that they didn't care. The reality was that death was commonplace. Back home, a scene like this would have sent people into a panic, or at least make them call a cop.

"Where to Rivera?" I yelled as I noticed him handing the transmitter back to Lackey.

"Back to French quarters," he ordered.

"Okay, men, let's move out," I said as I thought once again how predictable we were becoming. Actually I didn't mind returning there today. My uniform had already been covered in two weeks' worth of muck before last night's encounter. I was ready for a shower and a change of clothes.

Our shower was an empty napalm shell, a donation from Command, complete with a screw valve to release the cold water we got from a well located right in the midst of the rusted concertina wire surrounding our compound. As each man finished, he replaced the water he used. The locals loved "shower day" for two reasons. It meant income for the local mamasans who washed our utilities and socks for us and it drew a crowd of giggling girls and boys since we had no way of building walls around the shower. Large American bodies, covered with so much hair, provided quite a contrast to the typical Vietnamese body, with no hair other than on their heads and rarely exceeded 5' 5" in height.

I tried to ignore the local admirers as I completed my shower. I was tempted to grab one of the girls and have her join me, but I shoved the thoughts aside. I did not want to join the ranks of those who took advantage of the locals in any fashion, and I did not want to be taken in by a spy for the VC.

I put on my clean utilities and socks. Underwear was never worn due to the inevitability of jungle rot in all areas tightly enclosed by elastic bands. With an old rusty bucket in hand I began the chore of refilling the shell with more cold well water. Jones was waiting impatiently. "Got it full yet?" he quizzed.

"It's all yours my man. Just hold your breath when you get in."

"Water that cold?" he asked.

"The discovery is all yours," I yelled over my shoulder as I poured in the last bit. I laughed as I watched him look up at the shower valve as if he were thinking, "Do I dare?"

I decided to hunt down some breakfast. The search was brief. Hordes of locals met me at the gate with their offerings. The old standby of sour-dough bread with raw strips of meat was impossible to refuse. I heaped on some Nước Mặn sauce and settled down for a quiet morning meal. Occasionally bugs or weevils would crawl from the roll as I chomped down for a bite, and I would set them aside for the chickens that scurried underneath our feet. Johnston noticed my little ritual. "Trying to fatten one up for the kill, mate?" he asked as we watched two chickens fight for the bugs thrown them.

"Not a bad idea, my Australian friend. Not bad at all. How about yourself? Have you ever sunk your teeth into a tasty bit of fried chicken?"

"Why sure," he answered. "It's considered part of our primary diet back on the Island."

"Kind of sets you thinking doesn't it," I said. We both fixed our eyes on the nearest victim.

"Have to wait 'til we have time to cook the blimey thing though," Johnston added.

I was just finishing up the raw fish sandwich when Taan walked up, smiling from ear to ear and holding his hands behind him. I stopped chewing. "What's up?"

Taan didn't answer. He brought his hands toward me and revealed the prize he held behind his back. I couldn't believe it. There in his hands lay a neatly folded Viet Cong flag.

"You want?" he asked.

"You're giving this to me?" I was incredulous.

"Yep," he smiled real big, proud that I was affected by his generosity.

"Is this the flag from last night?"

"Yes," he said.

"Yahoo!" I yelled, elated with the thought that we had captured their flag. "It's great, Taan, just great!" I rubbed his head briskly with my open palm. He laughed and sidestepped to escape the attack on his scalp. I studied the flag, complete with bullet holes and bloodstains from the night's battle.

"Now," I said to myself, "how do I get this home?" I knew that men would kill for that flag. I also knew that if I just wrapped it up and sent it to the rear for mailing it would never make it home. I had to come up with a plan.

"I have it!" I exclaimed with a sudden burst of energy.

"What? Have what?" Taan asked.

"Come on." I urged him toward our storage building. When I found my duffel bag, I unlocked it and dug into its depths for a previous treasure from home—a fan. I laughed as I recalled the letter I had written home about how hot it was getting, and how my mother, being a good mom, decided to help me. The next thing I knew, I was opening a package that I was sure was cookies or some other sweet treasure. I rolled in laughter as my eyes stared at the fan in the box. Mendez had taken it and run around and around, forcing the blades to turn, yelling, "Look, it works!" We all laughed until we could laugh no more. I wrote my poor Mom with sincere thanks for the present and asked if she would mind sending a hundred-mile long extension cord. There was, of course, no electricity for miles. In fact, I had nearly forgotten what an outlet even looked like.

Holding the fan in my hands today, I explained electricity to Taan and we both had a good chuckle at my mother's expense. Then, using my knife as a screwdriver, I removed the back from the fan, wrapped the flag in a plastic bag that had at one time been a home for my socks, tucked the flag neatly inside the housing and replaced the back cover. I stuffed a note between the blades advising "whomever" that the fan was being sent home for repair because it did not work. I chuckled to myself. It was true the fan did not work—not without electricity. I wrote a separate letter advising my mother to remove the back of the fan and take out the contents before she tried to operate it.[4]

By then it was around 1500 hours. We had all settled down to clean our weapons with the government-issued cleaning gear that had finally arrived, which was a good thing because my Dad's cleaning gear had not made it to us. It took at least thirty days for a letter from us to reach home, and the same length of time for return mail. Packages took even longer. I imagined that somewhere in the U.S. Mail archives there was a package from my dad to me, marked "Urgent." I vowed again that when I returned home I would pay a visit to the company that had been on strike. I was forming quite a mental "hit list" to pay back those who had harmed us in one way or another. Hate was building a solid home within my soul.

Suddenly Lackey's radio crackled with an abrupt message. "CAP One, this is Command rear. Over."

Lackey grabbed the transmitter. "CAP One. Go ahead. Over."

The radio came alive with a voice neither one of us had ever heard before. "CAP One, we need your Victor November.⁵ We're paying you a visit in a matter of minutes. Over."

Lackey looked at me. "Could be the black guy and blonde guy that have joined the VC," he suggested.

"Yeah, could be," I answered. I looked around for Rivera. He was not in sight, obviously meeting with Sergeant Shôu again. I made my decision.

"Whoever it is, bring them in. We'll be ready for them."

"Roger," Lackey smiled. He keyed up the transmitter to advise them of our location. I left him with his chore as I rounded up all of the rest of the men. I was just finishing my plans with them as Lackey came trotting up. He caught my eye. "They'll be here in about fifteen minutes."

"Okay, let's take our positions," I ordered.

"Where's Rivera?" Rodriguez asked.

"Who knows?" I answered, "Just take your position. Rivera will show up if he hears any gunfire."

Minutes rolled by slowly as we waited for our "unknowns" to arrive. Suddenly in the distance, toward Chu Lai rear, we heard the telltale roar of a jeep fighting its way down the blacktop. I breathed a sigh of relief as it came into sight. "I guess the traitors wouldn't be paying us a visit in our own jeep," I thought as I watched the jeep make its way. "Relax guys," I yelled out. "Looks like one of the good guys."

The jeep rolled to a stop. A young man jumped to the ground, emblazoned with polished captain's bars on his shoulders and his cap. He was so polished that I almost threw him a salute.

He stuck out a hand. "Howdy. I'm Captain Anderson of the Entertainment Corps."

I shook his hand. "The what?" I said as my men gathered around.

He acted equally shocked. "Why, I'm your Entertainment CO in charge of making sure you guys are happy and content." He seemed serious.

I thought my men were going to embarrass themselves as they literally rolled around on the ground in uncontrollable laughter. I was not amused. "Look. No offense, Captain, but we just finished a hard night with Charlie and we don't need someone from the rear out here telling us he's going to entertain us."

"Wait a minute," he answered, holding his hand out like a traffic cop. "Do you mean to tell me you don't know anything about me?"

"Not hardly," I answered, "and if you don't mind me saying so, the very idea of entertainment out here in the bush is ridiculous."

He didn't even hear me. His thoughts had taken him someplace else. Finally our visitor spoke. "Look, every week for the past six months I've been sending two cases of iced-down beer and four cases of soft drinks to you guys. And now you tell me you've never heard of me?"

It was my turn to react. "Soft drinks? Beer? Look, I don't know what you're up to, but we pay the local mamasans a buck a piece for drinks and they are rarely iced down. So who's pulling whose leg?"

Anderson simply shook his head and searched the ground for answers. The answer became obvious to both of us simultaneously.

"Black market," he said.

"Yeah, looks like it," I agreed. "I'd say you've been entertaining the black market goons for the past six months, making them rich."

"Yeah," he agreed. "Look. . . ." He was suddenly alive with energy. "Let me make a call to the rear."

"Be my guest," I said as we turned back to his jeep. He grabbed the transmitter of his radio, stopped for a moment and looked at me. "Whoever is responsible, I'll nail him to the wall," he said. I walked away to allow him to do what he felt he had to do. I stopped in front of my group of thirsty marines and decided we could all use some levity. I looked them over and took on the role of an enraged general. "Men," I said as I paced back and forth in a mock ritual, "I want to know what you have done with six months of beer and soft drinks." I stopped, studied them with my most fierce look, then continued. "Jones, step forward. Lively now."

He did as ordered and stood at full attention, stifling a grin. "Sir! Yes, sir," he yelled.

I walked around him in mock inspection, then stopped in front of him. "Let me smell your breath," I bellowed.

"Sir! Yes, sir," he yelled again as he blew in my face. I grabbed my throat and nose and fell to the dirt. "It's him! It's him! Grab him!"

Lackey and Mendez quickly subdued our marine. We all convulsed with laughter as Jones yelled: "They made me do it. They made me do it."

Anderson interrupted our little charade. Lackey and Mendez released their prisoner, sat back on their haunches and waited to receive the news.

"Corporal Goodson," he began, "and you men, please accept my sincerest apology. You and I are definitely victims of the black market."

"Hey, man, don't worry about it," Jones piped in. "We ain't got time for entertainment, anyway."

"Well, I'm going to make up for it today," he grinned from ear to ear. We waited for his plan. "A chopper is on its way with six cases of iced-down beer and soft drinks, along with assorted nuts and other goodies. So y'all have fun," he added.

"Yee haw!" I yelled.

No sooner said than done. We could hear the chopper approaching from the south. I looked at Captain Anderson and extended my hand. "Sir," I said, "you are a man of your word."

He shook my hand firmly. "I try to be," he said, showing that smile again.

I slapped him on the back and said, "Now get out of here before I start liking an officer."

He laughed and headed for the jeep. Stopping momentarily, he studied the ground, then turned back toward me. "I'll find out whoever is behind all this," he said, "and that's a promise."

I watched him go. "I have no doubt," I thought, "no doubt at all."

The helicopter settled down as Anderson's jeep vanished in the direction of Chu Lai. The crew unloaded our goodies—bags of chips, crackers, and nuts, along with beer and soft drinks smothered in ice.

Taan walked up just in time.

"Go get your friends, Taan. We're going to have a party," I said.

He laughed and then in all seriousness asked, "What is . . . party?"

I smiled and changed my approach. Grabbing an ice cold brew, I popped the top and shoved it his way. "Go show this to your friends and tell them there is more where that came from."

That he understood. He grabbed his prize and headed out in search of party animals. I reminded the men of our daily beer limit and then—the party began.

Taan returned with a dozen eager PFs in search of this thing called "party." We all settled down to some serious drinking and eating. About an hour later, we were laughing and sharing stories. Mendez was telling us about his home town high school days.

"What are you going to do when you get back home?" Jones asked him.

"Don't know for sure," Mendez answered. "I try not to think about it." He frowned and sipped his beer, suddenly serious.

L–R. "Rodriguez," "Mendez," "PF Dau" and "Lackey," standing in front of the old French headquarters.

"I'm going to get married and take a bath in this stuff," Johnston yelled out, holding his beer aloft for all to see.

"Who you going to marry, some Aborigine?" Rodriguez prodded.

"No way, mate. She's the most beautiful blonde in the whole blooming world. Here take a look." He held out a well-worn photograph. His display drew sighs from all the admirers.

Our moment with beauty was suddenly interrupted when one of Taan's other men came running up to us. Thinking he was going to join us, we offered him a beer. He waved it away as he pulled Taan aside.

Suddenly Taan dropped his beer and stared in my direction.

"What is it?" I asked, reaching out for my rifle.

"Come," he said.

I tossed my own beer to the ground. We left the rest of the men to their party and moved out of earshot. Taan turned to me. "Villagers find dead soldier, dead American soldier!" I understood his secrecy. He feared, as the villagers did, that we would blame the death on them and retaliate with anger.

I returned to the group. "The locals have discovered a dead American soldier in one of the huts down the road. Mendez, you're in charge. Y'all continue your party. I'm off with Taan to check it out. If you hear gunfire, it means it's a trap, so stay alert."

I looked around at them. The party had obviously lost its steam.

"We'll be ready," Mendez promised.

"Yeah," the others chimed in.

"So much for party time." I forced a smile, turned and walked away, joining Taan to search out the dead GI.

We entered the small hut alongside the blacktop about two kilometers south of our little party. Face down, sprawled out on the floor, was an Army soldier. Carefully I felt underneath his body to make sure it wasn't booby trapped. Satisfied that all was safe, I rolled him onto his back. I didn't know him, but I had not expected to. The army and the marines each kept to their own little world.

A brief inspection of the body revealed no visible reason for the man's death. There were no wounds of any kind. I asked Taan to check the surrounding villagers to see if they knew what had happened. One old mamasan stepped forward as Taan spoke. She was holding an object in her hand. Taan retrieved it and passed it over to me. It was weed—a joint of marijuana. "That couldn't have killed him," I said, more to myself than anyone else. I broke the joint open. White powder dusted the air. I covered my mouth and nose as the dust settled and disappeared into the dust of the floor. "Heroin," I said aloud. "I didn't know you could smoke the stuff."

"Number ten,"[6] Taan added as he looked on. "That bad stuff."

I looked around the room and then returned my attention to the deadly cigarette in my fingers. I fought back the rage boiling up inside of me. "Taan, send your men for Lackey and the radio. We need a chopper to get him out of here."

"No problem," Taan turned to his comrade and issued his orders.

Lackey and Johnston returned with Taan's PFs. Johnston perfunctorily checked the GI for vital signs. He looked up at me. "He's definitely a goner."

"Where did he come from?" Lackey asked.

"No one here seems to know," I answered. "He's probably from the firebase. Chu Lai is too far away. In fact, even Fat City is a little far."

I looked him over once again. He had no information, no papers or ID. Nothing on him but his dog tags.

"You don't think he could be one of the guys that's been working with the VC?" asked Lackey.

"Must admit the thought crossed my mind," I answered, "but if he was, that means there were more than two. This man has dark brown hair. The two descriptions we have were of a blonde dude and one black man."

"True," Johnston said.

We all stood looking down at our fellow soldier. Where did he come from, and why? His dog tags said he was Specialist Givens. All else was a mystery.[7]

The "chop, chop" of the approaching helicopters interrupted our thoughts. Within moments Givens was bagged[8] and loaded. I watched as the chopper disappeared behind the trees; taking the soldier on the first lap of his journey home.

"Wonder what they'll tell his parents," I asked the others. "He *was* killed by the Viet Cong, but no one will look at it that way. They'll say he was just a doper, and won't stop to think who put the heroin in that cigarette."

The mental picture of the dead Army soldier sprawled on the dirt floor of that hut haunted me as I made my way back to the party. Why had he been there? Had he been alone? Was he planted there after dying someplace else? What unit had he been with?

I shook my head sharply to escape the questions for which I had no answers. They immediately came back. I shook my head again, almost falling down. "Get out of there," I said out loud. "Leave me alone."

Taan placed a hand on my shoulder, with an understanding look in his eye. "Corporal be okay," he said. "Army soldier dead not your fault!"

I simply stared at him for a moment, then laughed and shoved the haunt into the already-crowded room in the back of my mind.

"You're right. Let's finish that party."

"It don't mean nothing," Taan said, repeating the words he had heard us utter so many times before. I wasn't sure he knew what they meant, but that was of no importance.

Taan didn't hesitate. We both felt in need of a drink. Indeed, except for one fact, we would have enjoyed getting stone-faced drunk. The fact? To be drunk in the bush meant death. Painful memories had to be dealt with in some other way. Our way was typically to cover one bad memory with another. Seek and destroy the Viet Cong; release our wrath on them. Create a memory to hide a memory. A vicious cycle out of control. It was just as well we weren't set on finishing the beer, because Lackey's radio crackled out a message as soon as we entered the old French compound.

"CAP One, this is CAP Command. Over."

"Roger, Command, go ahead," Lackey relayed back.

"CAP One, be advised that we are sending out Lance Corporal Thompson to spend the night in the bush with you. Over."

I stared at the radio, then squeezed the transmitter. "Who is Thompson —and why? Over."

"Be advised," the CO's voice was stern, "that Thompson is one of my top men and he has only three weeks left in country. I want to send all my men home with medals but cannot do so unless they spend some time in the bush. He is already on the chopper and should be at your site in a matter of minutes. Over."

I couldn't believe it. This idiot was sending a short-timer, an office pogue, into the bush, just to give him a worthless piece of metal. The idea boggled the mind. The poor man was probably scared beyond belief, and for good reason. The CO could have just signed Thompson's death warrant. The man had no combat experience and no time to learn it. We would have to protect him the best we could without endangering our own lives.

I squeezed the transmitter with all my might hoping to see it explode in my hands. As it had in the past, it ignored my death grip and awaited my last transmission. Vicious names and insults flitted across my mind as I searched for the proper retort to let the CO know how truly stupid I felt he really was. Words failed me. "Roger, Command," I snapped and threw the transmitter back to Lackey, whose hands shot up in defense against the projectile I had hurled his way.

"Sorry, man!" I apologized as I realized what I had done.

"No problem, man. I can't believe our CO can justify sending a short-timer into the bush. That's like handing the man a death warrant for his own body. How could the CO be so stupid?"

"Born that way, I guess," I proposed.

The sounds of the approaching chopper brought a sobering solemnity to our party. We all stood and watched as the lucky marine jumped from the hovering bird. He waved at the men still inside as if they were friends dropping him off at a party.

He was a clean cut, right-out-of-the-USMC-manual type of marine. Polished brass, spit-shined boots and a starched, heavily creased uniform.

He boasted the same gear with which his predecessors had been laden. I shook my head and stepped forward to greet him.

"Corporal Goodson," I stated as we shook hands.

"Yeah, figured so," he said. "I'm Lance Corporal Thompson. Just call me Ben."

"No problem," I answered. "One question, though."

"Yeah?" he asked.

"Do you have any idea of what you've gotten yourself into?"

He read my mind and laughed. "I think so. I'm a lowly Remington Raider[9] who's never set foot in the bush. I'm scared beyond comprehension and want absolutely nothing but to go home. Does that answer your question?"

I stood silent for a moment watching the chopper disappear over the trees. "Yeah," I said. "No offense, it just seems like a dumb move to make when you're so close to home."

"Boy, don't I know it," he answered, "but I have no choice."

I nodded. "Come on," I urged him forward. "I'll introduce you to your new friends."

After finishing his howdies, Thompson asked if he might address the squad.

"Sure," I said. "They're all yours."

He nodded and turned toward the men. His face grew taut and serious. "Men," he stated, then paused to gain strength for what he had to say. "I'm no coward and I promise you I'll do my part if we get in a firefight tonight. It's just that the CO has decided that the best feather in his bonnet is to send every man—even us office pogues—home with a medal. I must admit that I would only refuse one if I didn't deserve it." He paused again, obviously finding it difficult to say what he had to say. "The main thing I want y'all to understand is that I don't want to be a burden to you, but I also don't want to die in the three weeks I have left. I need you guys to protect me."

I stepped in. "Men, Thompson is with us for only one night. He's inexperienced, but I have no doubt that he'll carry his own weight." I turned to the short-timer. "Thompson," I said, looking him right in the eye, "the only way any of us have survived so far is by the grace of God and by each one of us learning to watch out for the other. We are one big happy family of which you have just become a part. You carry your load and we'll carry ours. The rest is up to God."

I turned back to the men. "Okay, guys, listen up. Tonight is a black night and I have no doubt that Charlie will be out and about. So make sure your gear and weapons are ready for action." With that I glanced at Thompson, smiled encouragingly and set out in search of Rivera.

I still had not decided what to do about our sergeant. He obviously knew by now that we had been in his footlocker, or at least that someone had. I hoped that maybe just knowing that we knew about his thefts would be punishment enough. It might be a good idea to let him stew on it for awhile. Maybe he'd go whacko trying to figure out when we were going to have him hauled off.

Rivera's curiosity about all the noise must have gotten the better of him. He was just entering the compound as I was leaving to find him. "What's going on?" he asked.

"We have a visitor from the rear," I stated. "One of your illustrious CO's men."

"Why?"

"He wants to pin a medal on him, of course!" I laughed. My answer made him back up against the gate post. I filled Rivera in on the day's activities and concluded with a suggestion to set up our night's ambush by Fisherman Village, the old chieftain's village.

"Good idea," he agreed. "That's probably our safest bet for no contact."

I checked my watch. It was 1815 hours. "We better head out now," I suggested. "Charlie will be active as soon as it's dark and I'd rather he walk into our ambush than have us walk into his."

"Sounds good," Rivera agreed as he turned and headed off to assemble his gear.

"Saddle up, men," I ordered. Most of them were already decked out and ready for the night—whatever it might bring.

I grabbed my rifle and made my way over to our newcomer. He looked nervous, real nervous. "Thompson, for your sake and ours, I'm going to have to ask you to shed all that extra gear. None of us carry food. The jungle and the villagers take care of that. And as for the entrenching tool, well, we never dig in. If we're not on the move, we're dead. When we fight the Cong we use natural cover and maintain an open back door. And one last thing," I knew he wouldn't like this one. "Get shed of that canteen. If your mouth gets dry, chew on a twig or a small stone. Canteens are too noisy, even the plastic ones, and they're just excess weight. There's plenty of water out there and some of it will make you sick. But sick is temporary. Dead is *dead*!"

Thompson did not argue, but instantly shed every item. He was more than eager to obey my orders in his attempt to survive the night. I looked around for Jones. He was giving his M-60 a final going over. I smiled knowingly and waved him over. He headed our way, 60 in tow.

"Jones, we need a couple of . . ." I began.

Without waiting for the order, Jones held out two belts of M-60 ammo. While he was helping Thompson put the belts crisscross over his chest, I dug out four frag grenades and handed them to Thompson.

"We only hunt Cong," I laughed, "but we go loaded for bear."

Rivera showed up ready for the night.

"Okay, men, let's move out," I ordered. I took the lead. Our route took us immediately off the blacktop, northeast into the jungle. The sun was just touching the tops of the tallest trees. The jungle shadows were already long and dark, setting my nerves on edge.

Taan was supposed to meet us about a mile into the jungle, close to the area where we had demonstrated our axes and our chopping ability to the locals. We made good time. The trail was relatively dry since we had not had any rain for a number of days. That made the going easy, but noisy.

Taan and his four men were in plain sight as we rounded a banana grove. "Good," I thought. "I don't want any mistaken identities tonight." Taan mingled his men with mine and then took over point. I didn't argue. Taan knew the land better than anyone and had a special sense, not only for booby traps, but also for the enemy.

Our destination was a trench between two paddy dikes right on the southeastern edge of the sand dunes that in turn led to the VC village about six kilometers farther west. A number of trails converged right in front of the trench, sort of a footpath interchange. If the Cong moved tonight and tried to head east, we had them. Fisherman Village was south and east of our final site. We decided not to take the action too close to the old chieftain so as not to risk his life.

By the time we reached the trench and positioned each of the men, it was dark. There was not even a hint of a moon, and you could not see your hand in front of your face. I put Thompson beside Jones, because I knew Jones was a strong survivor and I could depend on him to help our "newbie" if I bought it. We settled in for the wait. My thoughts turned to Thompson and the men responsible for his being placed in such a dangerous situation.

My heart went out to him. We had to be there, but he was someone else's pawn.

An hour passed. We were halfway into the second hour when I heard a noise behind me. I readied my rifle, but my sense warned me to wait. I let the man approach.

A hand reached out and tapped my boot. "Corporal Barry!" came a quick whisper. It was Taan. I lowered my rifle and he settled down next to me. "We need to leave," he urged. Experience had proved that Taan had an extra sense when it came to dangerous situations. I did not question him.

"Pass the word," I ordered.

Taan turned to one of the younger of his four men, a boy about sixteen, and ordered him to go from man to man advising them to prepare to move out by a gentle tap on the foot. It was a signal we always used and every man knew it. That is, every man but Thompson. I had forgotten to tell him about it before we headed out, and unfortunately, I didn't think about it now.

Taan and I had left the trench and were waiting for the others to gather. We were quietly discussing where he wanted to go when the night was interrupted with a long automatic burst from an M-16. In an instant, Taan and I knew what had happened. We ran to Thompson's position, hoping the shot had not met its mark.

We were too late. The sixteen-year-old boy lay sprawled out on the ground, full of gaping holes. Steam rose from the blood as it drained from his lifeless body.

Thompson sat staring at the boy. I could see that he realized his error. He gazed up at me. "He touched my foot. I thought he was VC," he muttered. I said nothing, but squeezed his shoulder with my hand. I understood more than he would ever know. Again, my heart ached for him. His only night in the bush and he had killed one of our own men. "God, help him," I thought. It was my fault, not Thompson's. I should have remembered to warn him. I knelt beside the dead boy and cursed myself for my mistake.

Suddenly the other PFs came rampaging forward, rifles threatening. Taan moved in front of Thompson, blocking their fire. Then I remembered. One of them was the boy's brother. We were about to see a lynching party. My men moved in behind them, weapons cocked and ready for my command.

"Dừng lại!" I yelled, not caring about the obvious danger we were in from the VC. At that moment, the VC were immaterial. "Taan," I ordered, "stop your men! You know it was a mistake!"

Taan studied me for a minute, as if wondering whether it truly was an accident. Satisfied, he turned back to his men and barked a vicious order coupled with a threat.

"Lackey!" I yelled.

"Yo!" he yelled back as he handed me the transmitter.

I squeezed the transmit button. "Command, this is CAP One. Contact. Over."

"CAP One, this is Command. Contact. Channel is clear. Go ahead."

"Roger, Command. Be advised that we have one man down and one for medevac. Send a bird to grid 438110. Over."

"Roger, CAP One. Bird is on the way."

Rivera moved over to me. "Why the chopper?" he asked.

"Thompson," I said as I motioned in his direction. "You can bet that boy's brother and friends will find a way to kill him if he spends another minute in the bush."

"Probably so," Rivera agreed.

"I figure we'll set the chopper down in those dunes back toward the ocean. We'll surround Thompson until he gets on board. They won't risk a shot with us on full alert."

Rivera nodded as we made our way to the dune area. Within minutes, a Huey arrived along with two Cobras to subdue any approaching VC while we concentrated on loading up Thompson. We popped a flare. The Huey settled down to a hover over the dunes, waiting for our man.

"Let's go," I yelled as we surrounded Thompson and backed our way to the hovering chopper. The sand from the prop wash blasted us from all directions.

"Sorry, man," Thompson yelled as he jumped into the chopper. "I really thought he was VC."

"Don't worry about it," I yelled back. "I should have warned you. It's my fault. We'll take care of everything here, but do me a favor."

"Name it," he yelled back.

"Tell the CO to let this blow over for a week or so before he sends another man out. The PFs would probably shoot him on sight."

"Roger," he answered.

The chopper lifted into the sky to join its friends. I turned to my men and Rivera as the dust settled. "Let's get out of here pronto."

We rejoined the PFs, who had settled down to a low growl with their threats. They were not pleased that I had taken away their opportunity for revenge.

Taan stopped us. "My men are very mad," he said. "They want to kill all marines."

I wasn't surprised. I figured the next few weeks would be touch-and-go until our Vietnamese counterparts were able to deal with their hurt and anger in another way. They too had shelves already overcrowded with bitter memories.

Since so much activity had let the Cong know our position, Taan and I decided to return to our original trench to wait out the rest of the night. We figured that the Cong would set up ambushes along the trails leading away from it, and the trench at least offered natural cover from all sides.

The rest of the night, however, passed with no further interruptions. The early dawn light seemed to somewhat lessen the tension of the night, but threatening glances kept bouncing our direction as we prepared to move out.

"Taan," I motioned him over. "We'll be glad to build a carrier for the boy," I offered.

He glanced back at his men. "No," he said. "They want to kill you now and would if you touch boy's body."

"Okay," I said. "Let's move out," I ordered as I motioned the men forward.

I turned back to Taan as we walked away. "Look me up this morning. We're returning to the old compound. We have to get this settled—today!" He nodded and waved us on.

"God help us," I thought. "Our illustrious CO has once again caused havoc and mayhem, and this time we may be doomed." The PFs had us outnumbered about eight to one. If they wanted us dead, our only chance was a prayer. Somehow, we had to convince them that it had been an accident. We couldn't just call out the choppers to haul us away. That would seem like admitting guilt. Besides, we would be deserting the villagers and the old chieftain, leaving them to the mercy of the VC. Everything we had fought so hard for would be overturned instantly.

"No," I thought. "We'll just have to figure another way out."

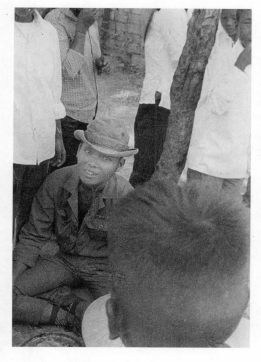

The boy wearing the hat is the PF that Thompson accidentally shot.

---

1 Heli-lift refers to helicopter transport.

2 Refers to "utilities," the marine field uniform. In the army, the same uniforms are called "fatigues."

3 F4 Phantom jets and Huey Cobras.

4 The flag did make it home and is still in Goodson's possession.

5 Victor November indicates the letters "V" and "N," which stand for "vicinity," i.e., a position on a map in terms of coordinates.

6 "Number ten" is marine slang for "poor quality" or "last," with "number one" being "the best."

7 There was a dramatic increase in the use of drugs among American forces in Vietnam during 1968–69. By 1969, about a quarter of U.S. soldiers were using marijuana on either a regular or occasional basis. In addition, American troops began using hard drugs by that year, especially heroin. George Donelson Moss, *Vietnam: An American Ordeal* 2nd ed., (Englewood Cliffs, New Jersey: Prentice Hall, 1994), 332; Ronald H. Spector, *After Tet: The Bloodiest Year in Vietnam* (New York: Free Press, 1993), 273–78.

8 "Bagged" refers to the body bag in which dead U.S. soldiers were placed.

9 Remington Raider refers to the fact that Lance Corporal Thompson was a clerical worker, Remington being a brand of typewriter. About one in six American soldiers in Vietnam served in a support troop.

## Chapter 10

# April 25—Bunker Day

**F**or a couple of weeks following the boy's death, the air was filled with tension, distrust and fear. During the day the villagers shunned us and refused our offers of help. They even refused our medical treatment for their sick and wounded. At night, Taan would arrive with fifteen or twenty of his fellow PFs in lieu of the traditional three or four. When we set up ambush, he no longer mingled his men amongst mine. Instead, we took opposite sides and simply sat staring at each other, waiting for the other to make just one wrong move. Our true enemy, Charlie, was completely ignored, and it seemed likely to me that he would soon collect the reward he had posted for our lives. I wondered whether the PFs would cash in on the reward or simply kill us for their own satisfaction.

Eventually, our good deeds of the past must have weighed heavily in our favor, because the fine line was never crossed. Time subdued the overt hatred and bitterness, but our relationship with all the Vietnamese people had changed. The distrust could not be shaken. The CO's quest for glory had almost destroyed everything we had spent all our time working and hoping for.

At the beginning of the second week in April, 1969, CAP Command dropped another bomb on our already shaky state. They sent out a chopper with a new replacement. Lackey was looking towards the southern horizon as I walked up.

It was a cool morning. The ocean breeze was gently swaying the slender palms bordering the perimeter of the old French compound. A spattering of morning clouds nestled among the mountain tops towering above

School House Valley. I followed Lackey's gaze, sheltering my eyes from the rising sun.

"Whatcha looking for?" I asked, still searching the horizon.

"Command just radioed that a chopper is dropping off a new replacement," Lackey said.

"Replacement for who?" I asked. "None of us are due for rotation."

"They said he is a 'Kit Carson scout.'"

The sounds of the chopping blades interrupted our conversation. We both stood in silence as the Huey circled in for the approach to their LZ. The pilot had decided to set her down right in the middle of Highway One.

As the bird dropped from the sky, the Vietnamese in its path fled into the protection of the jungle. Part of the roof of a nearby hut ripped away as the chopper settled to the blacktop. The papasan came running outside shaking his fist at the helicopter. I sent Taan to reassure him that we would immediately set things in order after the helicopter left.

I watched as a rider jumped out of the open bay door of the Huey. He was a short Vietnamese, approximately five-foot-two, dressed in the new style jungle utes and sporting a black beret for a cover. To my amazement he was followed by two other men loaded with gear. I waved all three over as the Huey lifted off.

I had heard of the new Chieu Hoi Program in which the rear air-dropped leaflets into the jungles with hopes of enticing the enemy to surrender to our side and help us fight against their own troops. It made absolutely no sense to me. Why would they choose to fight against their friends, the liberation fighters? If they truly believed in Communism, how could we possibly convince them to become traitors? The program seemed to me like an open invitation for VC infiltration.

I watched as they trotted towards me, and I looked directly at our Chieu Hoi. I did not trust this man. If he sold out his friends, how could we trust him?

The chopping sound diminished to a distant "thump, thump," as our new men gathered around.

"Chào ông," I greeted them all with a slight bow, my eyes never leaving the ex-NVA. He was small but extremely stout. He extended his hand. We shook.

"How are you?" he said. "I am Ton Tín Ho." He handed me his orders. Taan rejoined us and I asked him to make the new man feel at home. I turned to the other men and shook hands with each.

"Y'all are a sight for sore eyes," I said.

"I'm Lance Corporal Thomas, Frank Thomas," one man said. "Glad to be here, I guess."

I laughed and turned to the next man.

"Name's Paul Speck. PFC Speck," he said.

"Welcome to our country club, gentlemen," I said. "You're just in time for a field trip."

Johnston came waltzing up. "Hiya, guys," he yelled out. "Want me to show 'em around?" he asked me.

"Sure," I answered. "I need to study Kit Carson's orders." I waved toward Johnston and spoke to the new men. "Doc Johnston will take care of y'all."

As they gathered their gear and followed Johnston, I said to myself, "Two new men. That is definitely a pleasant surprise. I wonder about Mr. Kit Carson, though." I started reading through his orders.

According to the orders, Ton Tín Ho had been an NVA anti-aircraft gunner in the Ashau Valley and had been shot by "Puff" a few months back. The 7.62-mm mini-gun pumped seven rounds into his body and he lived to tell about it. He was captured by a marine patrol, nursed back to health, and convinced to join our side.

"Doesn't sound like a true volunteer," I mumbled.

"Say what?" asked Lackey.

"Our new man," I stated. "Let's keep an eye on him."

"Think he's a plant?"

"Could be," I said. "Could be."

During the days that followed, Ton Tín Ho did his best to fit in by catering to every request. He was likable enough and adamantly swore allegiance to us. Still, we kept a watchful eye, never allowing him to be alone.

On April 25, CAP Command told us that the temperature was supposed to reach 140 degrees with a hundred percent humidity. They advised us to keep to the shade. We took their advice and were lazing around the compound, basking in the sun, when Taan approached me.

"Corporal Goodson," he greeted me.

"Yo, Taan," I smiled back.

His words came hard. "Barry, we no longer blame you and your men. We know now the boy's death was not your fault. Many people sad. Some still not trust you." He paused. "I trust you and tell them they wrong. We friends, okay?" He stuck out his hand.

The words were like gold! "Friends forever, Taan," I smiled and shook his hand vigorously. I could feel the tension leave instantly. It would never be the same as it had been, but it was a start.

"Let's release some tension on Charlie, how 'bout it?" I suggested.

Taan never turned down a good fight. "Yes, let's go!" He set off in search of his men.

I found Lackey lying in the shade. "Hey, man, you can't get a suntan in the dark," I chided him.

"If I get any darker," he returned, "Jones will start calling me 'Bro.'"

I laughed. "Where *is* Jones?"

"Off praying," Lackey stated.

"Good. We'll need it."

"Yo, Mendez," I yelled.

He raised the banana leaf he had been using to cover his eyes. "Yeah, man, what's up?"

"Hunt up everyone. We're moving out in thirty minutes," I ordered.

"Roger," he said and set out to round up our strays.

"And don't forget Jones—he's praying," I yelled.

Mendez waved in acknowledgment and headed off.

Taan returned with three men. I smiled and nodded my head in a slight bow of reverence and acceptance to them. They understood and returned my greeting.

"On the road to recovery," I sighed. "Transmitter, Mr. Lackey." He handed it up and then laid back down. I chuckled at him and keyed up the transmitter. "Command, this is CAP One. Over."

Moments passed. Obviously they were once again up to their old tricks of delayed answer. I was considering joining Lackey in the shade when the radio finally crackled.

"Go ahead, CAP One. Over."

I fought back the urge to commend the operator for being so eager. "Command, be advised that we are going into School House Valley and the countryside on the west side of the valley in search of VC," I paused. "We'll set up ambush there tonight. Over."

Lackey bolted upright, eyes wide open, staring at me as if I had just signed his death warrant. I looked back at him and attempted a smile.

The radio was silent again. "Did you copy?" I barked into the transmitter.

"Roger," came back a reply. "You almost made me choke on my sandwich. Over."

"Okay, listen good, Command," I stated. "We'll be around the mountain about ten clicks southwest of Fat City firebase. Please advise Arty to not fire within 1,000 meters of Grid BT 452 075. Over."

"Roger," came a reply. A pause. "And, CAP One . . . good luck. Over and out." The radio fell silent.

My heart felt heavy and my hands were sweaty, the telltale warning signs my body and mind had developed to warn me that I was about to engage the enemy. I swallowed hard and issued a silent request to God, "Give me courage and strength, O Lord, and deliver us from the oncoming night."

I glanced at Lackey. He was still staring at me. "We'll get 'em," I encouraged him. A hollow, dry feeling rose up in my stomach. Death was in the air. I knew it. Lackey knew it.

"Let's gather the others," I suggested, more than ordered. Soon we were all together with the exception of Rivera, who had rejoined Sergeant Shôu. I had not checked with him before telling CAP Command of our ambush plans, but when I did find him and tell him, he said he would join us in the bush around 1600 hours. We would have to leave a PF runner to bring him to us. I didn't like the idea, but I had no choice. I looked at all of the men. I could tell that they already knew we had a difficult assignment. Except for the new guys, they all knew me and my expressions well.

"Men," I swallowed hard again. The feeling would not go away, but I did not want to show them I was afraid, so I tried again. "Men, we are going into School House Valley, and to set up ambush there tonight. We have only one chance of eliminating that Mortar Gang and that is to go in after them. To destroy them we must attack them on their own turf."

I watched "Kit," as I had dubbed him. His face showed no fear or surprise. The other men's reactions surprised me.

"Guess it's time to clean up the old backyard," Jones muttered.

"Yeah, those blooming gooks have been a nuisance too long," Johnston chimed in.

Even Rodriguez was positive on the idea. "Yeah, man, it's time to get them off our backs," he agreed.

Thomas and Speck looked quizzical. They had no idea of what lay in wait for them.

"I admire all of y'alls courage," I admitted.

Lackey laid a hand on my shoulder. "Hey, don't worry," he said. "We'll nail their hides to the wall."

I looked them over once again, soaking in the memories I shared with each, knowing without doubt that some of us, if not all, would probably not make it out of School House Valley, on foot anyway.

"Tonight," I began, "we need to at least double up on ammo and grenades. Don't overburden yourselves, but realize that an all-night battle like we had during Tết is more than likely. Make sure all weapons are clean and knives are sharp," I paused, "and if you have a prayer, send it on its way— Priority One!"

They all laughed then turned solemnly and went about their preparations. "Men," I yelled after them. They all stopped. "We move out at 1500 hours." They each nodded acknowledgment and turned back to getting ready.

Taan and I studied my map of the jungle. On it, School House Valley was just an innocent-looking, shaded green area with little black dots portraying farmers' huts. It could not tell us of the hell that awaited us. Taan and I agreed on escape routes and rendezvous points if we got split up. With the night planned, I handed Taan two belts of 60 ammo for himself and two for each of his three men. I had never asked them to share our load before. He understood my message without a word passing between us. "No problem," he assured me and turned to deliver his presents to his men.

I checked my watch. It was 1500 hours. "Okay, men, let's do it," I yelled. They were ready. We left the compound and struck out due west into the jungle that separated us from School House Valley. We crossed the old railroad track ruins in silence and chose a trail that led directly to the School House, where I had decided to wait for Rivera and the PF guide. I didn't like the idea of just the two of them crossing half a mile of rice paddies in open valley, unprotected.

The going was fast. The rain we had was very light and the ground was baked from the ever-increasing heat of the approaching summer. Since I knew exactly where we were headed, I took point to give Taan's mind a rest for the real challenge of the mountain terrain that lay ahead of us.

About halfway to the valley, as we were making our way through a small banana grove, I suddenly came face to face with the largest spider web I had ever seen. It was suspended between two seven-foot banana trees, with a span equally as wide as their height. The entire trail was blocked by monstrous strings of white that intertwined to create an awesome trap that glistened and sparkled in the sunlight filtering through the treetops above. My awe of the web was overshadowed as soon as I discovered that it was the home for the largest spider I had ever seen. We had no means by which we could measure him, so I could only guess about his size, but the monster was huge. His body looked to be about a foot long. He was as black as sin and covered with glistening, bristly ebony hair. His eyes looked like a multitude of black blisters clustered on the front of his head. His legs were a brilliant orange spotted with shorter, yet identical, ebony bristles. I waved the squad to a halt. I had heard of these spiders, but did not know they had them in Vietnam. South America had them—known generally as Bird Spiders. This one, I discovered later, was known as a Banana Spider and ate not only birds, but anything that was careless enough to stumble into its network of sticky cobweb.

Memories of old Tarzan movies filtered through my brain. Giant spiders were heading for Boy and Jane, who were caught helplessly in their webs. I laughed at the memory and checked the surrounding area until I found what I was looking for, a bamboo pole about ten feet long. The men had gathered behind me. Taan's men hung back with obvious fear in their faces. I laughed. "Afraid of a little old spider?"

"Ugly looking monster," Jones offered.

"Yeah," I agreed. "Y'all stay back while I knock him and his web out of the way."

They didn't argue.

*Blunk.* I swung as hard as I could in hopes of getting the spider and the web, simultaneously, with one sweep of the pole. Much to my surprise, everything went according to plan. The spider fell to the ground and the web ripped into two pieces, dangling on each side of the trail. Fortunately, the pole end had followed the spider to the ground. In response to my attack, the spider rolled onto its back, wrapped its ugly legs around the pole and set about sinking its fangs into the bamboo. Very soon I discovered that he was surprisingly strong as he pushed against the ground in an attempt to force his way free of the pole.

I was just beginning to wonder if I truly had the strength to crush the monster when I felt a hand shove hard against my shoulder. I stumbled to the side, dropping the pole. Just as I gained stability the silence of the jungle was broken by the sound of a fully automatic burst from a carbine.

One of Taan's PFs had seen my fight with the spider and had run up, shoved me aside and blown the spider into hundreds of pieces.

He studied the remains of the spider to make sure it was dead, then visually searched the area around the web as if looking for another one in the bush. Satisfied, he turned to me in disgust. "Anh beaucoup điên kiện dầu!" he muttered, and walked away shaking his head.

Taan walked up and together we looked at the monster's remains. I was almost mad at the PF for spoiling my fun. Taan looked back at me, shaking a finger in my face. "You are crazy. Spider Number Ten. Kill men with bite. Very bad, evil, spider. Walk along jungle path and leap on men, women, children, animals like tiger and kill them. Dâu save you life, Corporal Barry."

"You're kidding—aren't you?" I checked his face. No, he wasn't kidding.

We struck out toward the school house. Taan walked point with me to further explain why PF Dâu had so abruptly taken over. The Vietnamese both feared and revered the monster spider of the jungle, which they called the Jungle Devil. According to Taan, the spider had a bite equivalent to that of a King Cobra and was able to jump approximately fifteen feet, especially when provoked. It was believed that the spider would enter villages at night and carry away goats, dogs, chickens, and sometimes children. Taan assured me that they had found remains of children entangled in its webs. I did not doubt him and thanked God for once again saving my life.

Minutes later we came upon the palm grove that opened up to the area around the school house. We settled into the cover of the jungle. Taan and I had agreed that we should remain under cover until Rivera arrived. My eyes searched the building still nestled innocently among the palm trees of the tiny peninsula that jutted out into the rice paddies. It showed no signs of the battle we had fought. The doors had been replaced and the bullet holes painted over. Today the building was empty. In fact, there was not a soul around.

We settled back to wait for Rivera. "He should be right behind us," I said to anyone who cared. It was 1545 hours.

Dâu looked at me again. This time he smiled. "Beaucoup điên kiện dầu." He laughed and just shook his head.

Rivera didn't make it until 1645, which put our nerves just a little on edge. We didn't like hiding in such sparse cover at the edge of a valley boasting heavy Viet Cong activity. I had neither comment nor greeting when he finally showed up. I simply motioned Taan to lead out. Rivera could fit in where he pleased.

Taan led the way to a trail that disappeared directly behind the school house. The feelings of the battle previously fought tempted my mind as we passed it. We hadn't even bothered to check it when we first arrived, and we now assumed it to be vacant because of its silence during our wait for Rivera. Taan stopped at the edge of the last bit of bush cover, raised his hand to call us to a halt, kneeled down and studied the open terrain before him. There was no need for the signal, but it was just as natural for Taan to give it, as it was for us to automatically stop to investigate the opposite side of a clearing or valley before attempting a crossing, especially this one.

Being in School House Valley was like stepping over the dare line we used to draw in the dirt as children when challenging someone to a fight. The mountain side of the valley was a stronghold of the enemy. The valley was their dare line. We accepted their dare. I quietly made my way to Taan's position.

"See anything?" I asked.

"Nothing," he answered. "Only nothing, but I don't like it."

"Neither do I, my friend," I said. "Neither do I."

We both studied the bush of the opposite side until our eyes hurt from the strain. The crossing was a good half-mile and would take fifteen or twenty minutes due to the zigzag pattern we would have to take.

Taan was ready. "We go!" he exclaimed.

I patted him on the back and watched intently as he stepped out on the dike. I motioned for three men to follow him. Then I stepped in line just ahead of Jones and Lackey. Johnston, Rivera, Rodriguez and PF Dâu followed up the rear. Mendez was in front of me. "Kit" fell in step beside me.

Taan led a fast pace with a constant change in direction. Had we chosen to cross at night, our crossing would have been different. We would have crossed on line, straight across the paddies, keeping to the water. The Cong typically set booby traps along the trails snaking across the dikes. Rarely were the waters of the paddies booby trapped. One exception was the placement of bamboo sticks so that they would stab you in the leg as you tried to step out of the water onto a dike.

At night there is a risk of a booby trap escaping even the most scrutinizing eye. Since the Vietnamese had trained us, booby traps stood out like stop signs during the day, and we easily avoided or deactivated them. We kept a watchful eye out as we crossed the valley with only an occasional glance to our rear. What was behind us did not concern us, at least not as much as what stood before us. "Surely they're watching us," I thought. "You just don't walk undetected into someone's front yard."

The main thing that bothered me was that as far as the eye could see in any direction there was not a person to be seen—or an animal, for that matter. Had it not been for the well-worn path under our feet, as well as the blatant markings of Ho Chi Minh sandals, we might have thought the place was dead.

Fifteen minutes passed and Taan stepped from the last dike onto a trail leading into the bush of the adjoining mountain. We quickly, quietly joined him. The crossing completed, we continued up the mountainside, breaking into two small groups spaced about fifty feet apart. I took the lead of the second group. The going was rough, in rocky terrain covered with a multitude of vines and vegetation. We never used machetes or any other trailcutting tool because of the noise they created. In addition, a cleared trail left an equally clear message of our presence and provided the enemy the opportunity to sneak up on our flank with relative ease.

We continued straight up the mountain until we reached the peak. No signal was used or needed. We automatically stopped to see what lay before us. A beautiful, serene farm nestled in a small clearing about a hundred yards down from the peak. A crudely constructed hut sat against the bordering jungle. Bamboo pole corrals revealed pigs and a water buffalo quietly, lazily milling around seeking shelter from the sun. Two dogs were lying on their backs under a small banana tree growing at the rear corner of the hut, at the opposite end of which stood a large clay pot filled with water. "Good," I thought. "I could use a drink." A drab-colored cloth hung limply over the opening of the hut.

The cover of our approach to the farm was fairly thick until within a hundred feet or so. On the side facing us was a large garden and potato patch. Leading to the rear of the house was a grassy clearing surrounding a long mound of earth covered with a bamboo growth. Keeping a watchful eye, we silently moved forward. The dogs had not yet detected us. Only minutes passed before we finally closed in on the unsuspecting farmer. I stopped my group and spread them out along the bamboo mound. Taan's group quickly, silently made its way to the front of the hut.

I heard a menacing growl from one of the dogs, then silence. Suddenly I heard talking, a full-blown conversation. I waited, watching the rear of

The School House Valley hut where the farmer who was hiding the Mortar Gang lived.

the hut. Nothing. Not a creature was stirring. Sweat from my forehead soaked into the dusty ground below me. I wiped my hands on my already soaked utilities, then checked my watch. Over two hours had passed since we left the compound. It was now 1705 hours.

I heard steps. Mendez came waltzing around the corner of the hut. "Come on out, guys," he yelled. "The place is clean except for the farmer and his family."

We followed Mendez to the front of the hut. There stood Taan, engaged in a discussion with the farmer. Surrounding them, with intent expressions, were two small children, a girl and a boy, their mother and an older girl, eighteen or nineteen years of age. She was pretty and showed only slight signs of the wear and tear of the bush which were bound to come upon her like a plague in just a few short years as she took on the responsibilities of the farm and family of her future husband.

Temporarily satisfied, Taan let the questioning drop and the farmer and his family stepped back inside. That bothered me at first. Normally, the children would mill around us, at first in awe and then, more boldly, in search of bits of food or candy. We never carried food, but we did try to carry C-Rat[1] chocolates or cookies to help make peace with the kids. I didn't like the smell of it, but chalked it up to our being strangers to them and their area.

Taan and I agreed that we should set up around the farmer's hut until dark to make sure neither he nor any member of his family would sneak off to inform their VC friends, if they had any. The wait would not be long. Dusk was only about two and a half hours away, giving us plenty of time to give our weapons one more going over before the inevitable battle.

I pulled out of my pocket a small 35-mm camera one of Taan's friends was trying to sell to me. I had borrowed film from Jones and decided to take it on a trial run. Taan and his PFs were keeping a watchful eye on the family as well as the surrounding area. Rivera and the others settled down in the clearing behind the bamboo mound. I set out to take the pictures that would prove or disprove the camera's capabilities.

"Hey Rivera," I yelled out. He looked up. "I'm going to wander around and snap a few pictures."

"No problem," he said as he settled back down against the banana tree. With camera in hand, I took a winding path back down the side of the

"Kit Carson," "Jones," and Goodson in School House Valley the day Goodson was hit.

L–R. "Rivera," "Thomas" (in back), "Rodriguez," "Kit Carson," "Speck," "Jones" and "Mendez." Taken in School House Valley the day Goodson was wounded.

L–R. "Thomas," "Mendez," "Rodriguez," "Kit Carson," "Jones," "Johnston," and "Lackey." Taken in School House Valley the day Goodson was wounded.

The photo Goodson took just before the CAP unit and the PFs discovered the Mortar Gang. He was standing near here when he was wounded.

mountain. I don't know why, but I felt fairly secure, even cocky. I found a place where I could take pictures of the valley we had crossed. Satisfied, I began a slow easy climb up the mountain to search for promising, photogenic creatures I could photograph on my return to the farm. I wished that I'd had the camera loaded when we first discovered the spider. *That* would have been one for the family back home to see.

My trek took me to the edge of the farmer's potato patch, where I followed a bamboo fence with rusted barbed wire wrapped around each pole. At one time the fence may have had a purpose. In its present condition I doubted it kept anything out. Rounding the fence, I slowly circled the farmer's hut and corrals, snapping pictures I felt would be interesting. A few of the men came over to see how the camera was doing. We took turns taking pictures of each other in small groups.

Leaving the men to their own discussions I walked to the center of the potato patch. PF Dâu and another of Taan's men walked around the hut, making their way toward me. They had just stepped onto the soft, freshly tilled earth of the patch as I attempted to focus my camera on them.

Without warning, one of the men tripped and fell to the ground. Through the viewfinder of the camera, I could see the other man grabbing for his rifle. I left my camera dangling from the strap fastened over my shoulder just as the sound of an AK-47 broke the stillness of the jungle around us. I grabbed my M-16 and crouched low, searching for the source of the fire. The man who had fallen rolled rapidly away from the area he had fallen into and yelled, "VC! VC!" I followed his pointing finger. He had stepped on the trap door of a Viet Cong bunker. We had found our notorious Mortar Gang.

Within seconds Taan, Rivera and the others had joined us. PF Dâu and I crawled up to the bunker opening, dropped a couple of grenades on the trap door and then hugged the dirt to be clear of the inevitable shrapnel. The grenades blew simultaneously as the door disappeared in a puff of flame and smoke. The explosion shook the ground, making my ears ring. We converged on the opening, firing as we approached and tossing more grenades. Muffled booms ripped from the hole as the undetected grenades found their mark.

Suddenly a hand shoved its way through the smoke filtering from the hole. I opened fire, hoping to force the man out. My bullets found their mark but not before the hand tossed a projectile in my direction. A shiny gold can came to rest at my feet. I looked at it as seconds ticked away, my mind confused with battle. "Why would he throw out such a beautiful gold plated can?" I thought. Then realization penetrated. "Homemade grenade!" With a war whoop, I dove backwards to escape the wrath of the oncoming explosion. I rolled as I hit the ground, readying my weapon to continue the attack. Hours seemed to pass as I waited. Nothing! The grenade was a dud.

AKs broke the silence again as the VC tried to force their way out. Fire came out the bamboo cover behind us as the VC attempted to escape from back door hatches. We lobbed concussion grenades into the gaping hole of the bunker and rolled to the shelter of a shallow drop-off at the edge of the potato patch. The AKs were growing in ferocity as more VC emerged from hidden holes.

We returned fire with equal ferocity and were joined by Mendez's trusty M-79 grenade launcher. The explosions opened the bamboo thicket just enough for us to see the black PJs of our enemy. "Give 'em hell," I screamed. We cut loose with everything we had. Suddenly the battle was interrupted by the telltale explosion of 105 rounds from Fat City dropping on the mountainside below and north of our position, then progressively advancing up the side of the mountain.

"Give me that transmitter," I yelled at Lackey. "Everyone hit the deck. They're bringing it in on top of us." No one hesitated as I stood there like a brazen fool calling in a "check fire," hoping to stop their assault before it reached us.

"CAP Command, this is CAP One. We need check fire now," I screamed into the mike.

"Roger, CAP One. Stand by. Over," came the reply.

Seconds passed as the next volley ripped apart the jungle just a hundred yards below us. The VC had stopped firing, no doubt seeking cover themselves. The radio crackled again, interrupted by the exploding HE rounds.

"CAP One, this is CAP Command. Over." It was the good old CO's voice.

"Yes, Command. Call in a check fire right now. We've got Arty on top of us!" I yelled.

A round exploded at the crest of the mountain just as I finished, as if for added emphasis to my transmission. The radio crackled again.

"CAP One, that incoming is mortar rounds from the VC you are engaged with. Over."

I couldn't believe my ears. "Look, CO," I screamed. "I know 105s when I hear them. Now get me a . . . " A scream echoed in my ears. I never finished the sentence. A barrage of 105 HE rounds ripped apart the jungle around us. One round landed between PF Dâu's legs, ripping him into a thousand pieces. Another PF was ripped in half by a single piece of shrapnel.

I felt a hot iron slam into my left side as I was catapulted into the air for all to see. The shrapnel felt like a red hot poker as it shoved into my side and ripped through my body. I felt my body slam to the ground. Lackey came half crawling, half running over to me, radio in hand. Johnston was beside me.

"How's it look?" I asked, dreading his answer.

"How do I know, mate? I'm just a bloody corpsman," he answered.

I knew. I knew all to well. Blood was already soaking the two compression bandages he had secured around my waist. The sulfur compound he had dressed the wound with did not even burn. I guess the pain from the gaping hole in my side overpowered it. My mind played back memories of the men I had held in my lap, men with stomach and chest wounds. Most of them died within minutes. "Oh my God," was my only thought. I could feel the cold blood trickle down my side and onto the ground beneath me, no longer mine to keep. My life was draining away. I knew it and so did Johnston. I could see it in his eyes.

Lackey was on the radio screaming at the CO. "Get us a check fire, you idiot, and now a medevac. My squad leader is down and two other men are dead!" No answer came back. Suddenly the world was silent for a moment. The CO must have decided to call in a check fire. Smoke and the smells of battle filled the air. Taan and his men chased down the remaining VC, filling the air with the sounds of gunfire again. I closed my eyes as I heard the faint chopping sound of the approaching Huey medevac. I was weakening as I laid there listening to the reassurances of Lackey and Johnston. I opened my eyes. Mendez and the others had gathered around, leaving Taan and his men to seek out and destroy the remaining VC.

"What about the others . . . PF Dâu and . . ." I trailed off, the pain jolting my side.

"They bought it," Mendez answered. "All of us are okay, though. Just the two of Taan's men."

"Great," I said as screeching pain stabbed through my side. "More PFs killed by 'friendly fire.' More trouble to deal with."

The medevac set itself down right in the middle of the potato patch, its blades throwing sand and debris in all directions. I hardly noticed. My mind grew fuzzy as someone grabbed my arms and legs and loaded me into the chopper. Lackey squeezed my hand as they prepared to lift off. "See you in the world," he yelled over the noise.

The chopper rose into the air like a giant bird, hovered momentarily, and then struck off for Chu Lai, gunships following behind. The menacing jungle became a blur of vegetation hundreds of feet below.[2] I stared down into it as the wind whipped around me. A shiver crept up my back and a chill settled into my bones. "Where to now?" I wondered. "Dead or home?" More blood flowed from the wound, soaking the floor of the helicopter. I wondered what time it was. My arms were too weak to lift. I gave up, deciding "it don't mean nothing" anyway. Life meant nothing—time meant even less. I closed my eyes again to wait, simply wait. The pain was beginning to take its toll.

For once I was going to find out what happened when a wounded man was loaded onto a medevac. Far too many times I had watched the choppers disappear over the tree tops carrying a friend I would never see again, never knowing whether he had lived or died. This time was different. This time it was my men on the ground watching me disappear behind the tree tops. This time I would know what happened to a wounded marine.

The fuzziness was taking over as blood, my blood, continued to flow from the holes in my side. All I could think about was sleep.

The medic kneeling beside me took my hand in his and began slapping it, commanding me to stay awake. "You can't let yourself fade away, man," he said. "We need you awake."

" . . . and alive," I thought. I forced what I thought was a smile. Sleep tried to sneak in. The loss of blood, the drone of the engines, and the chop of the blades all fought to put me to sleep. My new friend and I fought back. As usual, sleep in Vietnam spelled death, if I succumbed.

"We're almost there," I heard him say.

My mind drifted away as we approached our destination. I was already home, drinking a brew with all of my old buddies. Suddenly a marine, blown apart at the waist, was kneeling down beside me. He had a strange, scary smile on his face. "Looks like you've joined the rest of us," he yelled out as he grabbed my hand, attempting to drag me from the chopper. "Come on man. Join us!" He laughed hauntingly as he continued to tug on my hand. I looked over his shoulder. Countless others were standing behind him, each one mangled and torn. Each one beckoning me to join their ranks. I tried to scream but could not. "Come on." The words echoed in my mind. I closed my eyes.

"Come on man. Wake up." I opened my eyes. The chopper corpsman was kneeling beside me, slapping and tugging at my hand. He smiled down at me. "You're going to make it corporal. Keep fighting that sleep. We're going in now."

I felt the medevac tilt as it dropped for the landing zone. "You're going to make it," I told myself as I tried to raise up on one elbow to look outside. The effort was futile. "Home. . . . Please God, let me go home. Alive."

---

[1] C-Rat is a C-Ration, a standard marine field ration.

[2] The day Goodson was hit, the CAP unit was at approximately Grid #452 075, putting them in the foothills near a village known as Kương Tho 1. It was west by northwest of the old French compound, which Goodson believes must have been along the roadside surrounded by Kương Long 2 to the east; Kương Hiệp 2 to the northwest; and Kương Quảng 3 to the southwest.

## Chapter 11

# MASH Chu Lai

**I** assumed I was on my way to a MASH unit.[1] I knew I was in trouble. I didn't need a doctor to tell me that. Extensive blood loss, internal bleeding, weakness, dizziness, and hard breathing were all telltale signs of the death that awaited me if the chopper was late. "When is late?" I thought. I wondered what death was really like, wondered if I would start floating around in the air, looking down at my lifeless body like I had seen in so many movies. I was afraid to dwell on that thought, afraid that it might come true all too soon. As if in answer to my thoughts, the chopper began a long descent to a concrete pad boasting a bold red "X."

"Made it this far!" I gasped as I strained to look at the ground below. For some reason I had to see, to soak in everything that was going on around me. There was so much I had never seen. I suppose I was afraid that if I stopped observing the events and places around me, death would sneak in, undetected, and my soul would be captured without my knowing it.

The medevac touched down. Doctors and nurses gathered around like ants on sugar as they transferred me onto a stainless steel table with wheels. "On the slab already!" I thought. The air from the swirling rotors of the helicopter rushed around me, sending another chill to my bones. I could see sweat on the brows of the people around me, yet I was cold, very cold.

A doctor leaned over me while a nurse checked my pulse. She looked up at him as the orderlies covered me with a stiff blanket. She shook her head. "Get him to OR fast," the doctor yelled. He headed off to wash up while the nurse ran alongside the gurney, reassuring me that I would be all right. Her eyes told a different story.

The gurney crashed through the doors of the OR. I barely felt the impact. My "bed on wheels" stopped next to an all-white table covered in white sheets. The nurse held up a long needle for me to see. "IV," she said. "Now this may hurt a bit." I almost laughed as the pain in my side gave me a jab to emphasize what pain was all about. "Top the pain I already have, lady."

She wrapped my arm with the plastic tube to get the veins to raise up. "Come on," she rapped her fingers down hard on my exposed flesh, encouraging the sunken veins to fill with the blood that was no longer there. I tried to help by clinching my fist tightly. No response. "Oh, well, I'll have to get it in anyway," she stated.

"Great!" I thought.

She stabbed the needle into what she thought was a vein. A frown came to her face. "That definitely won't work," she murmured to herself. "Have to try another spot." Eight attempts later, I had new holes in my body. My arms and hands looked like a doper's. I was getting weaker, not because of her failure with the needle, but because time was closing in.

The doctor appeared beside her. "What's the problem?"

"Too much blood loss," she explained. "I can't get the needle into a vein."

"Get out of the way!" he yelled. Quickly, expertly, he stabbed the needle into its appropriate home.

"Ninth time's charmed," I thought as I sensed more than felt my head return to the pillow.

"I'll have to cut you open from your solar plexus area down to your crotch," he explained to me.

"No way," I breathed out, thinking of the scar that would make. "Just patch me up, Doc." My breathing was becoming labored.

He ignored me. "Nurse, get me some oxygen," he ordered.

She left, returning in an instant with a small cylinder complete with an oxygen mask. "This will help you out," the doctor stated as he placed the mask over my face.

I didn't argue. The bush of the mountainside of Kương Tho loomed before me, outlined by a strange haze. The potato patch battle was in full swing. Within a few moments, the gas had put me to sleep. I could hear the distant thunder of the exploding howitzer shells as they stalked up the side of the mountain. Suddenly all was black.

Three days later I woke up in a recovery ward in a naval hospital. The same doctor was standing over me, as if he'd never left. I looked at him for a moment and tried to move but the weakness had not left me. He laid a hand on my shoulder. "Just lie back and rest, corporal. You've come through a tough battle and it will be awhile before you'll be able to do much. You're a lucky marine."

"Why's that?" I asked.

"Well," he began, "by all rights you should be dead. We almost lost you during surgery but you fought to survive all the way. I'm still surprised you made it."

I had no comment. I looked around the room, which was about forty feet long and half as wide. A wounded soldier lay in every rack, each bandaged in accordance with his own wound. Many were missing an arm or a leg; some were missing both legs. A window at one end of the room offered a view of the distant jungle bordering the airstrip. I looked back at the doctor.

He continued. "When they brought you in, your vital signs were down to nothing and your body functions had all stopped with the exception of your heart and lungs." He fumbled in his pocket and brought out a small plastic bag with a piece of metal in it about the size of a half dollar. "This is what we found inside you," he explained. "From the report it looks like the round that hit you landed about ten feet behind you. Your men said that you were thrown about fifteen feet into the air."

I forced a smile. "Pretty close, huh!"

"I'd say," he agreed. "The shock wave alone should have ruptured every organ in your body. You should have died on the spot."

"You're kidding!" I exclaimed. "So, what's my condition now?"

"Your vitals are back to the safe zone," he said, "and I couldn't find a single thing wrong inside other than a bunch of ripped up muscle. This little critter missed your left kidney by about a half inch." He held the piece of shrapnel out for me to see. "I have to attribute your being alive to your being in this country for so long that your muscle tone was maxed out. The muscles must have absorbed all of the shock that should have killed you." He stopped and studied for a moment. His brow wrinkled with thought. He continued. "Now, I can guarantee you only one thing."

"Yeah? What's that?" I asked.

"Your left side will remind you of this war for the rest of your life. The nerve endings in the muscles received permanent damage. Your side will be extremely sensitive until the day you die."

"That's better than dead," I smiled.

"You got it!" he smiled back and then turned to leave. "Oh, yeah," he said, turning back, "you'll see that you got your wish. I only cut you open enough for a frontal exploratory. I'm not sure what the organs in the back look like. X-ray showed they were okay!"

"Thanks, Doc," I smiled

My thoughts took me away. "Great!" I thought. "Alive and no bad scar."

Doc had left the bag with the piece of shrapnel lying on the stand beside my bed. I picked it up, studying the deadly piece of steel. Its edges were serrated where the explosive had ripped it away from the larger shell. I wondered why I had only been hit by one piece. Of course, we knew from experience that an exploding round is unpredictable. I saw one man in a similar situation cut in half because the round that exploded behind him blew into two halves. One half whistled harmlessly away. The other hit him in the back, ripping him in two. I was lucky . . . more than lucky. I wanted no part of the steel. I tossed it into the trash can beside my rack.

The doctor returned later with a couple of other officers. I didn't catch their names, but I noticed one was a general and the other a colonel.

"Corporal Goodson, we'd like to ask you a few questions," the general began. "We understand you are doing okay and that you are wanting to file charges against the army." I remembered that as I had lain in the bush waiting for the medevac, Lackey and I had plotted against the ones responsible for the friendly fire. I had assured him that if I made it, I would see to it that he and the other men would have no more trouble from our CO. Obviously, Lackey and the others had been talking to the Brass about "our problem."

I stopped him. "No sir, not the army, or at least I don't think so. I just want the guilty party taken care of, and in my mind, it's our own little CO."

"That's a pretty strong accusation," the colonel joined in.

"If I was strong enough right now, he'd be dead—sir!" I half yelled.

"Now calm down, Corporal," the general urged. "We'll have a full investigation into this screw-up and I assure you the guilty party will fall.

First, we need your side of the story. Please make it accurate to the last detail, starting with April 25th early morning."

I told him the entire story up until the moment the chopper lifted off to Chu Lai, with me in tow. I left out nothing.

"Well son, are you sure you've included everything?"

"Yes sir," I replied, "everything."

They left assuring me that the matter would be resolved.

A short while later a nurse arrived to give me another dose of pain-killer. She said nothing but simply cleaned my arm, stabbed the needle into muscle, patted me on the shoulder, smiled and walked away. Soon I was asleep. At 1600 hours, the nurses woke us all with advice to stay awake because the Army Engineers were blasting away jungle for a longer runway for the airport. I obliged, gladly. I didn't care for any surprise explosions.

Days passed and my first week in the hospital reached a close. Lackey and Mendez had dropped in for a visit along with Johnston. They assured me that the investigation was indeed going on and that each one of them had been quizzed in private. "They warned us not to discuss it with anyone until the investigation is over," Mendez said.

"Yeah," Lackey added. "You wouldn't believe the Brass we've been talking to."

"I can imagine," I said as I filled them in on my own brush with the Brass.

Having brought me up to speed, they headed out to get back to the bush before dark. Part of me—a major part—wanted to go with them. I felt a little like a traitor, being there in a nice comfy bed and knowing they were going out to face the enemy again. I wept at the thought of losing the family I had grown to love. Then the morphine took over again and I drifted back to sleep.

"Kaboom!"

I bolted upright, ready for battle. Fists clenched, eyes searching for my weapon. Searching for the enemy. Suddenly I noticed a nurse running toward me. I was still in the hospital. The engineers were blowing away jungle again.

"You were sleeping so peacefully, I thought I'd wait until almost 1600 hours," she explained. "I'm afraid I lost track of the time." In the same breath, she gasped, "Oh, my God!"

For the first time, I felt it. The point of the IV needle was jutting out of my upper arm, the clear, life-giving fluids mingling with the blood that was flowing from my arm. I ripped off the tape and yanked the needle out. In disgust, I tossed it to the floor.

She grabbed a swab from a nearby tray and applied pressure against my new wound. "I'm so sorry," she said. "I only meant to help you."

"Let's not make a habit of that," I urged her.

She forced a smile. While I held the pressure on the bandage, she began to clean up the mess. Mission accomplished, she applied a fresh bandage and enough tape to hold down a tank. "There, that ought to do it," she muttered.

"I'm certainly not going anywhere," I quipped.

"Careful, marine, or I'll tape you into that bed," she said as she let go a laugh. I laughed with her as she carried away the mess "we" had made.

Moments later she returned with a new IV package in her hands. "No way," I ordered, memories of the nine IV tries slipping through my mind. "I'll pass, thank you."

"Now, don't be a baby," she purred. "I'll make it quick and clean."

"Yeah, just like they did in OR! I'm not about to let you stick me again!" I backed up against the headboard as far as I could and prepared for a battle.

"Now look, corporal. The doctor says he wants this in until you can eat solid food," she yelled back. She wrestled with me, then took a few steps back to plan a different strategy. I watched her eyes, waiting for her to move in once again. That needle was not going back into my arm.

The doctor walked in during the yelling. "What's going on here?" he demanded.

"He won't let me put this IV back in," the nurse complained, her frustration showing.

"And why is it out?" he asked.

He turned and stared a hole through me as the nurse filled him in on the events leading up to the fight over the needle.

"Well, for crying out loud, woman," was all he could say. He turned back to me, but I could see no hope for sympathy. He was just as intent as she was.

"Don't even try it," I told him.

"Calm down, corporal," he urged. "You've got to have an IV until you're ready to eat."

"I'm ready. Put it in front of me—steak, potatoes, the works."

"You're kidding," he stepped back. "Are you really hungry?"

"Starved!" I said. "Just put it in front of me."

"You don't feel nauseous?"

"Only when I think about nine more tries with that needle," I stated, pointing at the sinister object he held in his right hand.

"Okay, nurse," he said, handing her the needle. "Get the man something to eat."

"Yes, sir," she replied and turned to go.

"And don't forget the ketchup," I yelled after her.

The doctor laughed. "You get back in bed."

Mission accomplished, I settled down for the wait. A short while later she returned with a steaming bowl of soup.

"What is that?" I asked.

"Now don't start, marine. It's potato soup. The doctor says you'll have to eat soft food for the next few days and that's final."

I could not argue. Potato soup certainly beat anything I had eaten up to that moment. "Bring it on," I said. "Can I at least have some pepper?"

"Sure," she replied as she reached into a pocket and fished out a pepper shaker. Taking it in my hands, I rolled it over and over, observing its beauty.

"Are you okay?" she asked.

"What? . . . Oh yeah, sure," I stammered. "I just never thought I'd see anything from civilization ever again."

She laughed. "You'll be okay." I watched her walk away. She was something else I thought I would never see again: a good old American woman.

I finished my first week in the Chu Lai naval field hospital by graduating from potato soup to the steak and potatoes I had pleaded for. Recovery was proceeding nicely, so I figured they'd send me back to the bush. I was anxious to rejoin my fellow marines, but the doctor had a surprise for me.

Fourteen days had come and gone. I was looking out the window at the jungle just visible over the distant rows of concertina wire. "Here's your orders, corporal," he said. I looked around, startled by his abrupt statement. The doctor was standing beside my bed holding out a stack of papers. I took them from him.

While I was reading, he said, "Pack your gear. We're shipping you to Cam Ranh Bay,[2] then on to Yokosuka, Japan."

I folded the papers and laid them in my lap. "I thought I was healing nicely," I said. "Surely I'm ready to return to the bush."

"It will still be awhile before you're completely healed. All torso wounds have to go through a long healing process. We're not set up for that here. Japan is the place for you. You can forget about returning to the bush, for a long time, anyway."

I was alternately happy, then sad, about his news. I had longed for the moment I would leave Vietnam, but now that it was here, I knew I would never see my men again. To simply be shipped out like a hunk of beef seemed wrong. Good-byes had to be said. Pacts had to be made. Addresses back home had to be exchanged. There were a million things that had been put off until tomorrow. Now they would be lost forever in the bush, and I was miles away about to be shipped off to some other "Godforsaken place," with no way of letting them know.

Again, I had no choice. In the military, you are not given choices, only orders. Before I knew it, I was once again lying on my back in a medevac chopper, heading for some place called Cam Ranh Bay. "It's so quiet and beautiful there," the doctor had said. "It has become known as the R and R spot of Vietnam."

The very idea of rest and relaxation—of a vacation—in Vietnam, set me back a bit. "Incredible," I thought, "a little heaven in this hell." But I was destined never to know if the doctor was right about the bay area. All of my R and R was spent in a hospital bed with a view of the distant bay. The extent of my freedom was to answer the call of nature. The nurses kept pumping so much medicine in me that I slept almost twenty-four hours a day.

The week in Cam Ranh Bay went by too quickly. The big transport that carried me to Japan was loaded with wounded soldiers, each one of us on a canvas rack, stacked one over the other, three high. Nurses flitted back and forth giving shots to everyone. They wanted us all asleep for the duration of the flight. Before I knew it, we were being unloaded in the dark of night in a place I assumed to be Japan. The night air was cool and moist. I could hear waves crashing against an unseen shore somewhere behind us. Once again I was on a gurney heading towards a place I had never seen. I tried to recall the name of the place. "Yoko . . . something." Bright lights loomed through the windows ahead of us. "We can't be in 'Nam," I told myself. "The windows would be blacked out." All I could do was settle back and wait for whatever came.

During the first two weeks in the naval hospital in Japan, they kept me sedated most of the time. Events during that time period are more than just sketchy, they are practically nonexistent. The healing process was slow. The doctors continually opened my wounds from the outside to clean the inside as deeply as possible. I was beginning to relate to a rifle bore and a cleaning rod. It seemed like the doctors dealt more in pain than in healing, but the nurses assured me of the necessity of the process. I was in no position to argue.

During my waking hours, I spent a majority of my time reflecting on all that had taken place during my Vietnam tour. I began to make a mental list of all that had happened, the good and the bad.

On the good side stood the friends I had made in Vietnam. Jones, one of the best machine gunners I had ever met, as well as one of the nicest men. Mendez, one crazy Puerto Rican dude, fun-loving, yet ruthless to the VC. Lackey, a fine man, strong in many ways. Johnston, who kept me laughing when I felt like crying and made me long to go to Australia. Rodriguez started out rough but ended up being a good, honest fighter. Rivera had his problems, but he never shied from a fight. Ciminski, the only Yankee I had ever liked. He always had something good to say. Everett, one fantastic squad leader and fighter and the most honorable man I ever knew. Doc, predecessor of Johnston, a brave man with a great sense of humor. Speck and Thomas I knew only a few days. Smith, also, not with us long enough for me to get to know him, but he died bravely. Last, but not least, Taan, my Vietnamese counterpart who had saved my life and the lives of others countless times. A true friend. Without Taan, as well as the other Vietnamese, I would never have known the war as I did. They provided me with a reason for fighting that no one else had been able to provide. *Freedom* . . . from oppression, from the grips of terror, and happiness for their children. All else was meaningless. They had given a purpose to my intrusion into their lives. For that I was forever thankful. I could only wish that I had done more.

Other good things included the Vietnamese people and the help we had given them. Mamasan and Lín Tôu. PF Dâu, who had saved me from the spider, only to lose his own life to our friendly fire. The old chieftain for accepting us and making our job easier.

On the bad side was the process of taking areas away from the VC, then giving them back, then taking them again, time after time. Watching friends die from wounds so gruesome it etched a spot in your mind forever. The dismembering booby traps. The dictatorial, sadistic leaders; the egotistical leaders and the downright stupid leaders. The men who died or were

ruined for life because of them. The pungi pits. The senseless killings of
innocent men, women and children. The malfunctioning weapons. The
hordes of mosquitoes. The ever-present leeches. The black market. The
poisonous snakes and insects. The torture techniques of the PFs. My own
participation in all of it. Fighting an enemy for ten months and getting
wounded twice, not by the enemy, but by our own artillery. The fear gener-
ated by the slightest noise. The pitch black nights. The sound of explosions. The sound of gunfire. Ambushes. The desire to kill. The stench of
death. Body bags. The list was endless and included last, but not least, the
protesting by our own country, our own people, not just against the war,
but specifically against us. The audacity of people like Jane Fonda, visiting
and encouraging the North Vietnamese troops.[3] The worst one of all, the
supplying of weapons, by our own people, to the enemy. Too often we killed
a VC or NVA and found American, British and German-made weapons on
them.

The bad things were unforgettable, and at that moment unforgivable.
The bitterness and rage held back for so long was slowly, ruthlessly taking
over my mind. One thing was for sure. The nineteen-year old boy who had
left Fort Worth and ended up in Vietnam was gone—vanished—not even a
memory left of him. The only reminder was a shell, now hardened by combat and possessed by bitter memories and controlled by a seemingly irre-
versible rage. The boy was gone, not just replaced by a *man*, but by a crazed
animal trained and ready to kill. My days of killing the VC and the NVA
were over, set aside to concentrate on another enemy. In my bitterness and
rage, I was actually plotting the deaths of politicians and business leaders
who had perpetuated the war and benefited from the deaths of my friends.

I had no idea how to accomplish such a feat. In combat it had been
easy: just a simple squeeze of the trigger and your enemy was blown away.
I knew deep down inside that I would never carry out my plans, but only
because I still had enough sense to know killing them was wrong . . . dead
wrong. I struggled to find some way of expressing my feelings. They simply had to come out.

"Hey, nurse!" I yelled one day. "How about some paper and pencil?"
She obliged. I felt a strong desire to draw, something I had not even thought
about for eleven months or more, although I had always enjoyed drawing
cartoon-like figures. With pencil in hand and rage in full flow, I let my
mind do its thing. Within moments my creation lay before me, a monstrous looking beetle standing on its hind legs, erect like a man, perched on

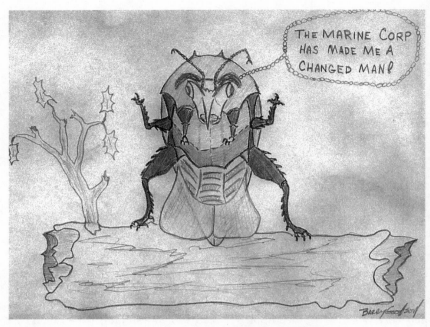

The first of two drawings Goodson made while in the hospital.

a log as if looking for some unsuspecting prey. Above his menacing head I wrote a caption that read, "The Marine Corps has made me a changed man." I looked it over. It was a self portrait of the feelings locked away inside of me. I stuffed it away in fear that someone would wonder what prompted such a crazy drawing. I wasn't ready to talk, not yet, not to anyone.

At my feet, waiting for me to take it up and review the events of the world, was an editorial magazine bulging with political statements and overtones concerning the war in Vietnam. I bent forward to pick it up. The pain in my gut made me hesitate momentarily, wondering if it truly was worth the effort. I had not seen a magazine of any sort since leaving the states. The pain subsided to a bearable throb as I stretched the last few inches.

There were probably hundreds of other magazines that would have been better for me to read at that time, but I had this one in hand, searching through it for a tangible, justifiable reason for the death and destruction the politicians had created in Vietnam. I found it: money. The American

"*I think I won!*"

Goodson's second
drawing while in
the hospital.

economy was booming. Companies manufacturing everything from explosives and aircraft to clothing and food were raking in fortunes as a direct
result of the war.

I turned another page. Lying before me was a political cartoon of a
crazy-looking soldier standing in the middle of a battlefield—alone. The
caption under it basically patted America on the back for "fighting the
battle alone." In other words, for being basically the sole supporters of the

war in Vietnam. It wasn't true. There were Korean soldiers, Australian soldiers, and probably many others involved in the war. American politicians were trying to claim any and all glory for themselves.

I set the magazine aside and searched out my pencil and paper once again. I recreated the caricature into a scene more real, more expressive of me. I re-drew the lone—no, the lonely—soldier from the magazine. I changed his clean utilities for tattered and worn ones, placed a CAP insignia on his chest, turned his face into a battle-worn, kill-crazed look. The ground around him became a ravaged field. My caption read, "I think I won" with a question mark emphasizing the doubt of it all.

It was obvious that I had indeed survived the war. Yet had I truly won? CAP marines would no doubt soon leave Quảng Tin Province forever. From what I read and heard, I believed that the government was ready to pull out, leaving the Vietnamese villagers on their own. When they left would they leave a legacy of freedom and happiness? I had my doubts. In truth our impact, our influence would be only momentary. The growth of Communist oppression and terror would regain its hold as soon as our troops left. In reality we were inevitably going to give up the territory. We had not won. *I* had not won freedom for my Vietnamese friends. I knew it and they knew it. Taan had told me so many times. "Someday you go home. No more fight VC. No way for me, my family to be free. We will fight and die forever." The words resounded in my mind. Tears rolled down my cheeks. "You were right my friend," I said, "You were right." I placed the picture in the album alongside the other. Using the corner of the sheet, I wiped away the tears and the pain I felt for Taan and his people. Closing my eyes, I tried to shut out the memory and the knowledge of the unending terror that they faced. "God help them," I prayed.

Many days passed and with each one I grew stronger. Finally they let me participate in minor work details to stimulate the rebuilding of the destroyed and weakened muscles. I had gone from a solid 180 pounds to a weak 150 pounds. I wanted desperately to regain that weight before they shipped me out again. I ate like a starved animal and as often as they would allow, devouring such food as I had neither seen nor envisioned for what seemed like years. During the day Vietnam was put on shelf as I kept my mind occupied with varying details. Along with the night, the terror returned.

I had put off calling home. I guess I was a little scared of what I would hear. Crazy thoughts filtered through my mind. Would they still want me home even though they knew I was one of what people called "baby kill-ers"? Would they be proud of me for volunteering for this political war instead of waiting to be drafted? Would my parents even want to talk to me? I had not written them in more than two months, wanting to wait until I knew I would live.

Finally, courage up, I asked a nurse to place the call. I nervously waited for it to go through. My mother finally answered, full of joy and tears. Yes, they wanted me home, she said, as soon as possible. I assured her and my dad that my wound was healing nicely and that I would be shipped to Okinawa[4] for recuperation for a few weeks. I hung up the phone thinking how my physical wound was healing but my worst wounds were festering inside me with rage and bitterness.

I picked up the drawings and decided I had wrongly accused the Marine Corps of changing me. In reality they had done what they could to keep me alive. They had taught me to survive, in spite of the adversity. The real change in me came from my feelings about my fellow Americans and their constant verbal destruction of the American soldier. That, coupled with the effects of the war, had changed me irreversibly.

To keep my mind occupied, I began visiting the other wounded men in the hospital. One day when I was making my rounds, a particular man caught my eye. He was covered with small bandages—almost like band aids—from head to toe.

"Hey, man, it looks like you have the market locked up on bandages," I chuckled. My attempt at humor faded as he turned to me with tears in his eyes, holding out a picture for me to see.

"Now, that's a beaut," I encouraged him.

He produced a weak smile. "She was my fiancee! But now. . . ." His voice trailed off.

"A Dear John?" I asked.

"No, not yet," he returned, "but look at me."

I did. He had bandages from head to toe but he had not lost anything. His legs, arms, hands, fingers, feet, toes—everything was in its God-given place. "Okay," I said, "so what?"

"Come on, man," he returned. "I'll be scarred for life. She won't want me now. I'll look like some kind of freak." He began to cry.

As I laid my hand on his shoulder, my thoughts turned to my previous concern for my own scars. I thought about how stupid I had been. My heart went out to the man. "What unit were you in?" I asked.

He looked up, gaining control of the sobs. He stared at me for a moment. "Seabees,"[5] he answered. "Cam Ranh Bay."

"Really?" I asked, somewhat taken aback. "I heard that Cam Ranh Bay was a resort area. People were taking R and R there."

"They were," he said. "But a few weeks ago the Cong launched an attack against Chu Lai and Cam Ranh Bay. Guys were getting shot in their racks, even in the hospitals."

My heart sank. I didn't want to hear it, but I listened anyway. "How did you get it?" I asked him.

"I was asleep in my rack at about 0100 hours, when a B122 rocket struck within a few feet of me."

My mouth fell open. He noticed. "Does that mean anything? Are you okay?" he asked.

"Huh? Oh, yeah. I mean—are you sure it was a B122?" I asked.

"Yeah. At least that's what they tell me."

"Incredible!" was all I could say.

"What's the big deal?" he asked.

"Nothing, really," I answered. "It's just that you have not only survived an attack by the largest explosive in Charlie's arsenal, but survived with every finger, toe, leg, arm—you name it—intact. It's hard to believe."

"What's the big deal about a B122?" he asked.

"Big deal? It's just a rocket made in the Republic of China[6] that's about six feet long and about a foot in diameter. It has enough explosive power to turn that hooch of yours into nothing but a puff of smoke. Charlie humps it on his back for miles and then builds clay launching pads. He uses bamboo sticks as aiming aids, launching the rocket against unsuspecting bases like yours."

"You're kidding!" He shook his head in disbelief.

"Not hardly," I answered. "You not only survived the attack, you came through with flying colors. I'm impressed! Are you any kin to Superman?"

He laughed. "Well, I guess I am alive," he beamed, "and if an old B122 can't get me down, nothing can!"

"That's right, and that woman of yours will be proud to have you back and even more proud to hear your story."

He laughed. I shook his hand. "Keep the chin up, man. If you can survive a B122 attack, you can survive anything," I assured him.

"Thanks," he said. I turned to go, gratitude swelling in my heart that another one of our guys had been delivered from the clutches of death.

The next morning they put me on a plane headed for Okinawa. I had been assigned to doctor's care until my wounds had sufficiently healed. The transport wheels thudded against the dry pavement as we taxied to the assigned stopping place. I was tagged "ambulatory" and that's exactly what awaited me at the airport. I felt kind of silly climbing into an ambulance to be delivered like a piece of meat to my next locker. I'll grant you that my wounds were far from healed—in fact, I could feel the coolness of fresh blood against the bandages fastened around my waist—but I felt not only healthy, but excited.

The ambulance dropped their piece of meat off at the local hospital where I met my new doctor, Captain Garza. Within minutes, he had finished reviewing my files. He checked my wounds and replaced the bandages, assuring me the bleeding was normal for such a wound and that he would continue to use the "cleaning rod" method the doctors in Japan had used.

"Corporal Goodson," he said, "you are to report to my office at 0800 and 1600 hours every day for the next thirty days. After that, we should be able to ship you back to the states."

Home. I was almost excited, except for the longing I felt for my men back in 'Nam. I hadn't heard from any of them and had not written. I felt shame for neglecting to write, to them or anyone. But somehow I just couldn't bring myself to do it. I felt guilty for not being back in the bush. I was even too ashamed to write home.

My next assignment was to pick up my sea bag, which had been packed and shipped from my CAP unit to storage in Okinawa. I located the storage building about halfway across the base and obtained a driver and a jeep from my new temporary unit. Doctor's orders were "no heavy lifting or long walks." I almost felt like an officer.

The jeep rolled to a stop in front of a beige building. Its large doors sectioned the building into quadrants, with a letter of the alphabet above each door. A . . . B . . . C . . . finally, door G. The corporal in charge of the storage checked his papers once again to assure himself that Goodson definitely started with a "G." Satisfied, he stepped forward with key in hand, and unlocked the heavy padlock barring our entry. He swung the double barn doors open wide, revealing row after row of "G" bags, each boasting a large manila tag marked with the owner's name, rank, and serial number and its reason for being there. I stared, transfixed by the scene before me.

Simple pieces of paper portraying the lives of men. Everywhere I looked, the tags haunted my memory and jolted me back to the reality of the war. "MIA . . . KIA . . . WIA . . . ,"[7] the tags yelled out at me. A tear came to my eye as I watched the corporal toss the missing and dead men aside to uncover one wounded man.

"Here it is." He turned, holding it out to me. Noticing my momentary stupor, he handed the bags to my driver and closed the doors. The snap of the lock jolted me back to Okinawa. The corporal checked my face for a moment. "Did you see any bags you recognize in there?" he asked.

"What? Uh, well, no—not really. It's just hard to look at something like that without thinking about the men behind them." I continued, "It's sort of like you have the lives of men locked away, on hold, until someone arrives to reclaim their life."

He just stared at me. "I guess so," he answered, then turned and headed off for his air-conditioned office.

The driver dropped me off at my temporary home, another beige building. He showed me to my rack and then left. I never laid eyes on him again. I was getting used to that. I began unloading my gear from the sea bag. Everything was as I had left it except for one thing: my tape recorder was gone. I figured Slippery Fingers Rivera had taken it, since it was his responsibility to pack my gear and send it to the rear. For once his klepto problem didn't bother me. "Maybe they can all use it to send tapes home," I thought.

Gear in storage, I headed out to grab some lunch at the local mess hall. Suddenly, I became aware that everywhere I looked, there were large groups of black soldiers who seemed intent on keeping separate from the likes of the rest of us.

"What's the deal?" I wondered. I had long ago set aside any prejudice I had been taught as a child, as I fought side-by-side with all types of men. Race did not make or break a man in my mind. A man, who he was, what he was, came from inside. To judge anyone by his looks was asinine. We had no time for such things in the bush.

I was walking up the steps to the mess hall when a couple of guys rounded the corner of the building. They reacted at the same time I did. I let out a war whoop, "Yee haw!" Everyone stopped and watched as we ran to each other. I couldn't believe my eyes. It was Ciminski and Thomas.

"What are *you* doing here?" Ciminski asked. "The last time I saw you, we were fighting Cong during that wondrous night of Tét."

"Yeah," I smiled as memories of loading him onto the chopper invaded my mind. "How's your leg doing?"

Ciminski did a little jig as he demonstrated his regained strength. "Good as new," he beamed. "Takes more than any old VC to get me down."

We all laughed.

"Seriously, Goodson, your tour isn't up until next month, is it?" Thomas asked.

"You're right," I answered, "but friendly fire changed those plans." I filled them in on all the sordid details.

"I'd heard you were hurt," Thomas said, "but I had no idea how bad."

"Somebody ought to nail that CO," said Ciminski as we converged on the mess hall. Just as we reached for the doors, a half dozen guys, black and white, burst through the doorway, fully engulfed in their fight. We stepped aside to let them pass and continue their battle in a scuffle of dust.

"What's the big deal?" I asked.

Ciminski offered the information. "We have a weird war going on here," he said. "Can you believe it? The blacks are walking around in gangs and pouncing on unsuspecting white guys. New base rules require that white guys don't go anywhere alone, and short of a pass to the village we have a 2000 hours curfew."[8]

"Why?"

"Why?" Thomas repeated as if he couldn't believe I had asked the question. "Why, the blacks feel like the more whites they put in the hospital, the more seats will be opened up for them on the planes going home." That was his opinion. I could only wonder.

"That's right," Ciminski joined in. "Once your name hits the 'boarding list' for that week you might as well hole up, especially with that wound." He pointed to my side.

I winced at the thought of anyone hitting my side. "How can they get away with it?" I asked.

"Who knows?" Thomas answered. "Word has it the base commander is afraid of them. It's easier to just control us whiteys."

I had a difficult time believing that men could get caught up in racism after spending so much time together in the hell of the war. Fighting our NVA and VC enemies was hard enough; to fight amongst ourselves seemed a waste of energy. It was becoming obvious to me that our little unit was protected, in many ways, from other realities of the world. We had no radios other than our communication equipment and were landlocked to the limits of our APR. We never even associated with any Fat City personnel. Consequently, we knew nothing of Martin Luther King's assassination or of building racial conflict within the U.S. forces in Vietnam or back home in the states.

"Let's talk about something more important," I said. "Have you heard from our men in CAP One?"

"When I left, which was a few days after you did, everything was okay," Thomas offered. "The body count from the day you got hit was confirmed at fourteen Viet Cong."

"Any news about the investigation?" I asked.

"Not really," Thomas said. "Only a rumor that the Army CO in charge of the artillery was kicked out of the Army with no retirement pay or anything."

"What about our own illustrious CO?" I asked.

"No, nothing. They didn't touch him," he stated. "At least, not before I left."

"That figures."

We continued our meals, sharing ideas about what home would be like and how anxious we were to get there, and simultaneously agreeing that we weren't too sure that we even wanted to go home. Ciminski was the most excited. His mother had saved all the money he had sent home, and he planned to buy a big four-wheel-drive truck fully equipped with a power winch and snow-plow blade. He hoped to spend the winter of 1970 helping people out of snow drifts and ditches. I was happy for him.

We shook hands and parted company, agreeing to look each other up once we got back home. Ciminski and Thomas flew out the next day in search of home and their dreams.

The weeks flew by as I waited for my release from the doctor. I was ready to follow Thomas and Ciminski. The second week of June, I received my orders.

"Home. I'm going home!" I yelled. Then I unfolded the orders. I couldn't believe my eyes. "Destination: CAP One Unit, Chu Lai, Vietnam" was the bold heading. I was mad, then happy. I wanted to back and help my men, yet I wanted to go home. Then again, I didn't want either option.

Orders in hand, I sought out the only man who might have the right answers, my doctor. I entered his office. "Yo, captain," I half yelled, holding out my orders for him to see.

He took them. "What!" he exclaimed. "I'll see about that. . . . Private Herald!"

A slender young man came running into his office. "Yes, Sir." He stood properly erect, awaiting the order.

"Get the CO on the horn," the doctor yelled. The private turned on his heel and shot off to complete the duty. The captain turned back to me. "Your wounds are healed over, but you're in no shape for combat. I'm sending you home tomorrow," he stated.

"Tomorrow?" I stammered.

"Yeah," he smiled. "Go pack your gear. I'll work things out with the CO and have a jeep take you to the airport barracks. The jet will leave at 0800 hours." He stuck out his hand. "Have a safe trip home, marine." He smiled, shaking my hand.

I smiled back. "Thank you, sir," I said. "You've been a big help."

"My pleasure," he smiled. "Now get out of here!"

I did. As I stepped out of his office, I thought, "Rats. Another officer I have to like!"

The plane left at 0800 the next morning. This time I was sitting up in a real seat and in a real civilian type Boeing 727. I looked across the wings of the beautiful bird as the thrust from the twin jet engines catapulted us down the black stripe of the runway beneath us. The wheels rumbled to silence as the airliner lifted into the air. My gaze followed the jungle below as it changed from an overwhelming mass of towering trees to a rapidly shrinking blur of green passing beneath us. Somehow, being up in the air always seemed to diminish the gargantuan reality of the death that waited below. Emotion flooded my senses. I fought back the tears. No longer was it a dream. Finally I could set aside the "fear in the night."

I was going home.

---

[1] MASH stands for Mobile Army Surgical Hospital. The time between being wounded and being evacuated to a medical station for an American soldier in Vietnam was 2.8 hours (through 1967) as compared to 10.5 hours in World War II. Spurgeon Neel, *Medical Support of the U.S. Army in Vietnam, 1965–1970* (Washington, DC: Govern-

ment Printing Office, 1973); Ronald J. Glasser, *365 Days* (New York: Braziller, 1971).

2  Cam Ranh Bay was a major American military base on the South China Sea in central South Vietnam, about 250 miles northeast of Saigon. Yokosuka was the site of a U.S. military hospital just south of Tokyo.

3  Actress Jane Fonda, an antiwar protester who was at the time the wife of former Students for a Democratic Society leader Tom Hayden, visited Hanoi in July 1972. In widely circulated photographs and on film, she was seen posing on a North Vietnamese anti-aircraft gun singing antiwar songs. Some hawkish members of Congress accused her of treason. George Donelson Moss, *Vietnam: An American Ordeal,* 2nd ed., (Englewood Cliffs, New Jersey: Prentice Hall, 1994), 363; Myra MacPherson, "Women at the Barricades, Then and Now," in Andrew J. Rotter, ed., *Light at the End of the Tunnel: A Vietnam War Anthology* (New York: St. Martin's, 1991), 495–96.

4  Okinawa is an island in the extreme southern part of Japan and is the site of a U.S. military base.

5  Seabees are U.S. Navy construction troops.

6  Republic of China refers to the People's Republic of China.

7  MIA stands for missing in action, KIA for killed in action, and WIA for wounded in action.

8  Up until 1968, black and white troops in the U.S. forces in Vietnam got along relatively well. After the assassination of Martin Luther King, Jr., in April 1968, and the subsequent traumatic events of that year, racial conditions deteriorated. For a discussion of the beginning of the end of racial harmony among American troops beginning in 1968, see Ronald H. Spector, *After Tet: The Bloodiest Year in Vietnam* (New York: Free Press, 1993), 242–59; Wallace Terry, *Bloods: An Oral History of the Vietnam War by Black Veterans* (New York: Random House, 1984).

## Chapter 12
# The Trip Home

**I**t felt strange to be wearing a khaki dress uniform with a chest full of ribbons and decorations, sitting in a commercial airline 727 with soft cushion seats. I was euphoric, but I kept waiting for the dream to be over. "It's just a matter of moments before the crack of an AK will bring me back to reality," I suddenly blurted out. Embarrassed by my outburst, I looked around to see who had noticed. No one seemed to be aware I was on the plane.

A pretty stewardess passed by en route to answering some guy's call. I looked around me. The jet was full of marines, their faces long and silent. Only a handful were laughing and cutting up. The rest were like zombies waiting for their next job.

"Would you like something to drink?" a voice said.

I looked up. It was the stewardess, leaning over me with that million-dollar smile. She was a gorgeous blonde wrapped up in a skin tight, royal blue uniform. Part of me wanted to grab her and hug her. The other part wanted her out of my face. That part won. "No, thanks," I said, "think I'll just rest a bit." I settled back against the cushion of the seat and forced my eyes away from her tantalizing beauty. She had no idea of the longing I'd had for the past twelve months, just to look at a woman like her. To talk to her seemed . . . well, it was dangerous to talk to your dreams.

"Okay, just yell if you need something," she offered as she leaned over the next marine.

I knew it was their job, but everything was just too "peachy." The reality of the 'Nam would not allow such frivolity. I don't know what I expected. I was confused. My mind continually bounced back to the CAP, my men and the bush. "I have no right to be here," I told myself. "No right at all." I looked for a way off the plane, but of course there was none. I was trapped into facing a reality that my mind refused to accept. "This can't be real," I thought. "War is the only reality." Bewildered, I forced my eyes to focus on the unending blue of the ocean below us.

I closed my eyes—hard. Soon I was fast asleep. My mind took me back to Vietnam, back to my men, back to the bush . . . back to reality where I was comfortable. The plane I was on became the dream. We men of the bush had long ago stopped accepting thoughts of the beauty of the world we once knew. We cut the memory of it from our brains. Round-eyed women; soft, cushioned seats or beds; air conditioning; hamburgers—you name it— had become items you could have only in dreams. To even begin to think of them as real, much less touchable, was totally neurotic. Only a fool would ever believe in such fairy tales. The dreams became more like nightmares, continual hauntings of the past.

I had not even wanted to see "real" American women in Vietnam. They represented a painful temptation, a forbidden fruit, a tease that only brought feelings to the surface that I did not want to deal with. Women did not belong in our Hell. We lived in it and took it with us wherever we had to go. American women, I thought, belonged at home, safe with the rest of our dreams.

The smell of food brought me back to the plane once again. I awoke and looked outside. Darkness was setting in. The sun had already set, leaving an orange glow on the flat horizon. I grew tense as the memory of the dark nights prepared me for my enemy.

"Would you like a meal, sir?" a voice asked. It was the same stewardess.

"Sure," I said as I forced a smile. She placed a tray with some sort of meat and vegetables on the little fold-down table in front of me. The fragrant smell of her perfume tickled memories of days gone by. I looked at the meal. Somehow, I did not feel hungry. There was just too much flopping around in my mind. I took a few bites and I was soon fast asleep once again. It was my only escape.

The trip back to the states was long and fitful. The shooting pain in my side was constantly reminding me that it was tired of each position I placed it in. Finally, the sign on the panel in front of me lit up, advising us to stop smoking and fasten our seat belts.

I sat upright. A knot rose up in my throat. "Am I ready?" I thought. "What is waiting for me out there? Will they be glad to see us or not?" The questions were endless. The answers stood just outside the exit door of the plane.

A violent jolt vibrated through the body of the plane as the tires struck the runway. We taxied to a spot brightly illuminated by numerous floodlights. The pilot brought the plane to a full stop. I peered out the window into the night, my mind barely aware of the whining sound produced by the shutdown of the jet's massive engines. I tried to see what America was like, but the lights were too bright. I stood up, gathered my gear and lined up with the rest of the marines as the stewardess wrestled with the cumbersome door. Just outside, I could see an exit ramp being pushed against the body of the plane.

"Whoosh!" The air rushed in as the stewardess finally managed to swing the door open. "Watch your step, please," she advised, "and welcome home."

I forced another smile as I made my way toward the door. Multitudes of feelings bounced around in my mind. As I stepped from the plane, I was surprised by the brightness of floodlights shining directly into my eyes, making it impossible for me to see anything else. I knew that everyone out there could see me, however. I felt like a sitting duck! "Get out of the light, you fool," my mind screamed. Nervously, I looked around for cover, trying in vain to peer past the lights.

"Move along, sir," I heard the stewardess say. Her words forced my racing mind to react. Woodenly, I stepped forward and started down the gangplank. My eyes began to adjust to the brightness, and I could see a cyclone fence behind which a crowd of people stood. As I got closer to them, a girl started yelling out some guy's name. I stopped dead in my tracks. Yes, I had seen girls before, plenty of them, but this one was different. She had on the shortest skirt I had ever seen in my entire life.

"Move it, marine!" came a voice behind me.

I broke my trance again and continued down. Suddenly a handful of rocks hit the pavement just a few feet in front of me. "Thunk, thunk!" Instinctively, I ducked, ready to take on the enemy. A half dozen MPs quickly moved in and seized a group of young men and women. As they struggled to free themselves from the grasp of the MPs, they let another barrage go. These rocks hit their mark. "Go away, baby killers! Rapists! Murderers! We don't want you here!" they screamed. "Get out of our country!"

I did not need urging this time. I marched as fast as I could toward the top sergeant waiting for us at the main gate. The jeers and taunts followed us, digging into our very souls. I wanted to kill the protesters, and I wanted to cry. Neither desire won. All the rumors I had heard were confirmed in that one instant.

It was my first taste of my country's hatred for us and for our war, and it was a bitter one. "What do they know?" I thought as I fought back the rage and tears. I wanted to turn and re-board the plane. Emotional turmoil swelled up inside my gut. Memories of my dead and wounded buddies bombarded my mind. "They fought for you," I screamed.

My thoughts returned to a moment back in the hospital in Yokosuka when a man dressed in khaki attire, boasting no military insignia or identification, had approached me as I was completing one of my daily walks. He told me that he was part of a group that helped countries around the world fight oppression and Communism, and informed me that my record had been brought to his attention. He was there, he said, to recruit me, and could guarantee me a minimum of $100,000 per year. I waved him off, assuring him that I was tired of killing. As the insults from the civilians attacked my soul, I wondered if I had made the right decision. Maybe I did need to remain a killer.

Suddenly, I was standing with a group of marines, thoughts out of control. I checked their faces, drawn and taut in reaction to the slurs. I looked back at the people held at bay by the MPs. They weren't even long-haired hippies like I expected. Although most appeared to be college-age men and women, a few older, should-be-wiser ones were there as well.

"Listen up, men," the top sergeant's command made me momentarily forget our accusers. "If you have less than nine months left in the Corps and don't want to re-up,[1] step in the line on your left. If you have over nine months left or if you do want to re-up, step to the line on your right." For some reason, I did not hesitate. I suddenly found myself in the line on the left.

We all signed a roster to verify we were definitely back in the states, then boarded a Marine Corps transport bus parked just outside the airport gates. With a roar and a puff of smoke, the bus took us away from the verbal assault. As we pulled away, I couldn't help but look back at our attackers. They stood, waving fists into the air, screaming more profanity. I fought back the tears and rage once again. "Why?" my mind kept asking. I decided then and there to shed any and all relations that labeled me a "Vietnam veteran."

"Maybe I should look up that mercenary," I thought once again.

Before I knew it, I was loading my tired body onto a nice soft mattress in the staging barracks of El Toro.[2] It took them a week to complete all of the physical, blood, and urine tests, to make sure it was safe to release us into the real world. The only test they failed to run was one to determine our mental state. Many future problems might have been avoided if they had only had such insight. But they were not concerned with our mental health, only about moving us through the system as rapidly as possible, to make room for the mass of soldiers coming in behind us. The government had started a "limited" withdrawal, which meant that the Corps began offering "early out" options to anyone with nine months or less in their hitch.

During that time, we were not allowed base privileges or even phone calls. We were confined to barracks. Everywhere we went—testing, mess hall, whatever—was under armed guard, so no one would be tempted to go AWOL. I couldn't imagine someone getting that impatient, but that was their fear. I had my own fear. I had lived in the bush, eaten raw fish and raw pork, drunk the filthy water, lived among the people. Would the doctors find a rotten little bug in me that would keep me from being released to go home? The reports came through. The "rotten little bug" had remained undetected, locked away in the depths of my mind. We all passed. "Yeehaw!" I yelled.

Discharge papers in hand, I headed for the closest phone, but before calling I stopped to re-read my orders. They still read the same. "Corporal Goodson, U.S. Marine Corps, Honorable Discharge, 27 June 1969." I was about to bust a gusset with joy. Dialing complete, I waited for the voice at the other end. The ringing continued. Nothing! Nobody was home. I was enraged.

"Answer the phone!" I yelled. My fellow marines looked over at me from their phone calls. Some shared my frustrations. Others urged me to "quiet down."

I dug into my pocket and unfolded a piece of paper with my brother's name and number on it. Edd was still in the marines and lived in Oceanside, just a few miles from El Toro. I dialed his number. Two rings. His new wife answered. "Hello?"

"Hello to you," I said. "This is Barry. Would it be . . ."

"Barry!" the voice exclaimed. "You're home?"

"Yeah, well I'm in El Toro," I replied. "And discharged from the good old Marine Corps. Do you think I could spend the weekend with y'all? My parents don't seem to be home."

"You bet you can!" she answered. "In fact, Eddie would probably like for you to spend a week with us."

"Thanks," I said. "Is he there?"

"No," she answered, "but I expect him any minute. Are you ready?"

"You bet," I answered. "All I have to do is collect my gear. Tell him I'll meet him at the front gate."

"Great!" she said. "I'll send him on his way."

I hung up and headed toward the barracks, my thoughts in high gear. "A civilian again," I thought. I felt like screaming.

A car stopped to let me pass before it continued its own journey. A voice screamed out, "Hey, marine!"

I kept walking.

"Marine!!" The voice was belligerent this time.

I stopped, not even looking around. "Can't be talking to me," I thought, "I'm a civilian."

The voice sounded again, this time with a note of desperation. "Hey, you!" A hand reached out and touched my arm. I swung around ready for the enemy.

"Whoa, marine, don't you see that officer there?" A tall slender marine sergeant stood before me.

The fact was I hadn't. All I had seen was a car. I looked. Yep. He was right. The man was a full blown colonel. I peered through the windshield at him. "I believe you're right," I said. "He is an officer."

"Well, then, how about a salute?" the sergeant demanded.

For the first time I looked at him. He was definitely a stateside marine. He boasted only a "fire ribbon" on his chest, just like all the men who had graduated from boot camp with me. I held my orders up in the air, brazenly clutched in my fist. "Look, you idiot," I said. "I am no longer a marine. I have discharge papers in my hand, and only *you* between me and civilian life, so I suggest you step aside and salute the officer yourself!"

He abruptly stepped back. I glanced over at the colonel. He just laughed, leaned out the window and yelled, "Welcome back." The sergeant snapped out a salute.

I left him and the officer and headed out to rejoin the world I had once known, to pick up where I had left off. Vietnam was neatly packed away on its own private shelf along with the taunting from the airport. I planned to drown myself in everything civilian life offered and to blend in with the surrounding people. They would never know I was a Vietnam veteran. I would never hear the accursed accusation again. I did not have an inkling of how much I actually stood out. Hiding my association with Vietnam would prove to be impossible.

It seemed like eternity, but Brother Edd finally arrived at the front gate.

"Hey, bro!" I yelled.

"Hey, yourself," he yelled back. "Welcome home."

I jumped into his car, tossing my gear into the back seat. "Still have the old Volkswagen, I see."

He laughed. "Yeah, old reliable is sure enough alive and kicking." The cloud of troubles instantly lifted as I readied myself for the oncoming fun and games of my return to civilian life.

"How's the new wife?" I asked.

Edd just smiled. "How long are you going to stay in California?" he asked as he headed his car onto the highway in a beeline for Oceanside. The cool ocean air felt great, but the palm trees made me think of Vietnam. I suddenly realized Edd had asked me a question. I shoved Vietnam back on the shelf.

"Sorry, bro," I answered. "What did you say?"

"How long are you here?"

"I imagine just for the weekend," I assured him. "No offense, but I'm heading home as soon as I get a green light."

"Now *that* I definitely understand." He started telling me all about his new life and his new wife. The palm trees kept haunting me, aided by occasional choppers and military vehicles. I forced it back once again. My brother was filling me in on the things we could do over the next few days if I was interested. I hadn't heard a word he said.

"What do you think?" he asked.

"Hey, it all sounds great. I'll leave it all up to you. But don't go to any great pains. Just being back is enough for me. I could lay back and just soak it in for the rest of my life."

"Yeah. I know what you mean. Let's go to the beach." Edd did indeed know what I meant. Just the previous year he had returned from an over-

seas hitch in Okinawa, where he had been sent in lieu of his original assignment—Vietnam.

"Great," I answered. "Nothing better than a California beach."

For the next two days, we "took in the beach" as they called it. Everywhere I turned, "fun" surrounded me. I tried my hand at body surfing,
with a violent reaction from my still tender side. Everywhere you looked,
people were having fun. My mind kept telling me that I did not deserve to
have fun, that I should still be in Vietnam fighting beside my men. I tried
to shove the thoughts away, but they would no longer accept just being
swept into a corner. A tear forced its way to the surface. Secretly I wiped it
away, then checked to make sure no one had seen my moment of weakness.
They hadn't. Eddie and Linda were both chatting away about something I
never heard. The other people did not matter. They were having fun—
something I was going to have to try harder to do, but some other time.

My mind simply would not let me join in on the "fun." I excused
myself and set out for a long walk down the beach. I had to separate myself
from the crowds of people. Half-naked women walked by without even
coming close to diverting my troubled mind. My eyes were still in Vietnam.

By the time I returned to Edd and Linda, the sun lay low in the horizon, basking the ocean in an orange glow.

"Sorry! I didn't mean to run off and leave y'all."

"No problem," Edd said. "You'll probably need a bunch of walks like
that."

"Maybe," I mumbled. "Y'all ready to head back?"

"Sure," he said. "Are you okay?"

"Yeah," I forced a laugh, "just not much on crowds."

That night I tried calling my parents once again. This time a familiar
voice said "Hello."

"Mom?" I asked, just to hear her say so.

"Barry?" she asked.

We laughed. "Mom, I'm ready to come home. I'm a civilian again." I
heard sobs on the other end. "Mom, are you okay?"

There was silence. Suddenly my dad was on the phone. "Son?"

"Yo, Dad," I answered.

"Your mom can't talk right now." He hesitated for a moment. I could
visualize him turning to check on her. "When are you coming home?"

"Tomorrow, Dad!" I exclaimed. "Tomorrow!"

I caught them up on where I had been, including the weekend with Edd and his wife. They told me they had been at the farm but mom made dad come home early because she just knew they needed to be home. The thought of the old family farm brought a smile to my face.

The next day was Sunday, June 29, 1969. I thanked Edd and his wife, waved good-bye and boarded the jet for home. I endured the flight by studying the constantly changing landscape below us. Lake Powell[3] came and went. The circle pastures of West Texas followed closely behind. I grew impatient as I checked my watch. Finally, the little sign warned us of our approach to Love Field.[4] I was excited beyond measure. I didn't want to exit onto a ramp. I wanted to immediately step out, bow down and kiss the Texas soil I had longed to touch. I could see Dad, Mom, my younger brother Glenn, and my cousin Teri waving at me from the hallway. I fought back the tears, rushed out and dropped my gear to the floor. Hugs upon hugs, enclosed in the many arms of my family. I was finally home, away from the war, safe and sound in the country I loved.

But it wasn't long before I felt uncomfortable. My own hometown was different—Fort Worth had had a facelift. The flag that used to show its colors above the old courthouse was gone. Most of the old landmarks had been torn down. The styles had changed. The people had changed. Worst of all, I had changed. I found myself avoiding people I had known in the past. Old friends were shoved aside in search of new ones. My mind was ablaze with total confusion and pain.

My search for new friends was useless. Everyone seemed to have the same questions: What is war like? Is it as bad as they show it on TV? How many children did you kill? How could you be a part of something like that? Why couldn't you guys win the war?

The last question was one of the worst. People had no idea how many battles we had won, only to turn around and give the territory back to the enemy. Unlike previous wars, in Vietnam we were generally not allowed to be the aggressors. We could not march through the country and force the enemy back into North Vietnam. Nor were we allowed to invade North Vietnam directly. Instead, we were instructed to engage the enemy only when he entered our Area of Prime Responsibility. Even then, we were not to kill or shoot unless "shot at," or unless we saw a weapon on the enemy. We were more like a police force than a fighting force from previous wars.

We weren't in Vietnam to eradicate the enemy, only to fight him if and when he showed his face in the wrong area.

In Quảng Tin Province, fortunately, the story had been different. There were no officers telling us to give back the territory we had taken. The Viet Cong and the NVA knew that the territory was ours and that we were not going to leave and simply let them walk in and take it back. The local people knew it, too, and were glad to have us there. In the province, at least we were winning the war!

Unable to communicate my war experiences with my family and friends, I decided to write to my fellow CAP marine, PFC John Ciminski, who had been home about a month longer than I. I wanted to see if he was having better luck at fitting in. When a week went by with no answer, I sent off a second letter. Again, time passed with no answer. More than a month later, I received a letter with the return address: "Ciminski, Little Falls, Minnesota." I ripped it open, longing to hear from my old buddy.

"Dear Corporal Barry," it started out. "I'm John's mother and I apologize for not answering your letter before now. After John came home, he bought that truck he was telling you about and began helping stranded people. We get a lot of those up here. Well, anyway, just a few weeks after he got his truck, he was helping a young couple out of ditch when a crazy, drunken driver came flying around a bend in the road."

Suddenly, I knew what she was going to say. I stopped, swallowed hard, then read on.

"The car slammed into John, pinning him against the car that he was trying to get out of the ditch. Barry, he died on the spot. The drunk driver backed off, let John fall to the ground and then sped off. Since that day I have received threatening phone calls warning me to not even try to press charges."

The letter went on to say that she wanted me to come up and visit her for a while. I knew in my heart that I could not. I knew that if I went to Little Falls, I would seek out the person responsible for killing John, and I would kill him. Rage boiled inside of me as I recalled all that John had endured in Vietnam, only to return and be killed by a stupid-ass, drunken driver. I shoved the letter and John's memory on the shelf with Vietnam and took off on a long drive in an attempt to elude the pain that haunted me. My mother sent a return letter to Mrs. Ciminski, because I simply could not take pen in hand.

Days later I met up with a couple of old friends of mine who refused to
be set aside, Dale Cassidy and Bill Boomer. Together, we decided to move
into a large apartment over on the southeast side of Fort Worth which in
my absence had changed from a predominantly "white" area to a black one.
As we were walking home from the local 7-11 one night, a dozen or so
blacks surrounded us and demanded we give them our six-pack of beer. It
reminded me of the problems in Okinawa, and suddenly my mind returned
to the combat I knew so well.

I snapped out orders like the squad leader I had once been. "Dale, go
get your shotgun," I yelled. "Bill, get the security guard!"

In an instant, I was alone with all but two of the blacks. One had
chased after Dale and another after Bill. Their leader stepped forward:
"Why'd you send them for a gun, white boy?" he sneered.

"You're gonna die," I sneered back.

He swung at my face. The blow glanced off my forehead as I dodged
and drove home my punch. Suddenly a shot rang into the night air. I turned
and saw the security guard standing there with his .38 revolver pointed
into the air. The group scattered like BBs on a concrete floor, disappearing
into the night. Just as suddenly, it was quiet again. The firefight was over.
I checked my men for casualties, my mind still in Vietnam. I fought to
bring myself back to reality.

The security guard called the police. "Don't expect much," he said to
me as he hung up the phone. I wasn't sure what he meant until I had waited
more than an hour and a half for the police cruiser that finally pulled up in
the parking lot.

"You guys the ones reporting trouble?" the blonde one asked.

I looked at him, raging inside. "Yeah," I answered. "You guys stop for
a sandwich on the way?"

The blond guy just stared at me. His partner jumped in. "We were tied
up on another call," he offered.

"Well, you're here now. Let's go get 'em," I barked.

"Whoa, mister," he held out his hand. "We're here simply to report the
incident, and since no one was hurt, that's as far as we can go."

"You're kidding!" I glared at him.

"No, I'm not," he answered. "Now if you have trouble with them again,
there are things you could do . . . like give 'em swimming lessons." He
pointed toward the pool beside our apartment.

I looked into the depths of the clear water before I answered him. "Then you'd be back down here in fifteen minutes to haul me away to the slammer," I sneered.

"No doubt," he said.

Engulfed in rage and fury, I spun on my heel. The old urge to kill was bubbling to the surface. I had to get away from them—from everyone—to gain control. I walked around the dark shadows of the apartment complex, battling with my killer instinct. My logic told me I was not in combat any longer, but my emotions defied control.

The police officers completed their report with input from my two friends and then left. Dale and Bill thanked the security guard and sauntered up the flights of stairs, vanishing into the depths of our apartment. I hovered in the shadows of some bushes, trying to decide what to do. The enemy was out there, just across the street, in forbidden territory just like Cambodia, Laos and North Vietnam had been to us in Vietnam. Silently, slowly, I crept up the stairs to our apartment. I did not want any interference from Dale or Bill. Stopping just outside the door, I leaned forward to listen for sounds inside. It was silent. I dug out my key and slowly turned the lock. The door opened, revealing an empty living room and hall. Stealthily, I made my way to my bedroom, passing my roommates who were in the kitchen, talking loudly about our confrontation that evening. My rifle was in the closet. Slowly, I opened the door and pulled down my 30-30 Winchester, along with a box of shells. With rapid, smooth motions, I loaded the weapon with seven bullets and worked one round into the chamber. With the stealth of a cat, I left the apartment, leaving the door slightly ajar, not wanting to risk the sound of the latch.

The moon was half full, briefly shadowed by the low flying clouds. A gentle breeze met me as I crept down the stairs to the parking lot. The lot was empty except for one couple getting in their car to leave. I waited in the shadows of the hedges along the back wall of our apartment, watching as the last set of lights disappeared into the night. With a quick look around, I leaped from my cover and climbed onto the top of my car.

There I stood, glaring at the forbidden land, at the Cambodia we could never enter, where the enemy could come and go as they pleased. They could steal across the border in the dark of night, kill and maim, and then retreat back to a hiding place into which we were not allowed to venture.

I lifted my face to the sky. "Why?" I screamed, not caring who heard. I transferred my glare to the other side, to the hidden enemy, and I unleashed every obscenity held back in the depths of my mind. I screamed at every passing car and flung curses and invitations out to my enemy. "I dare you to try to sneak across tonight!" I screamed. "Come on, you cowards. Face your death like a man!"

My enemy remained silent. Life went on around me, oblivious to my very presence, oblivious to the relentless rage I was unleashing. No one took me up on my dare, which made me even madder. I wanted to kill. I had to kill. Yet the enemy refused to show his face. To this day, I have no idea how long I was engulfed in my madness. I stopped only because my throat was becoming raw from the continuous screaming.

I squatted down on my haunches, Vietnamese style, watching the traffic roll by. Tears began streaming down my face, my thoughts caught up in a whirlwind. A picture of the people at the airport in California, taunting and jeering, flitted through my mind. Memories of the countless bodies destroyed by the horrors of war forced their way in beside them. A vision of the look of horror on John Ciminski's face as the car pinned him against the one he was trying to help, crowded in among the other scenes. Rage was in full control.

With a vicious stroke of my hand, I wiped away the tears. "Welcome home, marine!" my thoughts screamed out. "Welcome home."

The rifle slipped from my hands, dropping with a metallic clatter to the roof of the car. I clasped my head, engulfed by the pain of the rage that haunted my brain. Tears streamed down my face as memories of the war flashed before me. The outcries from my fellow Americans crowded in beside them. I could resist no longer.

The sobs finally ceased as the emotion faded, allowing rational thoughts to regain control. I was unsure of the future that awaited me. One thing I knew without a doubt: the rage and bitterness had to be controlled. If not, I would end up like a caged animal for the rest of my life. I had no idea how to deal with my problems. There seemed to be nowhere to turn, no one who could share my burden. John was dead, after surviving the worst hell a man could survive. He was the only one to whom I could have turned. My parents would've helped if they could, if they had known—but they did not. Nor could they have understood. How could any civilian hope to understand the torment, the turmoil?

In truth, I did not want anyone to know what lurked deep inside my soul. Convincing myself that there were none who could possibly understand, I shoved the painful memories onto the already-crowded shelf. A demeanor of calm resolve took its place. The animal that had returned from the depths of hell would never be discovered. I vowed to discuss Vietnam with no one.

Picking up my rifle, I leapt to the ground below. I stopped momentarily, and turned back to face my enemy once again.

"Welcome home marine, welcome home," I said over and over to myself.

---

[1]   Re-up means to re-enlist.
[2]   El Toro is a U.S. Marine Corps base north of San Diego.
[3]   Lake Powell is situated near the south end of the Upper Colorado River Basin on the border between Utah and Arizona.
[4]   Love Field was the main airport for Dallas and Fort Worth in the 1960s.

## Chapter 13

# Welcome Back

**N**o one seemed to notice my rampage that night. I'm not even sure what I expected. All I knew was that my deepest self wanted to kill, to lash out at whatever evil was oppressing me. It wasn't the blacks. They were just handy, convenient for the release of the confusion and hatred that had carved out a home in my soul.

I wanted to kill "the enemy" as we had been so aptly trained to do. Yet the enemy had become intangible, lacking any substance I could grasp. I had wanted to come home, if not as a hero, at least as someone people would look up to with respect for having braved the good fight. Instead, I had to hide the fact that I was a Vietnam veteran or subject myself to verbal abuse. As I listened to the news media and other fellow countrymen unleash their constant condemnation of the war and the men who fought it, I wondered if other veterans felt the same pain and anger I did.

My "Vietnam" self was shelved, discarded for a safer facade. I resolved that no one would ever know of my true identify, my true self. Occasionally someone I met would make a statement or comment about how all of the Vietnam veterans seemed to have mental problems because of the war and how they were all dope addicts. Initially, I let it slide, but eventually my vow to silence had to be broken. I simply could not stand idle while fools attempted to pass judgment on a situation they knew nothing about. I had to set them straight.

"Do you know every veteran personally?" I would ask.

"Well, no," they would reply.

"Sounds like a pretty subjective opinion then," I would say.

The typical reply was, "Well, what's *your* opinion about Vietnam vets?"
"I am one."

Generally, they would change the subject or comment that I certainly
didn't act like a Vietnam veteran.

"How are we supposed to act?"

"Well, you're so clean cut and level headed," they would answer. "You
don't seem crazy at all."

This became almost a daily routine. People in night clubs didn't want
to buy you a drink to celebrate your return, as was the custom after other
wars. They just wanted to fight you to prove their own worth. Others wanted
to satisfy their own morbid curiosities, with no real concern for the people
involved. Although I continued to try to keep my Vietnam experiences on
the shelf, I could not hide the reality. I was a veteran, a combat veteran, and
I could not stand by while fools ridiculed and belittled us.

Three months after my return from 'Nam, I received two letters. The
first came from the Corps: "You are requested to appear at your local
Marine Corps Reserve office at 0800 hours on Thursday to receive the award
of the Purple Heart and the Naval Achievement Medal with Valor for wounds
received during combat and for outstanding performance of duties."

At first I was shocked and elated. Then bitterness slid back into control. The Achievement Medal, I had no problem with. I was glad and honored to receive it. The Purple Heart was difficult to accept. Still echoing in
my ears was the CO's voice from the first time I was wounded. It had been
a small wound, a scratch actually, from a small piece of shrapnel. The thought
of going after a Purple Heart never even crossed my mind. The CO, however, had to make sure.

"Corporal Goodson," he had stated as he stepped into the corpsman's
tent.

"Yes, sir."

"Heard you were wounded by our 105s. Just a scratch, huh?" he stated.

"Hardly even bled, sir," I answered.

He stared at me for a moment then continued. "Corporal, you understand, of course, that we cannot award you with a Purple Heart for this
wound. We simply do not award people for getting hit by friendly fire."

"No problem, sir," I said. "It's too minor to worry over, anyway."

"Good," he answered, "good." And he turned and disappeared through
the doors of the tent.

At that time, their rule did not bother me, although I did consider it a stupid technicality. Wasn't a wound a wound? Did it really matter which side inflicted it? And the phrase "friendly fire" was an oxymoron if there ever was one. Were you less courageous because of the source of your wounds? But I was willing at first to place the rule on the shelf of my mind along with other miscellaneous items marked "Stupid Rules," and I thought no more about it.

Then came my second bout with our notorious friendly fire. One day in Yokosuka, as I lay in my rack attempting to convince my body that there was no pain, an officer entered the ward accompanied by a PFC carrying an armload of dark colored boxes. The officer stopped at the first rack, and looked down at the marine lying in a multitude of bandages.

"Marine," the officer stated gruffly. I heard no comment from the bed. The officer turned and took a box from the PFC, then returned his attention to the wounded marine. "Well, fella, you've earned yourself a Purple Heart. We're proud of you for a battle well fought." He reached out and shook the man's hand, pinned the shiny purple and gold medal onto the man's pillow, stepped back, saluted, and turned briskly to the next bed.

This ceremony continued until he reached me. He looked down at his list, frowned, and then looked back up at me.

"Yes, sir?" I asked.

"Sorry, marine," he stated, "you were wounded by friendly fire. We can't give out Purple Hearts for that." He turned on his heel and continued to the next rack.

I wanted to scream. I had fought just as hard as the next guy. My wounds hurt, regardless of their source. I had been wounded in the thick of battle, yet according to the Corps I remained undeserving of the honor and respect the other marines were receiving. Instead of pride for a battle well-fought, I felt shame because I had been wounded by Americans rather than by the enemy. Hit twice and left with scars to remind me. No medals, only scars, some much deeper than others.

My parents were outraged that I had not received the medal so, unbeknownst to me, my mother had fired off a letter to our local congressman. Her letter inspired him to pursue the matter wholeheartedly, and he discovered I was due to receive a Purple Heart after all. The rule actually read that if you were wounded by friendly fire during a *battle*, you were eligible to receive the award.

As a result, on 12 September 1970, I found myself standing in front of a Marine Corps Reserve officer who was ceremoniously pinning a Purple Heart to my chest, along with the Naval Achievement Medal I had known nothing about. Somehow, though, the glamour just wasn't there. In my heart I knew the medal was rightfully mine, but my mind kept reminding me of the friendly fire. I shook the officer's hand and shared the moment with my parents. Then, back at home, I packed the medals away in a box and hid them in a small corner of my closet, along with the memories.

The second letter I received was even more of a surprise than the one informing me of the Purple Heart. It informed me that I was a possible recipient of rehabilitation assistance as a Disabled Veteran, and suggested I contact the VA Hospital in Dallas to determine my disability rating. I was amazed. On the one hand, they made me feel I did not deserve a Purple Heart, and then on the other, they wanted to label me "Disabled." I did not want that label, which I felt should be reserved for the elite group of men who suffered most from the war—men who had lost legs, arms, fingers, and in some cases, half of their bodies. My body was intact. Shot up a bit, but intact. I did not want to accept the label "disabled," yet my parents, friends, and government insisted that I "think of the benefits," especially the educational assistance.

The Medical Board poked, prodded, and examined me from head to toe and then asked me to wait in the hall. An hour later, they called me back in. "Mr. Goodson, we have determined that your wounds warrant a rating of thirty percent disability," the chief officer announced. "You will receive a monthly payment for the rest of your life, along with full payment for a four-year degree from any college of your choice."

I left the room happy but still confused. I had always longed for the college education that had so far been unreachable because of my income. Now, out of nowhere, the possibility was laid in my lap. Yet in order to accept it, I also had to accept the label of "disabled." How would I face other veterans who had given so much more?

The Vietnam shelf was beginning to overflow with memories I chose not to handle. They had to be dealt with, but I did not know how to do it. Somehow I had to uncover a way to fit in, a way to control the rage that boiled and festered within my soul. Maybe school would help. America was not prepared to accept the Vietnam veterans. It was up to us to shoulder the responsibility for our war while at the same time most people were trying to deny that it even existed.

It was easy for them. They had never seen the horrors endured by every Vietnam veteran and the Vietnamese people, so it was easy for them to say, "I was against the war in the beginning. It is your screw-up, so live with the consequences."

We did indeed live with it, daily. We each knew how deeply involved we were in the war. No one needed to remind us of our responsibility. America was wrong, though. Dead wrong. We *were* fighting against Communist aggression. We *were* fighting for the freedom of the people. We believed in our war. Believed in fighting for freedom.[1] Beyond that, well, we had no control.

---

[1] Some veterans, of course, opposed the war. See John E. Kerry and the Vietnam Veterans against the War, *The New Soldier* (New York: Macmillan, 1971); Ron Kovic, *Born on the Fourth of July* (New York: McGraw-Hill, 1976).

# Chapter 14

# A Slow Healing

**C**ollege! It finally hit me on that hot day in August, 1970, as I walked across the campus of Texas Christian University to attend my first class. I had signed up for the fulfillment of another lifelong desire, to become an artist, to nurture my ability to express my feelings on canvas. No one but the counselor knew I was a Vietnam vet. At least, that was what I thought. As it turned out, every one of my professors had been notified of the fact. I do not know why, but they knew.

One of my art professors had been a POW in World War II. He shared with me many stories of the horrors he had suffered at the hands of the enemy. My heart shared his pain. He was a kind man with a strong desire to help his students succeed. Unfortunately, I could not bring myself to open up to him, although I wanted to. My heart was aching to unload the pain it held inside. Yet I simply could not.

Every good person in your life always seems to be offset by a bad one. This situation was no different. My sculpture professor was an extremist who thought that being an artist meant being a radical—someone whose ultimate goal was to speak out against anything for which most common folks stood. He hated the war and everyone who was even remotely associated with it. He did not have any relatives or friends in combat, yet he was a standing authority on all the whys and wherefores of the war. A day did not pass without his offering his opinion of me and my war. I could see that a few of my fellow students had sympathy for me, but most were adamantly on the side of the professor.

In the beginning, I kept telling him to "back off," but he would not be thwarted. He was out for blood and come hell or high water, he was going to get it. My presence had given him the opportunity to vent his own frustrations. He outwardly detested me even being in his class, yet my being there allowed him to spout off every day.

For weeks, I tolerated his verbal attacks. The students came to know me as "the killer" and no doubt wondered if I had indeed killed babies and raped women. After all, my accuser was their professor. Soon most of them began to avoid me—politely, yet noticeably. I tried to dismiss them as poor, misinformed creatures who were not worthy of my time. It didn't work. I had an ingrained desire to stand up for myself and my fellow veterans. On one particular day, the professor unwittingly opened a door that allowed me to do just that.

The class was full. We were each deeply involved in our own creations, trying to prompt the clay to release the expression hidden deep within us. Suddenly, the hair on the back of my neck bristled as I sensed him standing right behind me.

Without turning, I asked, "What do you want?" A snicker reached my ears. Rage swelled up inside me. I swallowed hard to quench the fire by simply staring at the sculpture before me. My creation had nothing to say. It offered no assistance toward my need for self control.

"Just a thought I felt I should pass on to you, Mr. Goodson," he sneered.

"Get it over with," I said as I tensed for his next comment, my gaze transfixed on my masterpiece.

"Well, I've been studying the entire Vietnam situation . . ."

"War!" I corrected with a roar. "War!"

"Well . . . whatever," he continued. "Anyway, I have determined that the men who went to Canada[1] are the true heroes of this war, and that every man who went to Vietnam was—no . . . is—a coward."

His words rang in my ears. With one smooth stroke, I slammed my wooden ruler down on the edge of the table. Half of it went flying across the room. The other half, jagged and splintered, remained clutched in my grip. Before he could react, I reached back and grabbed him by the hair, forcing his head over the back of my shoulder. In an instant the jagged edges of the broken ruler stabbed toward his neck.

"Kill him!" my mind screamed. "Kill him!"

Something stopped me just as the first splinters reached out to plunge into the jugular hidden in the shallow depths of his neck. My hand hov-

ered, tensed, ready to sink my weapon deep. The creature inside me lusted
for the opportunity for revenge. Rage flared in full control, held in check,
momentarily, by a single thread of decency lingering somewhere in my
conscience. I looked around. The room, once teeming with students, was
empty.

I returned my attention to my enemy. He was shaking with fear. His
face was next to mine. I tightened my grip on his hair. He winced with
pain. "Don't do it, man," he whined. "I was only teasing you."

I glared at him while visions of the countless bodies of men, women
and children flipped through my memory, their deaths so grotesque that
the word "death" fell far short of describing the evil that had destroyed
them.

"This man is a sniveling, weak coward who deserves to die," my mind
argued. "Kill him!"

Once again swallowing hard, fighting back the rage, I looked him in
the eye. "Listen, and listen good," I growled into his face. "Never, ever
mention anything about Vietnam again." I tightened my grip on his hair.
Strands were breaking loose, one by one. "Understand?" He only whim-
pered and began to sob. In disgust, I threw him over the table behind us.
He fell backwards, crashing into chairs, rolling over the table, and smash-
ing the partial sculptures that lay in his way. Finally, he dropped to the
floor and rolled to a heap of sobbing cowardice.

I stood looking down at the man I had wanted to kill. "Never," I bellowed, then spun on my heel and left the room. A few of my braver fellow
students were hovering just outside the door. I stopped and stared at them.
They all turned away.

The rage slowly ebbed away as the magnitude of my rampage took
hold of my mind. I wanted away from my tormentors, my enemies, so I
took a walk to one of the picnic areas near the Fort Worth Zoo. It was quiet
there. A good place to think. To sort things out and return them to their
proper place. I had to get things under control, get back to reality. I was *not*
the animal I'd had to become in the war. Or was I? My thoughts were
caught up by the tornadic battle consuming my mind.

A squirrel searching the nearby grass for a tasty treat stopped momentarily to study the man who was intruding in his life. I smiled at his innocence. No condemnation in those eyes. "Don't worry, my furry friend," I
said. "You, I will not kill." But I wondered: would I indeed kill again? Had

I lost all sense of right from wrong? Maybe the professor was right. Maybe I should be caged up. The answers eluded me. There seemed to be nowhere to turn. No place to hide. And I did not *want* to hide.

"*They* are the cowards," I screamed. "Not me. Let them cower in the darkness." I looked around. Thankfully no one was near enough to hear me. "Pull yourself together," I said aloud. A memory filtered through the clutter engulfing my mind. "It don't mean nothing, man. Nothing." I chose what by now was my standard response. I shoved the entire event onto my memory shelf.

I looked back towards where my new college, my new opportunity lay waiting. It was there for the asking. I could not let them steal that from me. The pain in my left side reminded me of how much I had fought for such an opportunity. Somehow I had to get past the barrier. For years I had dreamed of a college diploma. My future depended on it. It had to be done. Failure was not an option. I turned to face the enemy that stood between me and my objective. With one swift stride I started the journey back to the challenge that waited in the halls of TCU.

Unknown to me that day, my future held a multitude of such confrontations. Hardly a day slipped by without someone confronting me with an opinion about me and my war. I tried to avoid trouble with such tormentors, yet some refused to leave it alone. Many wanted to fight, but I always managed to convince them it was a bad idea. Somehow that moment with my art professor made me fully aware of the monster that lurked deep inside my soul. Something told me that I had to keep it caged up, or end up in a cage myself.

It was my worst dilemma. On the one hand I hated killing and remained haunted by nightmares of the horrors I thought I had left in Vietnam. On the other hand, my very being cried out to "kill" in retaliation against my new-found enemy. I knew I could not do so, yet the desire never left, hovering just under the surface as if waiting for my one weak moment.

Graduation from college arrived just two short years after I returned from Vietnam. To help keep my mind off my problems, I had signed up for maximum hours every semester, including summers. The only thing left was to step out into the real world, start a career and finally put the war behind me. Once again I was to discover that Vietnam would always be with me. Shortly after graduation I began to experience severe pain in my wounded side. I tolerated it for a number of months until it became too intense to ignore. I finally called a clinic in Fort Worth.

A pretty, young voice answered the phone.

"I need to see a doctor, please," I told her. "I have an old wound that seems to be aggravated."

"A wound?" she asked. "Did you hurt yourself at work?"

"You might say that," I answered. There was no way I was going to reveal the source of the wound over the phone. I figured if I did she would tell me to call the V.A. Hospital and then hang up. I was able to make an appointment for that afternoon, and by the time I got there the pain was stabbing relentlessly across my left side and stomach.

When Dr. Sewell examined the small knot protruding from my navel, he said: "Looks like something in there wants out."

A short time later, after he had taken x-rays, he sat on the edge of his desk studying the pictures of my guts. He turned towards me with a fur-rowed brow. Peering over the top of his bifocals, he said, "Son, where did you get such a wound?"

Immediately my defenses flared up. "In Vietnam. Why? Does that make a difference?" I waited for the attack. The accusations. They did not come.

"Of course not," he answered. "I was just curious, because who ever did the surgery was in somewhat of a hurry."

"Why do you say that?"

"Your gut is full of foreign matter, Mr. Goodson. Trash."

"Full of what . . . ?" I was dumbfounded. "Trash!?"

"I've seen a little of this," he offered. "I suppose that's why they refer to it as 'meatball surgery.' They do what it takes to save your life and then go on to the next patient, leaving the clean-up work for doctors back here in the states."

"I suppose so," I answered. "I certainly can't blame them for that. At least they got me home in one piece."

"True, Barry. So when do you want me to clean you up?"

"I'm ready," I answered. "When can you do it?"

"How about this afternoon? I can have the nurse prepare the surgery room in just a short time if you think you can stand a local anesthetic."

"Let's do it," I agreed.

After a brief wait I found myself lying once again on a stainless steel table covered in white sheets. Bright lights radiated beams of concentrated light onto my stomach. Dr. Sewell leaned over to observe the work his nurse had done to get me prepared, then nodded his approval.

"You'll be okay," the nurse assured me.

Dr. Sewell looked at me as he reached back towards his nurse. "This may hurt for a little bit," he said, "but after awhile you won't feel any-thing."

"Get on with it," I urged.

The stab of the needle brought a wince of pain to my lips. Minutes later the doctor was studying my insides through the bifocals resting on the bridge of his nose. Droplets of sweat, created by the heat from the lamps, sparkled on his brow. I could just barely feel the slice of the knife. I watched as he folded back the skin to get to the "trash" hidden inside.

"My God," he cried out, glancing up at me.

"What is it?" I asked. "Worse than we thought?"

"No, not really," he answered. "I am just surprised. Do you want to see what I found?"

"Why not?" I waited as he dug around and then held up his first prize. It was covered in blood, but its identity was obvious—a small ball of hair.

"Oh great!" was all I could get out. The doctor dropped the mess onto a metal tray and then returned to the hole in my stomach. I could feel as well as hear the sickening sound of the moving flesh as he dug deeper.

"Wow! Look at this!" He held up another little piece of trash, captured between the tips of his fingers. I peered at it closely, but could not tell what it was. "What is it?" I asked.

"That, my son, is a rock. Evidently forced in by the explosion along with the shrapnel."

Suddenly I felt pale and weak. Sweat began to pour down the sides of my face. I was unsure which was making me sick: the sight of the "junk" or the memory of how I had received the wound. My mind was taking me back to the jungles of 'Nam. Back to reality. The battle with the Mortar Gang was still in full swing. A never-ending picture of gore. A light flashed as I heard the sound of the artillery exploding around us. Suddenly I was in a room, lying on a hard metal table. A doctor was standing, looking down at me. "It's all over marine. All over."

"What!" I shook my head.

"It's all over," Dr. Sewell said. "You're all sewn up and ready to go. Whenever you feel up to it. You had quite a bit of trash in there, but I think we got it all this time. Good luck to you." He reached out and shook my hand.

I shook my head again. "Thanks Doc," I stammered. I was still dazed by my lapse into the flashback. "Thanks a lot." Finally Vietnam returned to its proper place. I sat up, staring at the assortment of items lying in a neat row on the metal tray.

Dr. Sewell followed my gaze. "Do you want to keep all that stuff? I can have the nurse clean it up for you."

I laughed. "Not hardly. I've seen enough, but thanks."

I left the clinic and the physical pain behind. "If only the remaining pain could be dealt with so easily," I said to myself. "If only surgery could cut out the pain in my soul." I drove down the road as my mind searched for a way to handle the memories, the pain it seemed would never go away.

Because of the pain, I refused for many years to read books or watch movies about "my war." But inwardly, I yearned for a writer or movie producer who could recreate the horrors with such accuracy that Americans would finally hear the truth about Vietnam—that we fought the best way we could with the weapons and rules available to us at that time. We fought for the freedom of the oppressed. As individuals, we had no idea that the war was being manipulated by powers beyond our control. We only knew what our senses told us, that farmers and villagers were being beaten, slaughtered, raped and maimed in the name of the Communist "Freedom Fighters."

During all the turmoil of my healing years, I met a young girl full of the eagerness and innocence of youth. I really feel that is what made me fall for her. Somehow, I felt that her youth, her vitality, her innocence would rub off on me, or if not, at least her radiance would cover up the pain I felt inside. She tried to fulfill the role I assigned to her, she really did. But I was too messed up. Try as she might, she simply could not handle the creature lurking inside of me. She cringed when I even mentioned the war, and she refused to discuss it. After seven years of trials and failures, we went our separate ways. She filed for a divorce. I did not contest it. More pain elbowed its way onto the already crowded shelf.

The divorce finalized, I tackled the challenge of returning to single life. I discovered to my amazement that women were as eager for sex as men were, so they became easy prey. I wanted no part of their lives, only the challenge of seducing them. For once in my life, I felt like a free man.

Virtually overnight, I became a success with my new job. I took up new hobbies. Women were available day and night. Life could not have been better. Yet with all that, the pain I felt inside, coupled with the nightmares, would not allow me to forget Vietnam.

As if to increase the pain, the media in the late 70s began to revive the war. Movies began appearing, prompted by books of so-called experts. Stories erupted everywhere, once again portraying Vietnam veterans as drug-crazed "whackos" hiding in the depths of our country's forests and occasionally preying on America's innocent, helpless population. Before I knew it, people were bombarding me with questions once again.

"Boy, did you see *The Deer Hunter*?" they would ask. "That's some scary movie. No wonder veterans are mental cases."

Others would say, "What about that *Apocalypse Now?*[2] Was 'Nam really that weird? And the drugs . . . no wonder you guys couldn't win the war."

"Combat wasn't that bad, was it?"

"Did you ever kill anyone?"

"How could you kill your fellow man?"

"Did you have to kill all of those women and children? That's sick, man, sick."

The references to children always got to me the most. For some reason, children of all ages, shapes and sizes were always the stimulants of my most painful memories, so I managed, during those years, to twist that pain into what I thought was hatred. I avoided contact with children and swore an oath that I would never have any of my own. I could not explain my feelings to anyone. "Children are just brats," I would say, and I convinced myself that I believed it. It was only when I began watching movies and reading stories about Vietnam that I began to understand the reasons behind my emotions.

In the movies I watched, once again, children being brutally slain, destroyed by the ravages of war. My mind did not see the actors and actresses as they played their parts. Instead I saw the Vietnamese boys, girls and babies my subconscious had so aptly hidden from view for so many years. "No!" I screamed out as the horrors ripped through my brain. "No!" The tears flowed mercilessly, refusing to accept my commands to stop. Movie after movie. Story upon story released the painful reason why I had decided to "hate" the most precious form of life God ever placed in this world—children! I had shared in the taking of their lives. I had participated in the unforgivable destruction of their very beings, robbing them of the chance to see the beauty and glory of the earth, of the opportunity to grow, to run, to play. "How could you?!" I screamed at myself, "You are the one who should have died!"

Other movies brought other memories. In one, a soldier tried in vain to help a mortally wounded friend. The dying soldier screamed out in agonizing pain. "Shoot me! Shoot me!" he yelled. His buddy dropped to his knees before the half-man that lay drenched in the blood from his mangled body. His legs and midsection no longer existed, scattered somewhere by the mine he had tripped. My eyes welled with tears as I watched my own hands stretch out to help the man I knew was already dead. His blood dripped from my hands as I looked in vain at the remains of my friend. Once again he screamed out. "Kill me, man . . . please!" I watched helplessly as my outstretched hand squeezed the trigger of the .45 pistol held tightly in my grasp. "Boom! Boom!" The pistol sent forth its missiles of death. The smoke cleared. My friend was gone forever.

The smoke cleared once again. I stood grasping the hands of another friend as he lay in a pool of his own blood. "You're going to be okay," I heard myself say. "Don't worry. Help is on the way." The man smiled weakly at my efforts to reassure him. Bullets and explosions erupted without warning around us. I had to leave him as I turned to join the battle against the enemy that had tried to take his life. I watched as the medevac dropped to his side in answer to the smoke grenade I had left. I never saw them load him on the chopper, I never got to say good-bye. The battle grew too intense as our bitter enemy closed in upon us. I knew he would probably die.

It was a scene I would never get used to, but would have to live over and over until finally, the one loaded on the chopper was me. Even then I did not have a chance to say good-bye. There were so many valiant soldiers, men, friends lost in that war that I never saw again. They were whisked away in the heat of battle, never to be seen again. Gradually, because it was so painful to remember them, my mind even refused to recall their names. Yet their faces are etched in my memory forever.

Fortunately, just as Vietnam was once again becoming a festering wound in the country and in my mind, God sent an angel across my path. Cindy was packaged in a small, beautiful body. Within her soul, she had a heart of gold. A heart that looked past my facade. A heart that ignored the lies about Vietnam. A heart that wanted only to love me for who I was. She never asked the painful questions asked by so many others. She was so full of true love and understanding, it was difficult to believe. We dated for a couple of years and then moved in together for a couple more. The nightmares never ceased, but I finally had someone who would listen and try to understand. She had never been cursed with the memories of any sort of bloodshed, yet she understood the pain. What she didn't understand, she quietly kept to herself until I was ready to explain.

In the early 1980s, the media came up with a new label to describe the Vietnam veteran—Delayed Stress Syndrome.[3] Everywhere veterans were forming therapy groups to find a way to release the pain. New movies began portraying previously quiet, well-mannered men exploding with pent-up emotions from the war. Psychiatrists surmised that most veterans had tucked the war away in some corner of their brains. Now suddenly we were all erupting like violent volcanoes. People were urged to be careful around the likes of us. Movies like *Rambo*[4] began a rampage on the box office as men who had never seen combat began to portray their one-man armies and rake in millions of dollars from our war.

Veteran centers were established everywhere to help the hurting vets. Monuments were built by Vietnam veterans and others to commemorate their fallen buddies. For some reason the monuments always glorified the dead, the survivors seemingly forgotten. To gain any positive recognition as a Vietnam veteran, you had to be dead. Killed in a war that America wanted to call simply an "experience." Everywhere people were supposedly trying to help and understand the "whacko" veterans.

Cindy finally married one. I didn't want to go through with the wedding ceremony at first. I still feared the monster that lurked inside of me, feared that eventually the media would be right and I would "erupt" as they had so aptly shown. Deep down inside, though, I knew that if I lost Cindy I would lose part of me. Without her, the media would have their moment of glory saying, "See, we told you so. There's another one." Cindy became my wife, my rock, my friend.

As we grew together, Cindy, as well as other friends, began to urge me to write down my memories. "You've got a real story there," they would say. "No one has ever heard of the CAP Marines. You should write a book about it."

Finally, I sat down and put pen to paper and let my past flow out. Vietnam once again became a reality as the painful memories stared back at me from the pages before me. The time had come to empty the shelf that stored so many pains. The progress was slow and in many cases, too painful to put to paper.

Until the writing of this book, most of the memories, the pains, were locked away in the depths of my mind. Gradually, with every word I wrote, with every movie I finally watched, with every book or story I read, the dungeon doors swung open and the memories burst forth with bold recognition demanding their final day in court. My mind screamed in pain as the tears and rage flowed from the depths of my soul. At long last they each had their say. No longer did I have the opportunity—or the requirement—to shove them back on the shelf to be dealt with later. The excuses had left. There was no escape from the reality that lay before me.

Throughout the world there are veterans, not just from the Vietnam War but from all wars. Each one is dealing with the pain and memories in his own special way. Hopefully, this story has given its readers some insight into their feelings, thoughts, and fears.

In Chu Lai, and in the Quảng Tin Province, the people were, without a doubt, oppressed beyond comprehension. We fought to obliterate that oppression. Unfortunately, the pullout of Allied troops gave the Communists the victory they longed for.[5]

Sadly, Quảng Tin Province, along with the rest of Vietnam, fell into the clutches of their dreaded enemy. As a result, I know that the Vietnamese friends I fought with, shared many dreams and pains with, were either killed or taken to "concentration camps" where they were subjected to brainwashing tactics or suffered an agonizing death at the hands of their bitter enemies. Knowing the Communists as I know them, the deaths of my friends were tortuously slow.

Taan, my dearest Vietnamese friend, was no doubt the first to die. His hatred for the Communists was no secret.[6]

It was during the writing time that another experience helped me to heal even more. My brother introduced me to a religious leader whose words gave me hope of forgiveness. "Gary," I stated during an early morning prayer meeting, "I have killed." Tears tried to fight their way out. I fought them back. I wasn't going to let this man see the true pain I held inside.

Gary leaned toward me. "You mean during the war?" he asked.

"Yeah," I murmured, "and the Bible states, without question, 'Thou shalt not kill.' Is there no hope for a killer?"

Gary studied my face for a moment. "You know, Barry, God says you must obey your authority in your life and that includes your fighting for your country."

I stopped him. "I wasn't fighting for my country. Well, maybe in the beginning, but not toward the end. I *wanted* to kill. I hated it, but I wanted to kill."

Once again Gary studied my face, and he must have sensed the pain behind it. "Barry, regardless of your sin, God has forgiven you. Don't you know that? God's word says that all of your sins are forgiven. It's that simple. The hard part is forgiving yourself."

I could not believe my ears. For once, a man—a man of God—was offering me hope and freedom, instead of condemnation. My heart nearly burst with relief.

The process has been slow. The path has been difficult and painful. Yet today, thanks to my wife, Cindy, to Gary and to God, I can honestly say I am a new man. Still, war memories linger in my daily life, taunting me with smells and sounds of the past. I sometimes catch myself standing in the rain while others make a mad dash for shelter. Or I find myself lying awake at night listening intently to the hypnotic drum of the raindrops pounding against the roof of my home. I look around as my wife and children remain gently calmed by the melody of the tiny drops of rain. Their sleep continues uninterrupted by the noise.

With one smooth, quiet move I slide out of bed and make my way to the dark shadows of the bedroom. Silently I move from shadow to shadow throughout the house checking for the hidden enemy my memory assures me is there. My muscles grow tense as the rain intensifies. Try as I might I cannot shake the memory of what rain meant in Vietnam. I long for the feelings of my childhood, when the gentle sounds of rain soothed me and filled me with joy that always consumed my mind regardless of the severity of the storm. Then, the pitter-patter of falling rain seemed to transcend all of my problems and fears. But that was yesterday. The childhood friend has turned into a bitter enemy which can no longer be trusted.

The healing is not yet complete. Few memories are easy to deal with. Some of the pains hidden on the Vietnam shelf are in such far dark corners that they only come out in dreams. Eventually, I hope, all will be released. When that time comes, I'm going to burn that shelf.

At least I finally understand the reason for some of my feelings. The "why" has finally been revealed. Most of the pain has been released. My life can begin again.

*The Beginning*

---

[1] Many young Americans of the Vietnam era who were drafted into the Army avoided induction—and prosecution for failure to report—by fleeing to Canada.

[2] *The Deer Hunter* (1978), directed by Michael Cimino, and *Apocalypse Now* (1979), directed by Francis Ford Coppola, are antiwar films about the Vietnam War. George Herring, *America's Longest War: The United States and Vietnam, 1950–1975*, 2nd ed., (New York: Knopf, 1986), 275.

[3] On Delayed Stress Syndrome and the problem of veterans' readjustment in American society, see Michael S. Perlman, "Basic Problems of Military Psychiatry: Delayed Reaction in Veterans," *International Journal of Offender Therapy and Comparative Criminology* 19 (1975), 129–38; Robert J. Lifton, *Home from the War: Vietnam War Veterans, Neither Victims nor Executioners* (New York: Simon & Schuster, 1973); John Wheeler, *Touched with Fire: The Future of the Vietnam Generation* (New York: Avon, 1984).

[4] *First Blood* (1982), directed by Ted Kotcheff, starred Sylvester Stalone as a former Green Beret named Rambo. A sequel, *Rambo: First Blood II* (1986), was directed by George P. Cosmatos.

[5] United States combat troops withdrew from Vietnam in early 1973. The North Vietnamese Army defeated the Army of the Republic of Vietnam in April 1975. Herring, *America's Longest War*, 257–67.

[6] Generally, the Communist crackdown on those known to have supported or suspected of supporting the South Vietnamese government was quite severe. Gary R. Hess, *Vietnam and the United States* (Boston: Twayne, 1990), 150.

# Index

*Names with asterisks are not real names

AK-47. *See* weapons
Alverti, PFC,* 162
Amerasian children, 183
ammunition, 8, 29, 56, 96, 99, 101,
    183, 212; B-122, 130, 262; HE
    (high explosives), 121, 122, 123,
    144, 145, 245; Howitzer 105,
    157–58; quality of, 78, 153, 257;
    sounds of, 44; tracers, 115, 120–
    21, 210; VT (variable time
    explosives), 123; white phospho-
    rous ("WP"), 39, 48, 69, 144
Anderson, Captain,* 216–18
Andrews, Colonel,* 101, 103–106,
    107
Andrews, Sergeant,* 197
*Animal Farm*, 166
APR (Area of Prime Responsibility),
    40, 43, 45, 81, 114, 190, 266,
    278
artillery. *See* United States Army,
    artillery
Australia, 58, 260
axes, 40, 62, 63–64

bathing, 213
beetle nuts, 133
Bennett, Sergeant,* 78, 79
Bentley, Top Sergeant,* 1, 10
black market, 183, 217, 257
Bledsoe, Staff Sergeant,* 8

body count, 35–36, 105, 266
booby traps, 2, 15, 45–46, 69, 85,
    119, 148, 150, 189–90, 238–39,
    256
Boomer, Bill, 279–80
Bradley, Robert ("Doc"),* 29–35, 39,
    45–53, 56, 58, 256
buffalo dung, 2, 15, 79, 96, 142. *See
    also* water buffalo

Cam Ranh Bay, 254, 255, 262
camouflage, 16, 69, 79, 96, 142, 208
CAP (Combined Action Platoon
    program), xi–xii, 10; Command,
    14, 26, 40, 56–57, 70–80, 96,
    121, 141, 152, 172, 189, 202,
    204, 207, 215, 222–24, 227,
    232, 233, 260; insignia, 25;
    training, 15–19, 24
CAP One, 266; bounty on, 59–60, 88,
    169; casualties, 98, 246; com-
    mand base, 131–32, 153, 159,
    162–63, 189; firefights, 35, 48–
    50, 52, 69, 88, 94–104, 120–23,
    143–45, 204, 206–212, 244–46;
    interaction with Vietnamese
    people, 33–34, 39–40, 53–54,
    111–12, 146–48, 169, 256; meal
    with enemy, 92–96; movement of,
    31–33, 40–41, 43–52, 69, 83–
    85, 96, 115–16, 138–39, 146,